THE FIGHT FOR QUIET

By Theodore Berland

The Scientific Life

Your Children's Teeth
  (with Alfred E. Seyler, D.D.S.)

X-ray—Vanguard of Modern Medicine

How to Keep Your Teeth After 30

The Fight for Quiet

THE
FIGHT FOR QUIET

by

Theodore Berland

$(((((((((((\cdot)))))))))))$

Prentice-Hall, Inc., Englewood Cliffs, N.J.

The Fight for Quiet by Theodore Berland
© 1970 by Theodore Berland

ISBN 0–13–314591–3

Library of Congress Catalog Card Number: 74–121724

Printed in the United States of America *T*

Prentice-Hall International, Inc., London
Prentice-Hall of Australia, Pty. Ltd., Sydney
Prentice-Hall of Canada, Ltd., Toronto
Prentice-Hall of India Private Ltd., New Delhi
Prentice-Hall of Japan, Inc., Tokyo

For Cynthia
who, quietly, was always there

ACKNOWLEDGMENTS

A book such as this, which contains countless facts from medicine, science, social studies, and the law, plus the opinions of many people, is really an assemblage in readable form of those facts and opinions. One needs help in such assemblages. The suggestion that I write this book came from my literary agent, Julian Bach, Jr., of New York City, in part, because like many other city people he objects strongly to noise, and, in part, because he had confidence that I could write it. For his confidence and his support during these four years of researching and writing, I thank him.

Another principal architect of this book was Alexander Cohen, Ph.D., of the U.S. Public Health Service, with whom I consulted at the very beginning for direction. I did so because I felt he has the most thorough knowledge of noise research in the world. He guided me to experts and sources

vii

in Europe and North America which all proved rich in information. I thank him deeply for his guidance as well as for his role in organizing the National Conference on Noise as a Public Health Hazard, held at Washington, D.C., in June 1968, which served as another rich source of information.

I also thank each of the men and women I interviewed in six countries in Europe in April 1968 and those I interviewed in the U.S. at various times, as well as all of those who so kindly and courteously answered my queries by mail and by telephone. Because they are all mentioned in the text, I won't again repeat their names here.

Much of my data was provided to me by self-appointed scouts—friends who gave me information as they found it. Among these particularly were Julian Bach, Jr.; Leon Frederick Block of Michael Reese Hospital and Medical Center in Chicago; Jack Sloan, M.D., also of Michael Reese; and Sheldon Garber of the Blue Cross Association (now with Charles R. Feldstein and Co.). Information was also most kindly provided by the library of the American Medical Association, through the good offices of Roy R. Keaton of the Communications Division; by the John Crerar Library; by Eugene H. Kone of the American Institute of Physics; by the Insulation Board Institute, through the good offices of Gordon Lawler of Daniel J. Edelman Inc.; and from the Library of Congress through the help of U.S. Representatives Sidney Yates and Roman Pucinski, both of Chicago. A blanket thanks to everyone else who helped, such as Richard Mann and David Raskin and Harvey Posert. Thanks, too, to General Radio Co. for the use of a sound-level meter.

Special thanks go to the American embassies in Stockholm, Sweden (especially Argus J. Tresidder), and West Germany (especially Ilse-Dora Abel), for help in arranging my jet-fast days of interviewing in those two countries; to the French Embassy information office in New York; and to the West German and British Consulates in Chicago.

Dr. Laszlo Stein of the Henner Hearing and Speech Clinic at Michael Reese Hospital and Medical Center, Chicago, not only supplied me with information on noise deafness, but was also kind enough to review part of the manuscript and make suggestions for improvements.

My thanks go to the three valiant ladies who typed the manuscript, in sequence, Dawn Marshall, Evelyn Kidd, and, especially, Edith Lovinger.

Finally, my heartfelt thanks to my wife, Cynthia, to our three children, Leslie Myra, Elizabeth Ann, and David Reuben, and to my other relatives and friends who all suffered with me the agonies caused by separation and sedulity as I researched and wrote this book.

T. B.

Chicago, Ill.

CONTENTS

The day will come when man will have to fight noise as inexorably as cholera and the plague.

Robert Koch

$$((((((((((\,\cdot\,))))))))))$$

To me
High mountains are a feeling,
But the hum
Of human cities torture.

Lord Byron
(*Childe Harold's Pilgrimage,*
Canto III, Stanza 72)

1

WHAT NOISE IS
AND DOES

(((((((((((•)))))))))))

1
INTRODUCTIONS
AND DEFINITIONS

$$((((((((((\cdot))))))))))$$

Sound is to air what waves are to water. The analogy is more than rhetorical: sound waves do indeed break upon the eardrum much as the waves of the ocean break upon the shore.

There is no sound in a vacuum; a vacuum, by definition, is nothing, and sound requires something to carry it. This "something" is usually referred to as the medium. It can be cast iron: apartment dwellers banging on cold radiators or pipes make use of this principle. The medium can be water: submarines are located by listening to the sounds of their engines, and by beaming short bursts of sound toward them and measuring the time it takes for the echo to return; since sound travels at a known speed in water, this time is translated into distance and coupled with compass direction to form a picture called sonar. The medium can be earth: American frontiersmen learned from the Indian scouts that they could put an ear to the ground and hear the sound

3

transmitted by the hooves of horses miles away. The medium can be the body: Laënnec, who invented the stethoscope in 1819, in France, knew that an ear placed against the chest could hear the sound of the heart beating and the lungs breathing within. The medium can be wood: Laënnec had been inspired by watching children scratch one end of a wooden beam with a pin while listening to the transmitted sound at the other end.

Thus, the sound-transmitting medium can be anything. But it almost always is air. Sound travels through air by squeezing unseen molecules of air together in very orderly ways. As the sound source vibrates—be it violin string, tuning fork, loudspeaker, auto muffler, or whatever—it pushes against the air, then returns to its original position. Then it pushes again, and returns, and so forth, until it is spent or is turned off. This vibration produces alternating dense and sparse bands in the air. The result is cordon after cordon of dense air spreading outward from the sound source, much as ripples do on water after you throw in a pebble.

The waves in the air are sound and hence are called sound waves. Because of the physical nature of air, they travel at about 1,100 feet per second or 344 meters per second or about 760 miles per hour. This speed of sound, now exceeded by jet planes, is expressed as mach 1 (after Ernst Mach, 1838–1916, professor of physics at the Universities of Prague and Vienna, who made important discoveries about sound and the ear). When aircraft exceed mach 1, or go through the "sound barrier," the air molecules are not vibrated but are shoved faster than they would normally travel. The result is the explosive shock wave known as the sonic boom or sonic bang.

The rapidity or slowness with which a sound source vibrates, or makes the air vibrate, determines a basic quality of the sound known as *frequency*. Each push against the air and then relaxation is called a cycle. Frequency is expressed as cycles per second (cps) or hertz (Hz). At higher frequencies, sound waves are jammed closer together than they are at low frequencies.

The highest frequency a good human ear can hear is the shrill of 20,000 Hz; frequencies above that are ultrasonic. The lowest it can hear is the groaning 15 Hz. Below that is the infrasonic range. The low-frequency sound waves are long and far apart, whereas the high-frequency sound waves are short and packed closely together. You can get some idea of this by comparing the smallness of an ultrasonic dog whistle with the largeness of organ pipes, and, among the organ pipes, the relative smallness of the angelic pipes with the hugeness of the rataplan pipes. Some more specific examples: middle C on a piano is 261 Hz and has a wavelength of 4 feet; the very high F''' of a professional soprano is 1,408 Hz and has a wavelength of but 0.78 feet; the D of an operatic bass at 74 Hz has a wavelength of about 15 feet.

Bear in mind that no matter how long or how short the wavelength is, it still travels at the speed of sound. Thus high-frequency sound waves arrive quickly one upon the other, while low-frequency sounds are more sluggish in repetition.

It is important to understand that it isn't the air that moves in waves; it's the *sound* that moves in waves through the air. The best analogy is the effect of wind on fields of wheat or on water. The wheat and the water stand put, merely bobbing up and bending down. But the waves whip across them at many miles per hour. The concepts of frequency and sound waves are necessary to an understanding of how noise, or unwanted sound, affects hearing, but they're not easy concepts to grasp. Robert Bruce Lindsay, professor of physics and dean of the Graduate School at Brown University, well understood this in his essay on sound in the *Encyclopaedia Britannica*. He wrote,

Realizing that in open, still air it is possible to hear a cricket chirp at a distance of half a mile, the sceptic asks how it is possible that such a small insect can move the mass of air in a hemisphere with a radius of half a mile (over 1,000,000 tons) so that the air in the vicinity of one's ear may move sufficiently to lead to hearing. The fallacy of this reasoning lies in the assumption that the sound producer must move *all* the surrounding air *all at once* in order to produce the sensation of sound. It ignores the fact that air is a compressible elastic fluid, *i.e.*, can be squeezed, so that it is possible for motion to take place in one part without appearing simultaneously everywhere else. . . . This kind of motion, communicated in time from one part of a medium to another, is called wave motion. We'd say that sound travels in air as a compressional or squeeze wave.

Because of their nature, these waves of sound which radiate out from a source do interesting things when they meet solid obstacles like walls. They bounce off, and so are reflected, and scattered. They turn corners. They are refracted. They come back as echoes or noise. If the wall or obstacle can itself vibrate, some of the sound is transmitted through to the next room. If the obstacle is a heavy velvet curtain which completely absorbs the sound waves, the sound dies.

Unless you are taking a hearing test, you are not likely to hear pure frequencies. You usually hear fundamental frequencies plus their multiples, which are called harmonics. Also, what you perceive are not pure frequencies, but frequencies at certain loudnesses; this is *pitch*. The loudness affects your perception of that pitch. Thus, if you hear two sounds of exactly the same frequency, you'll say the louder one has the higher pitch, or is the higher note. This is very important in noise because pitch and its components, frequency and loudness, seriously affect our psychological reactions to noise, as well as the effects of noise on our ears.

The "loudness" or intensity of a sound depends on the

pressure its sound waves exert. Thus, faint sounds are weak while loud sounds are strong pressures—weak and strong, relative to each other, that is. Actually, the amount of power in sound and in noise is rather puny compared to the hundreds of horsepower in car engines and the hundreds of watts of electricity used in homes. For instance, noise that is loud enough to pain the ear has the energy of but 0.01 watt. Compare that to the 60- or 100-watt bulb that may be providing the light by which you are now reading. Sound waves spend most of their energy in traveling. Still, even the power of sound sources is paltry. For instance, the voice of an opera singer at the highest notes and most power generates about 1 watt, whereas the peak power of a piano is less than half (0.4 watt). The peak powers of some other musical instruments are: triangle, 0.05 watt; trombone, 6 watts; cymbals, 10 watts; organ, 13 watts; and large bass drum, 25 watts. The peak power of the total sound of a full orchestra in crescendo, the output of many musicians and their instruments at their loudest, is 70 watts.

One of the fascinating aspects of noise is that such relatively weak levels of power can provoke such strong auditory, psychological, and bodily effects on us.

The *range* of sound energy that the human ear can hear is fantastic. Sharply painful sound is 10 million million times as powerful as the faintest audible sound. In technical terms this is 2,000 dynes versus 0.0002 dyne per square centimeter. The dyne is a physical unit of pressure which is approximately equal to a microbar, or millionth of an atmosphere. The dyne has been called equal to the push of a healthy mosquito. But the dyne is too unwieldy to use as a measure of sound level because the range of the pressures of audible sound is so extensive.

Enter the decibel, or dB, the universally adopted unit for measuring sound intensity. It is not really a unit, but a ratio. Based on the dyne (a decibel is 0.000204 dyne per square centimeter), it is a logarithmic scale. It is related to the bel, which is named in honor of Alexander Graham Bell, who invented the telephone and worked with the deaf. Because it's logarithmic, the bel is not a constant unit as are inches and pounds, or centimeters and grams. It is more like the f stops on a camera lens. Thus, one bel is tenfold the power of a decibel and two bels means tenfold and tenfold again. If tenfold is 10 dB, a hundredfold is 20 dB. *Double* sound pressure is not 20 dB but 6 dB. Also when two sound sources impinge on you, the total decibels are not simply an addition of the two. If one source is 60 dB and the other is 60 dB, the total sound pressure is not 120 dB but 63 dB.

Artificial and arbitrary as they are, decibels are seldom computed; instead they are read from charts or from sound-level instruments which measure them. The advantage of the decibel is that it makes it possible to show on ordinary graph paper and ordinary meters a vast range of sound pressures in such a manner that small variations are as accurately portrayed as are large variations. And decibels can rather readily be converted to watts if necessary. Thus 120 dB is 1 watt, 60 dB is .000001 watt (10^{-6}), and 0.0 dB is .000000000001 watt (10^{-12}).

Noise is usually measured in the field by sound-level meters. Thanks to solid-state electronic circuits, these are made quite small and portable. For example, the General Radio Type 1565-A, which I used for a noise survey of America and Europe (presented in a later chapter), weighs less than 2 pounds and can be carried on a neck strap like a camera and operated with only one hand. Yet it is extremely rugged and versatile.

Sound-level meters essentially measure sound pressures. They consist of a microphone to convert sound into electrical energy, electronic circuits to analyze the sound and measure it, and a meter to display this information. Sound-level meters analyze the pressures of groups of frequencies.

The larger and more complicated of these instruments analyze the pressures of octave bands, or one-third octave bands, or even narrower bands of frequencies. Smaller and simpler instruments measure the pressures of groups of sound frequencies arranged in three scales.

The scale that most closely approximates what the human ear hears is the A scale. It covers a frequency range of 400 to 12,000 Hz; like the ear, it is more sensitive to the higher rather than the lower frequencies. The B scale, seldom used, covers the frequencies 124 to 12,000 Hz and is somewhat more sensitive to higher frequencies. The C scale has very few special sensitivities over its frequency range of 25 to 10,000 Hz. In practice, the noise level measured on the A scale can be compared with that of the C scale to make a rough analysis. Thus a higher reading of the same noise on the C scale than on the A scale means that the noise has a heavy component of low frequencies which the ear would not perceive. Decibels and scales are written like this: dB-A, dB-B, and dB-C.

There are also instruments that record the accumulated duration of exposure to noise. One kind I use is the Unico Mark VI Noise Exposimeter. The decibel minimum is set and the instrument does the rest. Whenever the noise in its environment meets or exceeds the setting, say 85 dB, a small electric clockwork is activated. The instrument is small and light enough to be worn on the person, or can be set anywhere noise exposure is to be counted. After the desired time of study has elapsed, the meter's scale tells the number of minutes during that time the noise level has exceeded the set level.

When I left for Europe in April, 1968, I left a Unico Mark VI set at 85 dB sitting on a shelf near the ceiling in the breakfast room of my house in Chicago. When I returned three weeks later, the meter indicated that my family had created and been exposed to this level of noise during my travel for at least 162 minutes—perhaps more, since the battery died sometime during the study. This was not a weighted reading, incidentally, but was a small matter since the shrill shrieks of children are bound to fall in the A scale. Nevertheless, Unico had an A scale weighting available after this small study.

Impulse sounds such as that from guns and sonic booms last only thousandths of seconds and so need different instruments for analysis and measurement. Special (usually small) microphones feed electronic circuits which work in thousandths and millionths of a second and display their data on TV screenlike oscilloscopes. The shape of the sonic-boom wave displayed on such screens is like a stretched-out N; that's why it is often referred to as an N-wave. The wave form comes from the sudden burst of overpressure followed by the comparatively slow return to normal pressure, then the rarefaction as the pressure falls below atmospheric and finally and suddenly rises to atmospheric again.

2

HEARING AND DEAFNESS

$(((((((((((\cdot)))))))))))$

"What has passed unnoticed is that many noise levels encountered in the community exceed standards found injurious in industry," noted John D. Dougherty, M.D., of Harvard University, and Oliver L. Welsh, Ed.D., of Boston University in *The New England Journal of Medicine*. "Hearing loss, formerly thought to be a hazard of aviators and boilermakers, occurs with age (presbycusis) after lifetime exposure to noise at community level." That the average 70-to-79-year-old American has trouble understanding speech is a result not of aging *per se*. It is the result of his having lived so long in a world that has become noisier each year. The steadily intensified sonic attack on his ears has left him little to hear with. The hearing of people of all ages is affected by noise pollution of our environment. This is due partly to the unique and fascinating sound-sensing construction of the ear.

The human ear is a marvelous and sensitive organ. It can detect the very weak energy that is sound, of a rather wide range of frequencies, and convert it to bioelectrical signals which are transmitted to the brain, where it is perceived. Aram Glorig, M.D., of Southwestern Medical School, Dallas, Texas, wrote in his book, *Noise and Your Ear,*

> Under favorable conditions man can hear sounds so faint that they might have been produced by the thermal motion of molecules; sounds that cause an excursion of the drumhead of about one-tenth the diameter of a hydrogen molecule. Yet he can also hear, without undue distortion, sounds that contain a million million times more energy. . . . Under optimum conditions frequency differences as small as two or three cycles per second and intensity differences of half a decibel can be detected. More than 300,000 tones of different frequency and/or intensity can be distinguished in the auditory area.
>
> With binaural hearing man can, from auditory clues alone, determine within a few degrees the direction from which sound comes to his ears.
>
> The ear is more sensitive than the eye in detecting temporally disbursed stimuli. Under favorable conditions the ear can detect pulsed stimuli up to pulse rates as high as 2,000 per second.

A Northwestern University noise expert, Edward R. Hermann, Ph.D., associate professor of civil engineering, said, "the ear can discriminate between slight differences in sound pressures and frequencies as well as or better than most of our electronic equipment. However, as with the other human sense organs, the ear does not possess absolute calibration."

The ear does its wonderful job in ways not completely understood. Small though it is, it still holds some big secrets, despite the massive amount of research done on it.

Anatomically, the ear is divided into three parts. The evident outer ear consists of a fleshy shell originally designed to gather sound. It lost that function many evolutionary eons ago. Also in the outer ear is an external auditory canal for carrying sound waves to the eardrum, or tympanic membrane.

The middle ear, which is more complicated, starts here with the eardrum. The waves of invisible sound beating upon it cause it to vibrate. The translucent pearl-gray eardrum is tough and flexible and not stretched flat like the skin of a drum at all. Instead, it is constructed much like the cone of a loudspeaker.

Attached to the inside of the eardrum is the *malleus* or hammer, one of the three tiniest bones in the body. As these linked bones—the ossicles—move in a pea-sized space, they transmit sound to the inner ear. Actually these three bones (the others are technically called the *incus* and *stapes*, and popularly known as the anvil and stirrup) do more than that. As they move they modify the sound they carry from the eardrum. They can either amplify or diminish it so as to protect the inner ear. The foot of the stapes, which is the other end of the link-up, transmits sound directly to the inner ear. It is about one-thirtieth of the area of the eardrum. This 30-to-1 ratio favors the efficient transfer of sound energy to the dense liquid filling the inner ear. In other words, the middle ear serves to intensify the sounds which it transmits from the outside.

The middle ear also serves to protect the inner ear. First of all, its 2-cc.-or-so volume of space is filled with air (kept at atmospheric pressure by the tunnel to the throat known as the *Eustachian tube*). The presence of air serves to dampen the heavy rocking of the well-balanced ossicles which comes with low frequencies. More importantly, there are two muscles attached to the malleus and the stapes: the *tensor tympani* and the *stapedius* muscles. They work against each other to stiffen the eardrum and the movement of the ossicles, thus reducing the efficiency of their transmission of sound. The muscles do this in an important reflex action on command from the brain a few hundredths of a second after the loud sound reaches the eardrum. This is known as the *acoustic reflex.*

The inner ear, the most complex part of the human ear, is filled with fluid which closely resembles the sea water that circulates through the rudimentary open ears of fish. Lying deep and well-protected inside the temple of the skull, it is a system of boney caves that is so complicated it is known medically as the *labyrinth.* The inner ear has component parts which have nothing to do with sound or hearing. One is the *utricle,* which is our sensor of gravity and acceleration. Another is the system of three semicircular canals which sense our orientation in space and are responsible for our sense of balance; when they go awry, we get dizzy and fall.

We hear in the snail-shaped part of the inner ear known as the *cochlea.* As the foot of the stapes bone rocks against a wide opening in the cochlea known as the *oval window,* sound is transmitted to the liquid inside. Just below the oval window is the *round window,* an elastic membrane that is the end of the pathway of sound into, then out of the inner ear.

(As an aside of interest, a frequent cause of hearing loss is *otosclerosis,* in which the stapes becomes attached to the oval window by bone growth. Thanks to surgery performed with the aid of a microscope, this can be corrected: the stapes is broken off and replaced with a plastic or metal part; the oval window is reopened and a new membrane made of blood vessel wall or plastic is stretched across it. These techniques have returned hearing to untold thousands.)

The oval window is the beginning of the vestibular canal which makes a two-and-a-half turn snail-shell spiral. Unlike a snail shell, the canal is widest at the center of the spiral;

there it connects with the thinnest part of the tympanic canal, which then doubles back around the spiral and enlarges as it does so, ending in the round window. Also unlike a snail shell, the cochlea has two stories. Stretched straight, the entire length would be about 35 mm or about 1¼ inches. Yet sound is sensed over an even shorter distance: the 30 mm of the *organ of Corti*, a microscopically bushy area on the "upper floor" or basilar membrane of the vestibular canal. Making this area bushy are hair cells or *cilia*—about 23,500 of them—evenly spaced in four rows.

As the stapes "raps" on the oval window, it sends sound waves through the fluid of the inner ear. The hair cells respond by bending, much like seaweed and other bottom plants bend with the rhythm of the waves above them. The microscopic hair cells are electrically charged. As they bend in response to sound they create bioelectric signals. Each hair cell is in effect one line on the auditory nerve "cable." The individual "lines" converge at the center of the spiral, where they become the "trunkline" running from the ear through the thick skull bone to the brain.

Although the cochlea is most sensitive to frequencies of 1,000 to 4,000 Hz, it can hear and analyze sounds within the range of about 15 to 20,000 Hz. Some of this is done in the cochlea itself. "Maps" charted by researchers (one of whom, Georg von Békésy, won the Nobel Prize in medicine for his work on the ear) show that the hair cells closest to the oval window are concerned with the highest frequencies heard, while hair cells closest to the center of the spiral are concerned with lower frequencies. The lowest frequencies we hear form what are called *standing waves* along the entire inside of the cochlea and are sensed by hair cells along the entire length.

So wonderful is this tiny inner ear that it can not only hear but analyze single frequencies and the far more complex sound we normally hear, composed of resonance, harmonics, overtones, and other combinations and interactions of sound. In addition, some of the analysis of what we hear occurs in the brain, since different parts of the brain are concerned with different frequencies.

Harbored safely in a healthy body, and furnished with an ample blood supply, the human ear can perform exquisitively and precisely for three-quarters of a century or more. But an ear assaulted by decades of noise in our mechanistic and crowded society soon fails in its ability to hear, just as certainly as do ears assaulted by diseases. In more ways than one, noise is a pathogen. Created by man, it suicidally destroys that part of him which brings him the joys of music, the enjoyment of nature, and necessary warnings—such as sounds of traffic—from his increasingly dangerous environment.

It is fitting, perhaps, that the one contemporary researcher best known for his studies of the relationship of quiet to good hearing is the same ear surgeon who gained fame for precise through-the-microscope operations to free "frozen" stapes bones and thus restore hearing to countless adults. He is Samuel Rosen, M.D., of Mount Sinai Hospital, and Columbia University, New York City. He has led several teams of medical and hearing researchers—including Dr. Gerd Jansen of Essen, Germany—into Sudan, Africa, near the equator, to study members of the Mabaan tribe, who are, he has written, "a pre-Nilotic, pagan, primitive, tribal people whose state of cultural development is the late Stone Age. They are a peaceful and quiet people, about 20,000 of them, living in small huts with straw-thatched roofs and bamboo sides, about 8 to 10 ft. in diameter. They have no guns, but hunt and fish with spears. They do not use drums in their dance and song but pluck a five-string lyre and beat a log with a stick. . . . In general, the sound level in the villages is below 40 dB on the C scale of the sound level meter except occasionally at sunrise or soon thereafter when a domestic animal such as a rooster, lamb, cow or dove makes itself heard. . . . The highest noise levels encountered during our stay occurred when the villagers were dancing and singing."

During his four trips to the Mabaans, starting in 1960, Dr. Rosen tested the hearing of tribespeople, for whom, he said, "Acute hearing is necessary for survival, so they have learned to listen since early childhood." He was amazed to see them converse 300 feet apart without raising their voices. "Hearing is significantly more acute in all Mabaans aged 10 through 70 years than in people of the same age who live in industrial areas of the United States. Except for the bleat of a goat and other sounds of nature, the Mabaans live in a dramatically quiet, almost silent atmosphere. The bombardment of excessive noise in our culture and the virtual absence of such in theirs could be one of the factors responsible for their superior hearing." He found that the average Mabaan man of 75 could hear as well as the average American man of 25 years.

In all fairness, I must say that absence of noise alone is not the only factor in preserving the fantastic hearing of Mabaans. Dr. Rosen found another important factor: the ample blood supply to the ear, even in the aged. This blood supply depends on the general health of the cardiovascular system, which itself relies on a host of factors, including diet, exercise, and heredity. One of these factors also is stress and, as we'll see later, noise adds a pertinent and dangerous stress on the body.

So noise both directly and indirectly affects hearing; and the reverse is true: absence of noise protects hearing directly and indirectly.

Another bit of evidence along this line came from Tulane University in 1968. There Dr. Clifton Istre, working under the supervision of Dr. Gerardo Gonzalez, placed caged guinea pigs at distances of 75, 150, 300 feet, and one mile from rocket engine test stands during six-minute firings at the Mississippi Test Facility of the National Aeronautics and Space Administration. The experiment left many of the animals with hearing losses and left some totally deaf. Dr. Gonzalez blamed this on blockage of the blood supply to the hair cells of the inner ear. These experiments thus help confirm the *indirect* effects of noise on hearing.

The *direct* effects of noise on hearing were confirmed by a strange case which came to the attention of A. J. Philipszoon, Chief of the Ear, Nose and Throat Clinic of the University of Amsterdam. It concerned an 82-year-old man who came to be fitted for a hearing aid because his hearing was worsening rather quickly. On examination, his right ear appeared normal, but his left ear seemed to be blocked by a wad of ear wax. Dr. Philipszoon found this "proved to be a dirty piece of cotton wool from which fibers could be pulled and which had obstructed the auditory canal completely." When asked how this plug of cotton had come into his ear, the patient became very angry and said that 32 years ago he had an ear inflammation and a doctor had placed the cotton in his ear. When the ear was better and the patient told his doctor the cotton was still in his ear, the doctor said no, it had been removed. Thus, the cotton had been in the ear canal for over three decades!

Dr. Philipszoon removed the cotton, then tested the man's ears. The right was deaf, the left had some hearing loss. But bone conduction hearing tests (to test the inner ear) showed the left far superior to the right. For 32 years the cotton had acted as an ear protector, Dr. Philipszoon said. "This case shows us 'experimentally' that for the onset of presbycusis [a general loss of hearing that comes with aging], the noise of every day is a very important factor. . . ."

In the absence of mechanical protectors, the ear has its own built-in ear defense called the acoustic reflex, described briefly a few pages back. The reflex is triggered by sound of about 70 dB. Studies by John L. Fletcher, Ph.D., psychologist with the U.S. Army Medical Research Laboratory, Ft. Knox, Kentucky, indicate that the reflex reduces sound reaching the inner ear by 10 dB on the average (that's a reduction in pressure by about 10 times) and up to 50 dB (for a pressure reduction of 100,000 times) in some people.

The reflex is so sensitively triggered that it can be used as an objective test to determine whether an ear hears or is deaf. Thus it is particularly useful in evaluating the hearing of mutes, children, suspected malingerers, and genuinely deaf persons. In practice, a weak sound signal is fed into one ear, and the instrument detects the sound which bounces back from the ear drum. Dials are turned and the instrument is adjusted so that the sound waves going into the ear and the echo coming out are in phase. Then the sound is fed more loudly into the opposite ear, and if it is heard, perceptual signals go to the brain and motor signals come back to the middle ear muscles, telling them to tighten. As they do so, both ear drums are flexed and moved from behind and the echo bouncing back is now out of phase, causing a needle on the instrument to flip. Since both ears' muscles are commanded by the brain, the sound can be used to test the hearing of each ear.

The reflex has three vital weaknesses as a defender. One is that these muscles of the middle ear can become fatigued with overuse. In an environment of sustained high noise level, they will gradually lose their strength, thus increasing the noise that reaches the inner ear. Second, again like most muscles, they are affected by drugs and other chemicals of the environment. For instance, Bengt Kylin of Karolinska Institutet (Royal Caroline Institute) in Stockholm, Sweden, found that the fumes of ether and other solvents have a narcotic effect that makes the middle ear muscles relax, temporarily negating the reflex. Third, the reflex requires the nervous circuit of ear-to-brain-to-ear to work; this takes time. Captain Fletcher found that "it takes the muscles at least 9 msec [thousandths of a second] to make this reaction to sound entering the ear; gunfire sound has already done its damage by the time the muscles can respond."

Kylin and his Karolinska colleague, Dr. Bertil Johansson, found that the acoustic reflex can be used to evaluate an individual's ears' susceptibility to noise. In tests on 50 subjects, they saw a high correlation of reflex action when low (500 Hz) tones were beamed into the subjects' ears. But when they used high-pitched tones of 2,500 Hz, 3,000 Hz, and 3,500 Hz they saw fatigue weaken the acoustic reflex of many subjects. Furthermore, those persons with poor acoustic reflexes showed extensive temporary loss of hearing after exposure to noise. So, apparently some people can keep their good hearing longer than others because they have a good middle ear reflex!

The temporary hearing loss mentioned above occurs in the inner ear and is the *one* of the one-two punch with which noise assaults our hearing. If detected early enough, it serves as a warning that unless noise is reduced or the ear is better protected from without, permanent hearing loss will follow. It is the *only* warning, since noise produces no real pain until destruction of the ear is well on its way. That sound level is very high—starting at 140 dB. Aural pain due to noise, incidentally, has been pinpointed as originating in the eardrum. When the noise level is high enough, the blood vessels in the eardrum become engorged and finally hemorrhage.

To the hearing expert, temporary hearing loss is known as *temporary threshold shift,* or T.T.S. An earlier name was *auditory fatigue.* Most people have experienced it; it's the difficulty in hearing after the noise of a firecracker, or the crack of a close firearm or the bong of a bell. It's analogous to spots before the eyes after the burst of a flashbulb. What happens is that the shock of the loud noise kicks upward the threshold of hearing. Once that happens, sound has to be louder to be heard.

There is another kind of shift that occurs. For some reason not yet completely known, the range of hearing that is lost does not cover those frequencies that offended, but instead, frequencies that are half an octave higher. This was discovered by a research team led by Hollowell Davis, M.D., of the Central Institute for the Deaf, and Washington University in St. Louis, and confirmed by Michael Rodda, Ph.D., when he was with the University of Canterbury, Christchurch, New Zealand. This phenemenon considerably dilutes the warning value of T.T.S., because by the time a person realizes that he has lost hearing, his hearing loss has spread and has become permanent. As Dr. Rodda explained it, T.T.S. occurs most commonly at the frequency of 4,000 Hz. "This means that the initial loss of hearing acuity occurs at frequencies above those mainly involved in speech (500 to 2,000 c/s [Hz]), and consequently considerable losses can occur before the effect becomes noticeable to the individual. It is only when the losses have spread out from the initial 4,000 c/s effect and begin to include the speech frequencies that most individuals become aware of their deficiencies, although critical musical enthusiasts may notice a loss of perceived quality in their favorite records, etc., prior to this. The danger is obvious, considerable damage may have occurred to the hearing mechanisms before the individual is aware of it."

The first sounds not heard are the fricatives—such as f, s, th, ch, and sh—which are among the higher-frequency sounds of speech. Thus the first words lost are those such as sick, thick, flick, or chick. The person suffering the first symptoms of noise deafness complains, "I can hear, but I don't understand." Then the explosive consonants fail to be heard—b, t, p, k, and d. An example of what noise deafness is like to the person suffering it can be shown with the

sentence: *Our office is on the twelfth floor.* The first losses
make it: *Our o__i__e i__ on the twel__th __loor.* Heavier
losses make it: *Our o__i__e i__ on __e__wel__ __loor.*

Most of the temporary hearing loss caused by noise occurs
during the first hour or two of exposure. Likewise, most of
the recovering in hearing comes in the first hour or two after
the deafening noise stops. By definition, temporary noise
deafness goes away after the ear gets a chance to recover.
But the length of the recovery period depends as much on
individual variation as does the level of noise which induces
the deafness. There are no rules that apply to everyone. The
only sure ways to tell is by monitoring the noise level and by
testing the hearing of persons exposed to it.

The deafness produced by noise is the result of the batter-
ing which the tiny hair cells in the cochlea receive. Microscopic studies of the inner ears of animals which were
experimentally subjected to noise show how these cells swell
and change shape. And the hair cells first affected are those
closest to the oval window, which are responsible for sensing
the higher frequencies heard. Apparently, if the noise stops
soon enough the hair cells suffer no permanent damage and
repair themselves. Thus mended, they go on with their
business of hearing. But if the noise doesn't stop soon
enough, or if there isn't enough of a pause between noises to
allow these cells to heal, they will stay permanently damaged and the noise-induced hearing loss will become permanent. Microscopic studies, again, show how the unrecovered
cells simply disintegrate and disappear forever. If the noise
is intense enough, and lasts long enough, and occurs frequently enough, the destruction of hair cells spreads and
with it comes a spread in the frequencies that are lost to
hearing. Depending on the nature of the noise exposure, all
the working parts of the cochlea can be destroyed in time.

Most of the studies which showed all this have been of the
inner ears of animals subjected to noise in the laboratory and

of cadavers of men exposed to industrial noise for many years. Even more frightening, though, is the fact that, as Drs. John D. Dougherty and Oliver L. Welsh of Boston point out, "Exposures to sound levels similar to that generated by home food blenders cause marked morphologic changes in the hair cells. They characteristically show vacuolization of the cytoplasm, swelling with compression of the nuclei, and change in the shape of the cells."

The noises that are most dangerous to hearing are those that are audibly the loudest, highest pitched, purest in tone, and longest lasting. Explosive sounds are also dangerous because they can cause another kind of damage: rupture of the eardrum. But this is in a way a blessing, because in most cases only the eardrum is damaged. It "gives," and thus protects the middle and inner ear. When the eardrum regenerates, hearing is usually restored. The other element in permanent noise deafness is individual susceptibility, now perhaps a predictable factor, as mentioned before.

That people vary so widely in their susceptibility to noise was pointed out by Dr. W. Ian Acton of the Institute of Sound and Vibration Research at The University of Southampton. "Many English people survived the bombing during World War II and didn't suffer any hearing loss at all, while others are affected by the noise of only traffic," he said. He further illustrated by telling of two cases with which he personally was acquainted. One was a 38-year-old man who had worked in a garage, at an oil refinery, and on a furnace, and had regularly fired rifles in the service in combat. He had suffered middle ear infection, malaria, and syphilis, and had been treated with quinine and tetracycline on different occasions. He had also been knocked unconscious a couple of times. In short, Dr. Acton explained, this man had been exposed to noises, diseases, drugs, and trauma—any of which *individually* could have caused significant hearing loss. Yet on testing he was found to have normal hearing!

The contrasting case was the student who fired a small (.22 caliber) rifle at camp and suffered temporary hearing loss immediately.

With noise deafness often comes the common hearing disorder known as *recruitment of loudness*. This is the phenomenon so often burlesqued in comedy situations where a hard-of-hearing (usually old) man says, "What's that ya said, sonny?" The younger man repeats what he said, in a yell. And the older man says, "Stop shouting son, I can hear you!" As an old-time radio comedian's wife used to say to him, " 'Tain't funny, McGee."

In recruitment, the zone between what is just audible and what is too loud for the ear is much narrower than normal. Recruitment ears not only have trouble detecting weak sounds, but also have difficulty with noises in the middle range. But at the same time, the recruitment ear keeps its sensitivity, or even has more sensitivity, for loud sounds. The irony is that noise-deafened persons with recruitment feel discomfort when anyone shouts above the din in a noisy environment.

Recruitment also poses problems in the use of hearing aids for the noise-deafened. The hearing aid has a microphone tuned in on the world which transmits sounds to an amplifier connected to a tiny loudspeaker built into an earplug and directed at the eardrum. A serious problem is that the hearing aid has to amplify sounds so that they are loud enough to be heard by the impaired ear; and at that level, the sounds can produce discomfort.

Hearing aids pose yet another problem, as was pointed out by Dr. Johansson of Stockholm. That is, if not properly fitted and electronically fashioned to the patient's hearing pattern, they can actually induce *further* hearing loss. "The output capacity of hearing aids is far above what is considered a hazardous noise, as defined in industry," he said. "Too many hearing aids are badly fitted by otologists. The loudest noise which industry is permitted for short periods of time is 120 dB, yet hearing aids can deliver 142 to 145 dB levels to the eardrum, and at frequencies of 1,000 to 3,000 Hz, which is the region most dangerous to hearing." He has designed a special kind of hearing aid which does not amplify sounds so much as it converts the frequencies of the voice, which may be inaudible to the noise-deafened, into frequencies that are audible (and usually lower). The problem with hearing aids, in Dr. Johansson's view, is that they use power where they should use finesse. "Hearing aids are bad instruments," Dr. Johansson stated. Drs. Dougherty and Welsh also expressed their displeasure: "Hearing aids for sensory deafness are not as successful as one would wish. . . . They make speech louder but do not clarify the distortion, especially if there is a wide difference in perception of high and low frequencies."

There are other damaging data on hearing aids. In 1967, for instance, two University of Connecticut researchers, Mark Ross, Ph.D., and Jay Lerman, Ph.D., after studying shifts in hearing acuity in children who wore hearing aids, concluded, "Hearing aids, therefore, should be limited in output to below 130-decibel sound pressure level. Children should be closely supervised in their use."

It is also ironic that the noise-deaf often have a problem in discriminating speech in noisy environments, as mentioned above. They have lost the ability to hear high frequencies or to hear them very well in quiet surroundings. But they also cannot hear people shouting against a noisy background; the ear becomes inaccurate in speech discrimination when sound levels reach about 80 dB, and these high frequencies just get swallowed up by the noise.

With noise deafness, as with other forms of nerve deafness, there often comes a maddening ringing in the ears, known medically as *tinnitus*. It has been described as being inside the head and sounding like a whistle or high ring. Dr.

Davis said it is "a pitch that corresponds to the borderline between sounds well heard and sounds heard poorly or not (at) all." He further suggested that it "probably represents a local irritation, the first stage of a degenerative process that has already destroyed some of the neighboring sensory cells."

Ringing in the ears is also often associated with dizzying and deafening Ménière's Disease (named after the Frenchman who first described it in 1861). But here the sound is more likely a buzz or a low-pitched roar. It usually comes and goes, and is not so likely to be steady as is the tinnitus of noise deafness.

Odd as it may be to consider, noise even has its effects on the ears of the totally deaf. In 1958, U.S. Navy and Southwestern Medical School researchers tried loud noise (up to 170 dB) on ten such people. Starting at 120 dB, the five men and five women reported feeling vibration and tickles, and experiencing warmth, pain, and dizziness. Somehow, the researchers concluded, the loud noise had its effects on inner ear structures which also generally affected their bodies.

Of course, there are other causes of hearing loss, which are not directly connected with noise: infections of the outer ear and impacted wax or foreign body in the ear canal; ruptured eardrum; those all-too-common middle ear infections (*otitis media*); general infections such as flu, mumps, and measles; pressures in the middle ear that come most commonly with flying and scuba diving; allergies that cause irritative reactions in the middle ear; otosclerosis or the overgrowth of bone around the foot of the stapes and the oval window that biologically welds them together; Ménière's Disease; blows to the head; reactions to drugs and particularly to those of the mycin series; certain growths such as cysts; the general loss of hearing that comes with aging and is known as presbycusis; and various congenital causes, such as German measles (*rubella*) infection during the first three months of fetal development.

This list is not exhaustive; it is just an outline. But thanks to advances in diagnosis, treatment, immunology, surgery, and other aspects of medical science and audiology, most of these other causes of deafness are being largely prevented or treated. Vaccines are used against flu, mumps, measles, and German measles, antibiotics for ear infections, and surgery for otosclerosis. Doctors urge better care of the cardiovascular system through diet and exercise so that the working parts of the ear don't get starved for vital blood with aging and consequent clogging of the blood vessels.

3

WHO GROWS DEAF—AND WHY

$$(((((((((\cdot)))))))))$$

That industrial noise could affect hearing has been known for more than a century. This is evident in archaic names such as boilermaker's deafness, miner's deafness, cannoneer's deafness, etc. Men in those occupations came to accept noise deafness as part of their wages. But even though the problem has been recognized for a long time, noise deafness is still a major health hazard of industry. Between 6 million and 16 million workers in the United States earn their livings under conditions that are hazardous to their hearing. What is incomprehensible is that many of these deafening situations have existed for so long. As long ago as 1830, an English researcher named Fosbrooke published his finding that blacksmiths as a group had hearing loss. Thirty years later another researcher named Weber published his reports with similar findings for boilermakers and railroaders. In

1926, a century after the English blacksmith report, scientific attention was directed at the fact that pilots of piston engine airplanes were suffering hearing loss.

In May, 1968, the U.S. Public Health Service published findings from its National Health Survey on the hearing levels of adults of different occupations, income, and educational levels. As may have been expected, American adults with more education and higher incomes (reflecting the quieter, professional nature of their occupations) had better hearing than those with less education and lower incomes (reflecting factory and other industrial workers who work in noise but who also may not get adequate medical care). But a surprising finding was that "hearing impairment was found most frequently among farmers." This seems erroneous until you think about how mechanized the farm has become. And, as a matter of fact, University of Nebraska researchers in 1968 reported that the farm tractor, in particular, "produces sound levels capable of causing permanent hearing loss when used over an extended period of time." These levels were 90 to 114 dB!

Two U.S. Public Health Service researchers, Charles D. Yaffe and Herbert H. Jones of the Division of Occupational Health, defined what high levels of noise do to the hearing of workers in Federal prison shops. They tested the noise levels of the Atlanta (Georgia) prison cotton mill; the Terre Haute (Indiana) prison woolen mill; the Leavenworth (Kansas) shoe, brush, wood furniture, and clothing factories, and printing plant; and the Lewisburg (Pennsylvania) clothing and metal furniture factories. Then they tested with audiometers the hearing of almost 2,000 inmates who worked in these plants.

The noise-level measurements were made in each plant annually from the same selected locations. The average exposures men received at the Atlanta plant over the whole sound frequency spectrum were 103 dB in the weaving department, 97 dB in the beaming department, 97 dB in the twisting department, and 96 dB in the spinning department. At the Terre Haute woolen mill, the noises were similarly loud and steady. At Leavenworth, the wood furniture factory noises were louder, but the noise was slightly less loud in the clothing, shoe, and brush factories and in the printing plant. At Lewisburg, the metal furniture factory noises ran mostly over 100 dB, but in the 80's in the clothing factory.

The inmates were in their twenties and thirties. Yaffe and Jones over a period of seven years examined the hearing of the men in each department of these prison factories to detect and record any changes. A typical finding of theirs: "One hundred twenty-eight men in the weave room showed very substantial increases in hearing level after three months of exposure." An increase in hearing level means that sound must be louder in order to be heard.

One of Yaffe and Jones's key conclusions was that "if a steady-state type of noise exposure is severe enough to produce eventually a marked adverse effect on hearing in the speech range, a definite elevation, or deterioration, of the hearing level in the test frequencies of 3,000, 4,000, and 6,000 cps [Hz] will usually appear within a few months after the exposure begins."

The most severe noise-exposure hearing-loss combination in the prison inmates study occurred among those who worked in the weaving sections of the textile plants. This finding was internationally consistent: in all of industry the world over, this situation is one of the noisiest and most destructive of hearing. Some of the most detailed studies along these lines have been conducted in the United Kingdom. In 1963 Dr. Michael Rodda published a report of the results of his study of 45 men and women who worked in two weaving mills near Christchurch, New Zealand. These fabric weavers were exposed continuously during their working day to noise intensities of 107 to 109 dB-A. Their hearing was tested with an audiometer and the results were adjusted for their age, to compensate for the effects of aging, or presbycusis. Dr. Rodda and his colleagues found that the longer the weavers had worked in the plants, the more loss of hearing they had. Furthermore, those workers who were most susceptible to noise left the factories for other kinds of jobs. "It would appear that after a certain degree of hearing loss is attained, then the workers no longer tolerate the impairment of their health," Dr. Rodda commented. He also found that "there was no significant difference in the hearing losses for males and females," as other researchers had thought there would be.

Some of the 3,000 weavers who work the looms of the jute-weaving machines in Dundee, Scotland, have been similarly intensively studied by Dr. William Taylor and his colleagues at the University of St. Andrews, St. Andrews, and at Queen's College, Dundee. They compared the results of hearing tests on 401 women weavers and 16 retired weavers with 25 school teachers and 32 office workers. The continuous noise the Scottish weavers were exposed to was quite similar to that which the New Zealanders experienced—about 100 dB. Some of the workers had had daily diets of such noise for 52 years. Subtracting from the hearing tests the normal slight losses which come with age, Dr. Taylor found that the weavers' hearing began deteriorating heavily in the first 10 to 15 years of exposure to noise; then, during the next 10 years, hearing deteriorated further, but slightly; finally, after 20 to 25 years of noise, their hearing further and heavily deteriorated. Their hearing was most severely affected at first at 4,000 and 6,000 Hz. Through the years, the hearing loss spread to 3,000 Hz, 2,000 Hz, and 1,000 Hz. Not so the teachers and office workers.

Dr. Taylor and his research colleagues delved a bit deeper and tried to assess the effects of noise deafness on the lives of 57 women of Dundee (average age 54 years) who had been

helping weave jute in the mills' sea of noise for an average of
34 years each.

Studying their hearing loss, Dr. Taylor found:

—Half of the women had to sit up front when they attended
church or any public assembly. Another 16 percent "found it
impossible to attend church, public meetings, and cinemas."

—75 percent "had a dislike of, and an inability to use, the
telephone."

—The effect of recruitment was evident in those weavers
who lived in households where "teen-agers listened to music
played at extremely high noise levels." The music could not
be tolerated by the weavers.

—Close to two-thirds of the women used lip-reading
and/or sign language—especially on the job.

Crossing city streets was not the problem which Dr.
Taylor and his colleagues thought it would be. They concluded that "hearing appeared to be less important than
sight and many weavers had benefited by the introduction of
pedestrian crossings controlled by lights."

We noted earlier that farmers who ran tractors suffered
noise deafness. What about the brawny men whose job it is
to operate those gigantic and powerful earthmoving machines that can, and do, level whole mountainsides? Two
California state public health researchers, Fred Ottoboni,
Ch.E., and Thomas H. Milby, M.D., "wondered at the sight
of men, rendered almost insignificant in size by the huge,
rubber-tired, earthmoving equipment that they operate.
. . . Certainly, there is no one among us who had not at one
time or another watched the ubiquitous bulldozer at work."
In the summer of 1965 they and three U.S. Public Health
Service researchers (including Alexander Cohen, Ph.D.)
studied the noise and hearing of heavy-equipment operators
at sixteen construction sites in central and southern California and found the weakness of these rugged individual-

ists. Every piece of heavy equipment the researchers surveyed (with the exception of one air-conditioned cab) "was found to expose the operator to excessive noise levels." These were in the area of 100 dB. On-site hearing tests performed on 66 of these men "showed systematic and statistically significant changes in the direction of poorer hearing with increasing age and for higher frequencies. These changes persist even after correction for aging."

The findings, concluded Ottoboni and Milby, show that there is "cause for considerable concern. These findings clearly imply that unless effective remedial measures are undertaken, the vast majority of heavy equipment operators of the future will be victims of significant, noise-induced hearing loss."

The British journal, *The Lancet*, in 1960 stated: "It is surprising how indifferent a man will be to the incessant rattle of machinery, to the high-pitched whine of a saw, or to the affront from a nearby pneumatic tool or panel-beater." It cautioned its readers, "Only by direct inquiry is the physician who suspects early deafness likely to learn that the patient is subjected to intense noise at work."

Denis L. Chadwick, M.D., otolaryngologist at the University of Manchester, found this out in a study of 160 patients with hearing difficulties—122 of whom, he found, had noise deafness. Only 4 of those 122 "said they considered noise to be responsible," he was amazed to learn. Most of these noise-deafened persons worked in noisy machine shops or factories or with noisy machinery of some kind. In addition, some had noisy hobbies—clay-pigeon shooting, game shooting, motorcycles, and sports cars.

Dr. Chadwick joined the chorus criticizing the Wilson Committee (appointed in 1960 by the Queen to survey Great Britain's national noise problem and recommend solutions, which it did in 1963) for "failing to lay sufficient emphasis on the causal relationship between noise and deafness" and

for, instead, concentrating on the psychological aspects of
noise. He sees, on the average, one noise-deafened patient a
week! Yet, he concludes, "That a noise hazard exists in many
factories is still often ignored, the introduction of satisfactory hearing conservation programmes tardy and effective
noise reduction expensive." (Since his 1966 report, England
has introduced new legislation to help protect workers
against noise. More on this later.)

There have been many other studies of deafness induced
by noisy working conditions. Here is but a small sampling:

—In one moderately noisy industrial complex, 20 percent
of the employees suffered noise deafness, according to
Northwestern University Civil Engineering Professor
Edward R. Hermann.

—"Some ear doctors have observed that the left [window-
side] ear of [American] truck drivers becomes hard of
hearing more frequently than the right," according to a news
release from the American Medical Association.

—Fifteen residents who lived near Northern Illinois University and who had low-noise occupations were asked to
mow their lawns for 45 minutes with their own lawnmowers.
Their hearing was tested with an audiometer in quiet rooms
of their homes before and after the mowing. The average at-
ear noise level of the mowers was 97 dB-C. All but two of
the subjects had temporary threshold shifts in their hearing
after mowing, and more than half reported that their ears
rang after the mowing.

—High-speed turbine drills used by most modern dentists
now produce shrill noise of enough power to affect hearing,
according to Dutch and Finnish studies.

As alluded to earlier, avocations—and especially those
involving firearms—can be just as dangerous to hearing as
factory and machine noise. The military establishments of
Great Britain, the United States, and other nations have
learned the benefits of protecting the ears of men who work

around big weapons. Slowly, the military is also learning of the danger to hearing of small arms, thanks to the efforts of men such as R. Ross A. Coles, M.D., of the Royal Navy, who also heads the Institute of Sound and Vibration Research at the University of Southampton. For instance, he pointed out, hearing loss is the second leading cause of the rejection of young men who apply for aviation service in the British navy (the first cause is eye defects). This is quite ironic because the hearing losses are noise-induced, often occurring when these young men shoot weapons while cadets! Another European military hearing researcher, Dr. Reinier Plomp, physicist with the Institute for Perception RVO-TNO, Soesterberg, the Netherlands, has done parallel studies, measuring the noise of arms on the firing line and assessing the amount of hearing losses thus induced. So has David C. Hodge of Aberdeen Proving Ground, Maryland. More recently, Herbert H. Jones and Alexander Cohen of the U.S. Public Health Service in Cincinnati conducted such studies among policemen in that city.

These studies show, first of all, that even hand-held weapons—pistols, rifles, shotguns, and automatic weapons—produce tremendously loud impulses of sound—from 130 dB up. The gun noise is lowest behind the weapon and highest in front of the weapon. Temporary threshold shift and permanent hearing damage seldom occur in the right ear of right-handed rifle shooters because that is the ear pointing backward, away from the noise and is also in the sound shadow created by the head. In out-of-doors shooting, such as hunting, the right ear seldom suffers, while the left ear suffers heavily. But the right ear can suffer heavily on a firing line—not from the rifleman's own noise, but from that of his neighbor. On indoor shooting ranges, both ears are in danger because the high sound pressure of each shot is reflected around the room and does not easily dissipate or attenuate, as it does in the open. Noise deafness from guns is most likely to affect those ranges of hearing that are not easily noticed. Because of the very high-frequency components of the impulse noise, hearing loss occurs at about 6,000 Hz and seldom below that, so that, as Dr. Plomp found, "speech intelligibility is affected only to a small degree."

Dr. Plomp's opinion well explained the results of a survey of sports hunters' hearing conducted by G. Dekle Taylor, M.D., an otolaryngologist; and Everett Williams, Sc.M., director of vital statistics for the Florida State Board of Health; both of Jacksonville, Florida. The survey involved 103 hunters and gun club members who answered a questionnaire. Almost none wore ear protectors. Interestingly enough, 58 of them, in answer to a question, said they were not suffering any hearing loss. Yet hearing tests showed that they did so suffer. "Thus a majority of sports hunters had some hearing loss in the higher frequencies of which they were not aware," concluded the Florida researchers. Also of interest was the fact that left ears were generally more impaired than were right ears. Commenting on this study, Dr. Coles said it added strong support to his "own efforts in Great Britain to bring about a greater awareness of the auditory hazards of sports guns and of means of their prevention." Particularly hazardous to hearing, he found, is the 12-gauge shotgun, although the .38 pistol is close behind in its deafening dangers. As with other kinds of noise, the persistence of exposure is one of the factors that can turn T.T.S. to permanent hearing loss. As a result, skeet shooters and weapons instructors are more likely to be noise-deaf than are once-a-year deer hunters.

Music is another pastime which sorely and seriously threatens our hearing. One wag has suggested that labels should be used on records saying, "Warning: Modern Music May Be Hazardous to Your Hearing." Unfortunately, the slogan would be true, but not only for modern music. It applies to any loud music, and even classical music gets loud. The orchestra musician who sits in front of a loud brass or reed instrument all of his professional life is exposed to very loud sounds, often for hours on end and often for days each week. He will just as certainly experience T.T.S. and then noise deafness as will the Scottish weaver or the weapons instructor. However, with today's electronically amplified music, the audience and dancers are now exposed to the same (or even higher) sound levels as the musicians. So the difference between classical and modern music is the number of people exposed to the hazard. The new sound of music is thousands of times more epidemiologically dangerous than is the old sound. In fact, one authority, James M. Flugrath of Memphis State University Speech and Hearing Clinic, told the Acoustical Society of America in November, 1968, "It is quite possible that due to modern amplified rock-and-roll music, we are raising a nation of teen-agers who will be hard-of-hearing before they reach what they consider old (30 years old)."

Charles P. Lebo, M.D., and Kenward S. Oliphant, E.E., of the Department of Otolaryngology at the University of California Medical School in San Francisco, in 1968 measured the sound levels of a symphony orchestra in fortissimo and compared their findings with similar data from rock-and-roll bands. The symphonic passages measured were "Bydlo," "Limoges—Le Marché," and "La Grande Porte de Kiev" from Moussorgsky's "Pictures at an Exhibition."

"The symphony was usually below 70 dB, while the bands were seldom below that level," Dr. Lebo and Engineer Oliphant reported. Conversely, "while the rock groups were usually louder than 95 dB in the lower frequencies, the symphony rarely achieved such levels."

Lebo and Oliphant, together with John Garrett, M.D., also conducted one of four 1967–1968 surveys of noise deaf-

ness and modern electronic bands which will be detailed
here. Theirs was made in "two typical San Francisco Bay
Area rock-and-roll establishments frequented almost exclusively by teen-agers and young adults, of whom many fall
into a group popularly designated as 'hippies.' " The sound
levels they measured at the centers of the auditoriums ran
from 100 to 116 dB-A. Their report concluded, "We believe
we have demonstrated that the noise levels produced by
some live rock-and-roll bands with the aid of high ampli-
fication unmistakably exceed those considered safe for prolonged exposure."

In interviews with a newspaper science writer, Dr. Lebo
revealed that he wore earmuffs during the experiment. Dr.
Garrett didn't and, as a result, he said, "I couldn't hear my
watch tick for three hours afterward." He had, of course,
T.T.S.

Flugrath measured the sound levels of ten rock-and-roll
bands which performed over a period of time in a dance hall
that catered to teen-agers. "When the music was being
played the chaperones could not be understood even when
shouting. They also complained of ringing in their ears
which lasted long after the dance was over. To an audiolo-
gist, ringing in the ears (called tinnitus) is an obvious sign
that the person's hearing has been damaged." Furthermore,
he said, "It is highly probable that many of the teen-agers in
the dance hall had their hearing damaged."

Momentarily casting aside technical measurement units,
such as the decibel, he explained that "The loudest dance
band tested played at a volume equivalent to the sound of a
loud horn at a distance of a few feet. Imagine having your
head under the hood of your car and someone leaning on the
horn for a couple of hours. I guarantee that you will have
ringing in your ears and your hearing might be damaged.
Try this a couple of times a week (teen-agers sometimes go
to dances two or three times a week) and soon you will

constantly hear the ringing in your ears and certain speech sounds will become very hard to understand. Eventually all speech will become difficult to understand."

Charles Speaks and David A. Nelson, of the University of Minnesota's Division of Speech Science, studied the sound levels of ten rock-and-roll bands in the Minneapolis area and the hearing acuity of the musicians. In a report to the Acoustical Society of America they said they found that the noise levels of the bands ranged from 105 to 120 dB—"only about 10 decibels less than the maximum noise level observed in a boiler shop." But not always, since the level varied over a 15 to 20 decibel range.

Speaks and Nelson gave before-and-after hearing tests to 25 musicians in these bands—the first an hour before playing, the second 30 minutes after a four-hour playing session. They found that six of the musicians already had some permanent hearing loss, ranging from mild to severe. Another five showed temporary hearing losses that ranged from 10 to 25 dB, considered "likely to incur some permanent damage after a few years of the same nightly exposure."

In all fairness, the Minneapolis researchers said, every one of the six with permanent hearing damage "revealed a history of other kinds of noise exposure, of which hunting and trap shooting were the most common." Some people, it seems, have suicidal tendencies toward their own hearing. Psychiatrists could well investigate this sort of behavior, which could be termed "suisonicidal" (sui, for one's self; sonic, for sound; cidal, for killing or destroying).

One night in 1968, George T. Singleton, M.D., chief of otolaryngology at the University of Florida College of Medicine, Gainesville, picked up his 14-year-old daughter Marsha at a dance. In the car on the way home, he was dismayed to find that she couldn't hear what he said to her. It was obviously some kind of hearing loss. He hoped it was temporary. He recalled the complaints of the loud music from the chaperones, then decided to study the situation seriously. He enlisted the aid of Dr. Kenneth C. Pollock and Dr. Everett Scroggie of the university's health center, and Dr. William Cutler, chief of audiology at the Gainesville Veterans Administration Hospital. Ten 14-year-olds were tested an hour before going to another dance, and then immediately thereafter. The researchers found their hearing was quite normal before; but after the dance, the teen-agers admitted ringing in their ears, a muffled feeling, and a state of exhaustion. Their average hearing loss was 11½ dB, with one boy registering a 35 dB loss.

The noise-level meter reading at the dance itself ran as high as 120 dB near the musicians and 107 dB at the center of the dance floor. Said the investigators, "It was necessary to move outside the building—some 60 feet from the band— before the noise level dropped below the 90 dB specified by the American Medical Association as being tolerable and safe for most persons." [Obviously, an old figure.]

Comments from the 14-year-olds revealed they like the noise in spite of the hearing loss dangers: "The sounds embalm you . . . they numb you . . . you don't want to hear others talk . . . you don't want to talk . . . you don't know what to say to each other anyway. . . ."

Dr. Pollack, together with a Houston Speech and Hearing Center research couple, Dr. James F. Jerger and his wife Susan, extended the music-and-deafness investigation by studying the hearing of three additional groups of young people. Group A consisted of five 17-to-23-year-olds who had played their loud music together for two years. Group B was four 14-to-16-year-olds who had been together for a year.

Tested before they played one night, three of the five older musicians showed permanent hearing losses; after four hours of playing, four of the five showed T.T.S. Every member of the younger musical group showed some T.T.S. after playing and one subject registered a high 38 dB loss at the 3,000 Hz tone.

Dr. Pollack and the Jergers also tested the before-and-after hearing of four young men (14 to 16 years old) recruited from the audience. Their temporary hearing losses were much less than those of the musicians, but their tests showed T.T.S. at 4,000 Hz, which, the researchers said, is "so characteristic of noise-induced loss in its earliest stages."

They concluded that "the prevalence of permanent hearing loss in the Group A musicians . . . should alarm those contemplating regular participation in this type of group. Further, parents of youngsters who regularly attend rock-and-roll dances should be alerted to the possibility that some degree of hearing loss might result."

Robert A. Larabell, architectural acoustic consultant in Phoenix, Arizona, also studied the loudness of pop music and the effects on teen-agers' hearing—and he didn't like the results. "I have two teen-agers of my own and although I try to be tolerant of what teen-agers consider quote music unquote, I have forbidden my kids to listen to loud, live bands, just as I would dissuade them from drag racing at 85 miles an hour on the city streets."

He said, "I wouldn't have the kids change their—pardon the expression—music, but I would have them turn it down. There should be governors on their amplifiers." A singer with one Phoenix band (John Fitzgerald of The Caravelles) had another solution: he secretly wore earmuffs under the flowing tresses of his masculine hair!

The reason that rock-and-roll bands are so much louder than the dance bands of old, and so much louder than orchestras, is that they are electronic. Their instruments are equipped with built-in microphones, which pick up the sounds and send them to electronic amplifiers, which then multiply the sound electrically and feed it to loudspeakers that blare out the amplified sounds. The loudspeakers are alongside the musicians on the stage and are aimed at the audience.

So there are really two reasons for the loud music. One is

that the teen-agers like it and want it (and who, except a teen, knows *why?*). The other is that electronics engineers have designed, and equipment manufacturers have provided, the devilish instruments by which the long-haired and swivel-hipped musicians can deliver this sonic mayhem. As organs and other instruments of "refined" music have gone electronic, so have the instruments of rock-and-roll. And the leading manufacturers of electronic organs, as might be expected, took the *grand jeté* into rock-and-roll electronic instrumentation rather effortlessly and quite successfully. One of the leaders has been Baldwin Piano & Organ Co. of Chicago, now not only a major producer of pianos and electronic organs, but of electric guitars and amplifiers. ("Musical Muscle for Today's Big Beat," says its *Yellow Pages*' ad.) The pianos and organs are kept sedately on the lower floors of the store. But upstairs are the pop instruments. There on display and ready for demonstration is the Baldwin Exterminator. Positioned against a back wall, and chest high, it boasts 250 watts peak power. On its back side is a red label which states, *"The Baldwin Company does not guarantee against loss or impairment of hearing due to use of this amplifier."* A sales manager of Baldwin explained that while the company is concerned about the potential of these instruments for causing hearing loss, they have to give the customers what they want. "The kids really go for the big sound. The bigger we make these amplifiers, the faster they go. Some of the teen-agers are dropping $1,200 and $1,500 for equipment," he said.

Perhaps to our new word, *suisonicidal,* we ought to add another coined word, *homisonicidal,* for the willful destruction of the hearing of others, especially by musicians.

Noise and hearing researchers at the University of Tennessee, Knoxville, have two unique and additional kinds of data to show how threatening our recreational noises are.

These are concerned with the hearing levels of teens and with the specific physiologically damaging effects of their music, their motorcycles, and their other noisy pastimes.

David M. Lipscomb, Ph.D., director of that university's Audiology Clinical Services, led a team of researchers who tested the hearing of 3,000 Knoxville high school students and 1,680 incoming freshmen at the university. "We were shocked to find that the hearing of many of these students had already deteriorated to a level of the average 65-year-old person," he said. His findings (15 dB loss at 2,000 Hz):

Sixth grade:	xxxx	3.8%
Ninth grade:	xxxxxxxxxxx	11.0%
Twelfth grade:	xxxxxxxxxxxxx	12.6%
College frosh:	xxxxxxxxxxxxxxxxxxxxxxxxxxxxxxxxxxxx	34.8%

Dr. Lipscomb's team found, as had Speaks and Nelson in Minneapolis, that the youngsters with hearing loss often had been exposed not only to loud music, but to motorbike and gunshot noises, as well. The noises worked synergistically on the youngsters' hearing, much as other poisons in our environment work villainously together toward destroying our health.

Dr. Lipscomb recorded on tape the music being played at a Knoxville discotheque, then played it back at the identical 120 dB level (138 dB peaks) at which it had been recorded. The subject this time was a guinea pig. Both of the animal's ears were exposed to the played-back music for 44 hours. Then the left ear was plugged and the right ear kept open to the blasting music for 44 more hours over the remainder of a three-month period. The listening sessions, incidentally, were spaced to simulate the exposure of a teen-ager—approximately four sessions a few days apart.

Dr. Lipscomb microscopically examined the cochlear hair cells of the animal after the test and found what he may have expected to find. It was obvious, he said, "that you don't lose a cell every time you listen to five minutes of this rock music. Apparently, however, a point is eventually reached where it seems the ear can take no more of the stress and it begins to deteriorate."

Under the microscope, at 1,000 times magnification, the cells of the 44-hour ear appeared quite normal. But the 88-hour ear's cells "had collapsed and shriveled up like peas."

Commenting on this two-pronged finding, Dr. Lipscomb said, "We have apparently reached the point that the young people are losing sufficient hearing to jeopardize their occupational potential. We must enter into a program of safety or the consequences are going to be pretty dire."

As a start, he suggested turning the volume controls down.

4

WHY NOISE ANNOYS YOU

$((((((((((\cdot))))))))))$

Even when it does not deafen, noise can invade sleeping as well as waking hours, distract attention from important tasks, so frustrate verbal communication between human beings as to be maddening. The major positive purpose noise serves—when it is not a real warning—is that it reassures us that we are alive. "A silent world is not possible, nor, on the available evidence is it very desirable," wrote Michael Rodda, Ph.D., of the University of Manchester. "Studies on sensory deprivation have indicated that for audition, as well as for other sensory modalities, a complete lack of suitable stimulus leads to a loss of orientation." This is something that the deaf struggle with daily, of course.

Richard Held, Ph.D., of Massachusetts Institute of Technology, an authority on spatial orientation, has shown how noise, like silence, acts to disorient us who hear by removing sound cues which our ears could use to readily distinguish parts of our environments. By masking these cues, noise produces the same effects as silence.

Whether noise annoys or not depends mostly on what it means to us, the milieu in which it is heard, our mood, and how used to it we are. Still, there are objective guides for predicting whether any noise will be annoying. The most annoying sounds are those that are:

> —Loud—the louder the noise, the more annoying it is;
> —High-pitched—upwards from about 1,500 Hz;
> —Intermittent and irregular—the more randomly the noise occurs, the more annoying it is;
> —Produced from a hidden or moving source—the more uncertain you are about where noise is coming from, the more annoying it is;
> —Inappropriate to your own activities—we seldom object to the noise *we* make;
> —Unexpected—like sonic booms, noise can startle.

The definition of noise most commonly used, in fact, expresses our psychological reaction to it, as has been pointed out by Australian Alan Bell of the World Health Organization (W.H.O.) Expert Advisory Panel on Occupational Health. In his book on noise, he stated, "Noise has been defined as any sound that is regarded or treated as a nuisance. The degree of annoyance is not necessarily related to the intensity of sound. . . . The noise of racing cars may be pleasant to their drivers but maddening to those living near the track. . . . Attitude of mind and environment are of major importance."

Neither are dissonance and noise synonymous. Most Occidentals consider Oriental quarter tones discordant and even noisy. Dissonant sound is more likely to be classified by westerners as noise, and consonant sound less likely. But, as Dr. Rodda pointed out, "The final classification, however, will be the additive effects of many systems, internal and external to the organism, and which are subject to temporal mechanisms. We can think of the human observer as having a variable tolerance level for sounds: if the sound crosses this tolerance level it is classified as noise, but whether or not this occurs is a function of the observer as well as the auditory stimulus."

What makes noise music? It depends on culture and geography, on time and adaptation, even on conformity. Wagner's first operas were received coolly by the critics, who considered his forceful and radically different musicodramas as so much noise. An even older master, Beethoven, had his First Symphony called "confused explosions" by a Leipzig critic in 1800. As Walter A. Rosenblith of Massachusetts Institute of Technology said, "Some of our contemporary composers have not yet been graduated from the noise category. In other words, one era's noise may be the next era's music." The truth of this comes easily when one remembers his parents' reaction to the popular music of his youth. If you are a parent, think about your own reaction to your children's favorite tunes.

"The annoying effects of a number of noises, all equally loud, will depend much more on the personality of the recipient than on the character of the noise," stated the 1963 report of England's Wilson Committee. Further, it said,

> The annoyance due to noise may perhaps be thought of essentially as the resentment we feel at an intrusion into the physical privacy which we have for the moment marked out as our own, or into our thoughts or emotions. From another point of view, the annoyance may be ascribed to the "information" which sounds may carry from the source to the recipient. The physical energy in the noise of a creaking door, a crying baby, or a distant party may be very small, and if distributed in the form of random noise probably would be quite unnoticed. But it may convey manifold suggestions of alarm, neglect, sadness, loneliness; and so

in some people it has an emotional effect all out of proportion to its physical intensity.

Francis I. Catlin, M.D., of the Johns Hopkins Medical
Institutions, Baltimore, explained that "certain sounds have
value judgments attached to them by virtue of cultural
factors. For instance, some sounds are considered unacceptable at the dinner table or in public places. Other sounds,
such as an airplane engine may be undesirable if one is
sleeping near the airport. During wartime, many of us found
the very same sound of an aircraft engine to be most com-
forting. Hence, the same sound may be desirable one day
and undesirable the next, depending upon circumstantial
factors."

An editorial in the *British Medical Journal* in 1965
pointed out that annoyance "can occur when a person becomes aware of even a very slight noise, such as a dripping
tap or when ice cream chimes are sounded in a housing
estate." Such reactions to noise are believed due to the
interference with one's privacy and are "akin to the reactions
of an animal to an intrusion into its territory."

This is apparently what happened in three instances reported recently in the press. The following appeared in
Chicago's American of March 6, 1967:

NOISE OF PARTY LEADS TO SLAYING

Gene F. Avant, 37, of 6216 Dorchester Ave., was killed
by four blasts from a shotgun last night during a
drinking party in an apartment at 6619 Blackstone
Ave. Other guests accused R— L. N—, 37, occupant
of another apartment in the building who objected
to the noise. N— was to appear in Felony court today
on a murder charge.

Something similar happened in this murder reported in
The New York Times of April 16, 1968:

INNIS'S SON, 13, KILLED IN BRONX

Negro accused of Shooting Boy
in Dispute over Noise
The 13-year-old son of Roy Innis, the militant associate
national director of the Congress of Racial Equality,
was shot and killed last night outside a Bronx apartment house a short distance from his mother's home.

The police quickly took a 49-year-old Negro man
into custody.

According to the police, the boy, Roy Innis, Jr., was
playing with his brother, Alexander, 12, and two other
boys outside 1142 Union Avenue about 7:45 P.M. As
the youngsters shouted, wrestled and raced in and out
of the three-story building, the police said, a man
leaned from his second-floor apartment and called:
"Stop the noise."

When the boys failed to heed the warning, the
police said, the man came downstairs with a pistol and,
as the boys started to run, fired a shot that struck
young Innis in the back.

And there was this item, carried by United Press International on October 28, 1968:

BLAMES SUICIDE BID ON 11 NOISY CHILDREN

Palermo, Italy, Oct. 27 (UPI)

Biovanni Gatto, 44, attempted suicide with an over-
dose of drugs today because his 11 children made too
much noise while he was watching the Olympic games
on television, police said. Gatto was taken to a hospital
where doctors pumped his stomach and placed him
under observation.

Actually, animals react less aggressively to noise than man
does. For instance, a movie made in Spain was threatened
with abortion because the filming location happened to be
near a big ranch devoted to the breeding of fighting bulls.

The location was chosen for filming Yul Brynner as Pancho
Villa. Norma Lee Browning reported in the Chicago *Tribune*
of October 30, 1967:

> Spain's famous fighting bulls are skittish about strange
> noises and the owners took a dim view of Pancho's 300
> clattering horsemen and the helicopter zooming down
> with a cameraman.
>   The producer pointed across the river at a cordon of
> armed sentries on the ranch property. . . . "They've
> got their guns pointed right at us, loaded with buck-
> shot, ready to shoot."

An English survey of the effect of aircraft noise on animals, commissioned by the National Farmers' Union, was
completed in 1967. The most common findings were that
such noise made cows abort and hens refuse to lay eggs, all
because of fright. One case involved a herd of cattle stam-
peded toward a ravine by some low-flying planes. The first
two cows fell into the ravine and consequently had to be
destroyed. A 5-year-old black and white sheepdog named
Bonnie received the fright of her life from Hunter (!) jets as
she was working her herd up a 1,250-foot mountain near
Radnorshire. She ran straight back to the farmhouse, her tail
between legs, and never again left home for the hills.

Animals on ten farms near Edwards Air Force Base, California, were observed for their reactions to the noise of
American subsonic and supersonic aircraft in 1966. A few
breeding race horses jumped up and galloped around their
paddock; some dairy cattle bellowed, yet did not alter their
output of milk; but chickens, turkeys, and pheasants flew,
ran, crowded, and cowered and apparently lessened their
egg production. Other studies showed that swine and mink
were little affected by aircraft noise. Federal agriculture
researchers thereby concluded that "the booms had very
little effect on the larger species of farm animals."

On the other hand, experiments at Stanford Medical Center, California, showed that noise affects at least one kind of behavior in animals, that of eating. Neurologist Irving Kupferman happened upon the effects of noise during some experiments with rats. He was training the animals to eat in response to visual signals. But the background din affected the way they sniffed their food, ran around, and came back to eat it. After being starved for two days, the rats were allowed to approach some food on the third day, while Dr. Kupferman and his assistants clicked, clapped, and whistled. Only 18 of 40 rats ate anything. On the fourth day, all of the animals ate something when noise was made. "Some animals ate only during the sound stimuli," Dr. Kupferman reported in the British journal *Nature*. "In general, low-intensity sounds (60 dB) induced chewing, higher intensities (70 dB) induced movements toward the food, and still higher intensities (80 dB) induced active eating (clicks and whistles measured with a General Radio 1551-B sound-level meter, room noise 54 dB). The vigor of the patterns was related to the intensity and duration of the stimulation. A series of clicks was sometimes associated with chewing motions in exact synchrony with the stimuli. . . . Some animals abruptly ceased eating on termination of the sound, and could be started and stopped repeatedly."

Human beings, like laboratory animals, who live in noisy environments soon become unaware of their noisy surroundings and so they never think of attributing any changes in their behavior or moods to the noise which invades their body and mind. One reason this is so is the interesting if not dangerous brain trick called habituation. Simply stated, this phenomenon is: if the noise is repeated over and over, the brain begins to lose its responsiveness to it. In other words, the brain does to noise what it does to odors, such as that of cooking gas, which we no longer smell after a few minutes of exposure. Immersed in a noisy environment, our brains soon stop alerting us to the noise—but only *that* noise. Thankfully, a noise does not dull our brain's responsiveness to all sounds. Even though you sleep in a noisy environment, certain distinct sounds can still alert you. This explains, pointed out Dr. Etienne Grandjean of Zurich, Switzerland, "why a mother can ignore all sorts of noise but is wakened up by any small noise of her child: through habituation she learns to distinguish between irrelevant traffic noise and the significant sound manifestation of her child."

Something similar happens to patients in hospitals. Robert M. Cunningham, Jr., editor of *The Modern Hospital* magazine, says "the noise out there [in hospital corridors] is just below combat level." Yet physicist Vern Knudsen tells about being treated some years ago for duodenal bleeding (probably an ulcer) in a hospital which was located near a trucking route. It was the sound of traffic on the roads and not in the hospital corridor which annoyed him. "I thought it would drive me out of my mind," he said. "When the noise would come, I'd feel a pain in my stomach." When he left the hospital, the former chancellor of the University of California at Los Angeles began a long career as a noise-fighter. (A British public opinion survey found that by itself traffic noise was as annoying as all the combined noises of aircraft, trains, industry, demolition and construction, domestic appliances, neighbors, children, radio, television, assorted bells, alarms, and pets. A Dutch survey of apartment dwellers found that 25 percent were annoyed by traffic noise, 12 percent by playing children's noise, and 10 percent by slamming doors.)

Street traffic provoked 25 percent of the noise complaints compiled from 114 patients during a survey at Royal Northern Hospital in London, England. According to Dr. Cecily Statham's study, the most annoying traffic noises were "in particular the sudden explosive acceleration of motorcycles." But in-hospital noises, and not necessarily loud ones, are the most annoying to patients: "other people talking, snoring, and calling out . . . banging of doors, clanking of bed pans, dropping things on the floors in wards and corridors, the noise of carts, bells, buzzers, elevator gates, and the scraping of chairs, tables, and beds on the floor or wall."

Another study of hospital noise in London, conducted at King's College Hospital by Drs. P. Hugh-Jones and A. R. Tanser, and the administrator, C. Whitby, found that 21 percent of 174 patients interviewed complained about noise. "Those who mentioned the source of the noise were particularly troubled by other patients who were very ill or mentally disturbed, and by the telephone ringing at night."

A study of noise at a 500-bed Birmingham, England, hospital found factory-loud noises at nursing stations and subway-loud noises in nearby service areas. Still, it wasn't just the loudness of the noise that was disturbing, but the environment in which it was heard. Thus, "sounds which may be almost welcomed during the day cannot be tolerated at night . . . a mere sound during the day becomes a noise at night and a noise during the day becomes a catastrophe at night." Voices, and not necessarily loud ones, often were the most disturbing, especially if from corridors. "The behavior of most people is noticeably different when in the presence of sick patients than it is in the hospital corridor, where the patient is out of sight and out of mind. Absurd though it may seem, many visitors and some members of the staff tend to forget that a hospital contains patients and is run solely for their benefit," the report stated.

An American survey of hospital patients' reaction to noise similarly found that noise can annoy simply by the disturbing *information* it conveys. The summary of the survey findings stated, ". . . the sounds noted as most annoying are caused by the use of television and radio by other patients. Second, and in fact prevalent in most hospitals, is staff conversation in the halls. In some cases, as evidenced by the comments, this was objected to not because of the noise level but because of the information communicated, such as discussion of other patients, operations, and symptoms. Third is the annoyance caused by other patients in distress, moaning, or calling for a nurse. Distress sounds, because of their nature rather than their loudness, are annoying to others. The most annoying sounds are not necessarily the loudest, as measured with instruments. Rather, it is their frequent repetition or their character which the patients find disturbing."

A metal pan dropped on the floor is louder but not as annoying to patients as voices which page doctors or talk about cases. Once patients are asleep, it takes high-intensity noises to awaken them: "the dropped pan, the shrill telephone bell, the sick patient calling out, and staff noise in corridors."

As an aside, this survey of noises, conducted in eight sample hospitals by acoustical consultants Lewis S. Goodfriend and R. L. Cardinell, for the U.S. Public Health Service, found that carts were "one of the most frequent noise sources." This included food, medicine, linen, and trash carts, as well as "hospitality" carts, which were found to be, inhospitably enough, "particularly noisy, because of lack of wheel maintenance."

Finally, outsiders were also a source of annoyance to American patients. Said the report, "During visiting hours at some hospitals, one might think the hospitals were resort hotels, judging by the noise generated in corridors and rooms. Despite various admonitory signs and posters requesting quiet, people are inclined to forget that there may be patients who are trying to sleep or rest during visiting hours. The same persons would not talk above a whisper in a public library."

The survey indeed showed the truth of the premise on which it was made: "Since comfort of an ill person is often related to a quiet environment, it was felt that noisy conditions might have an adverse effect on patients' comfort and morale." This can be applied to Florence Nightingale's admonition, ". . . the very first requirement in a hospital is that it should do the sick no harm." Thus, this comment from a Wisconsin psychiatrist (Dr. H. A. Denzel of Winnebago State Hospital) is particularly appropriate:

> While visiting several mental hospitals, as a psychiatrist, in Europe last summer, I was surprised to find that the noise level in these institutions was much lower than in equivalent hospitals in this country. Everybody talked in a subdued voice, double doors were common, and paging was done by light rather than by loudspeaker. It appeared to me that, as a result of this sedating atmosphere, patients were generally calmer.

(He must not have visited London hospitals!)

So much for hospitals, where people, because they are sick or injured, are particularly sensitive to and easily annoyed by noise. But whether we are hospital patients or not, the most annoying sounds are those that we feel have no good reason for existence. Research around the world shows that whether or not noise annoys us depends greatly on (1) our attitude toward the noise, and (2) our life style, or how used to noise we are. A 1948 study made in England showed that the sound of a delivery truck is less disturbing to the person receiving the delivery than to his neighbor; likewise, the noise of neighbors' pets are likely to be more annoying than your own. On the whole, we are more likely to be disturbed by others' noise than by our own.

Anders Kajland, a Swedish expert on traffic noises and their effects on people, has headed several studies, the results of which show the effects of attitudes on annoyance threshold. The studies were performed both in the field and at his laboratories at the Karolinska Institute in Stockholm. One study (unpublished as of this writing) involved 1,000 persons who lived in homes near highways. It was done in two parts. First, the noise level (or volume) was measured and recorded continuously at one-tenth second intervals just outside the homes. Second, the residents were asked questions about their life and their environment in what is known as a "masked interview," without their being aware of the goal of the researchers. Among the questions asked was, "In general, does anything bother you?" which gave an opportunity for the answer, "Noise." Later in the interview, they were asked whether specific noises—airplanes, traffic, etc.— annoyed them, and, if so, how much. Other questions were related to their state of health. One of the most interesting findings of this study is that a significant number of those interviewed who found traffic noise annoying also spoke separately of their own medical symptoms. Those annoyed mostly said the noise interfered with their viewing of television, their reading, and their general concentration. They also complained about bad stomachs, headaches, sleeplessness, and nervousness.

Other studies at Karolinska, and in the field, conducted with Kajland's colleagues, Erland Jonsson and Stefan Sörensen, showed that changing a person's attitude to the noise under laboratory situations can change his personal reaction to that noise. In the laboratory study, subjects listened to tape-recorded sounds of traffic or airplanes. When they were told that local traffic or air-command authorities were doing what they could to reduce the noise, they somehow found the noise less annoying than subjects who were told that these authorities were not interested in the public's problems. The field experiment was done in a residential community near the Swedish Air Force Station at Malmsätt. Those residents who were told about the military defense effectiveness of the aircraft (SAAB and F-3 jets) and who were given a book, *50th Anniversary of the Swedish Air Force*, found the sounds of the jets far less annoying than another group of residents who had not been so approached. "The results of the study show that by changing attitudes to the source, one can attain also a change in reactions," the researchers conclude.

Kajland and his co-workers collaborated with an Italian researcher, Bruno Paccagnella, in a two-country study of noise annoyance and attitudes. They interviewed people who lived in second-floor apartments which faced busy streets in both Stockholm, Sweden, and Ferrara, Italy. Measurements made in the apartments showed that the average noise level in Ferrara was about 6 decibels louder (dB-A) than in Stockholm. Despite this, the interviewers found, Stockholmers are more annoyed by traffic noises than are Ferrarans. "Summing up, we can say that the difference obtained in annoyance reactions between the Ferrara and Stockholm [residents] would seem to be due to differences in living conditions, and to different requirements and evaluations in respect of motor traffic noise as part of the physical environment," the investigators wrote.

Alexander Cohen of Cincinnati, Ohio, the U.S. Public Health Service's top noise researcher, said, "Complaints to noise in communities impacted by noise are more numerous in the evening, presumably because sleep and relaxation are being interfered with. Conversely, an individual will tolerate certain sounds if there is an advantage associated with them. The comforts derived from air conditioning apparently outweigh the noise produced by such units. The economic values to the community of nearby factories or airports may partially offset the noise-nuisance produced by such noise sources. Along with the above factors, there are many differences in individuals with regard to their ability to tolerate noise. Some individuals complain about all kinds of noise, indeed any kind of annoyance. One study has reported, for example, that many people who were greatly affected by aircraft noise were preoccupied with other physical problems in their communities including other kinds of noises, litter, air pollution. There is some support for the notion that people who have adjustment problems also seem to be more affected by noise than others."

Or to paraphrase Lincoln, as D. E. Broadbent, one of England's leading noise researchers, did, "some noises are annoying to almost all people, and probably any particular noise is annoying to some person." Broadbent has also stated two general rules about noise annoyance: the proportion of people who become annoyed rises as the loudness of the noise increases, and a noise believed to be preventable will produce more complaints from the community than one regarded as inevitable.

At the second meeting of the Committee on Hearing and Bio-Acoustics (called C.H.A.B.A.) jointly sponsored by the Armed Forces and the National Research Council, held at Armour Research Foundation, Chicago, in 1954, Dr. Howard C. Hardy of Armour noted that airplane noise is not complained about in some communities simply because the general noise background is already so high. Further, he said,

> Many household devices, including vacuum cleaners, kitchen mixers, air conditioners, refrigerators and fluorescent lights, make quite a lot of noise. Each of these devices appears to have its own maximum acceptable noise level. In other words, people will accept noise levels of 90 dB from a vacuum cleaner but will complain if a fluorescent light goes much above 40 dB. This presents a rather large sliding acceptance scale. In contrast to the acceptance of the Chicago Transit Authority at about 85 dB are the great complaints made about the 30 dB noise level produced by a power plant in Miami, Florida. Similarly, people accept truck noise to a considerable extent, and yet when

the very big and noisy trucks from the West Coast invaded the Middle West, many complaints were received.

That same C.H.A.B.A. conference heard from Col. Harry Shoup of Truax Field, near Madison, Wisconsin, that during the Korean War when a squadron of F-86 jet interceptors were stationed there, ". . . the complaint level rose precipitously, and continued until the situation became critical. Complaints were worse in the summer, and each day reached a peak just after lunch when babies were beginning to take their naps." Col. Shoup told how he and his staff began an intensive community education drive to tell Madisonians that the jets were there to protect the city and that he had taken measures to cut down jet noise, particularly at inappropriate times. "The more you educate people, the more you raise the tolerance factor for noise," he believed.

Paul N. Borsky of Columbia University noted fourteen years later (1968) that "if a person feels that those creating the noise care about his welfare and are doing what they can, he is usually more tolerant of the noise and is willing and able to accommodate higher levels of noise. If he feels, however, that the noise propagators are callously ignoring his needs and concerns, he is more likely to be hostile to the noise and more annoyed with even lower levels of noise. This feeling of alienation, of being ignored and abused, is also the root cause of many other human annoyance reactions. This is one of the major reasons cited for urban riots, discontent by minority groups, and more recently of student revolts. Evidence of its significance in explaining variations in annoyance with noise is found in all known community noise studies."

Relatively few people (somewhere between 10 percent and 20 percent) of a community ever complain about anything. And those that do, do so usually once but about more than one annoyance. A Boeing Company survey showed that of complaints of aircraft noise over a period of "several years," there were "approximately two complaints per complainant and two-and-a-quarter complaints per complainant household. The maximum number of complaints received from one person was 156, and all were telephone calls . . . but it appears that most of the complainants complained on only one occasion." Complainants must be articulate enough to express their annoyance, have some feeling that the community's leaders will listen to their complaints, and feel that their complaining will do some good. So while complaints in a community are some indication of annoying noise, they are of variable reliability.

5

WHAT NOISE
DOES TO YOUR MIND

$$(((((((((\cdot)))))))))$$

There are very specific ways by which noise grates on our nerves and affects our emotions and behavior. Some of these mechanisms lie so deep within our psyches that we are unaware of them. Essentially these are: interference with our communication, interruption of our sleep, and inspiration of fear.

Noise interferes with communication simply by getting in the way, interposed as it is between sender and receiver; in effect, it garbles the message. During World War II, for instance, the Allies searched for the cheapest and most efficient way to jam the enemy's communications. It turned out that the most effective way to do this was to use noise of the same sound frequencies as the human voice. This is technically called *Masking*. You can demonstrate its effectiveness easily by placing a microphone at a cocktail party and feeding it to a recording tape. When you play it back, you will hear many conversations at once, but will probably be unable to follow any one.

Had you been present at the party, you would have benefited from what has been called The Cocktail Party Effect. This is the human ability to hold a drink in one hand and an hors d'oeuvre in the other and carry on a conversation with the person facing you while a multitude of simultaneous conversations occur all about you. Your ears are receiving the same input of sounds as is the tape recorder's microphone. But somewhere in your brain the sounds of the voice of the person you are conversing with come to your conscious attention and the voices of everyone else fade into an indistinguishable background din.

Despite these marvelous workings of the brain, even when slightly sedated, the din of a growing party can finally intrude on speech communication. This happens when the party grows so that the density of guests reaches a critical stage. Then the background noise is so loud that you and your friend must raise your voices above a comfortable conversational level. Unfortunately, everyone else at the party has to do the same, and so signals and noise rise together. The result is that you soon find yourself shouting to be heard during cocktails and hoarse after you get home. Your hangover the next morning may be from din, not daiquiri. This raising of our voices to speak against background noise, called the Lombard Effect, is reflex in action. It has been used positively, at least in Australia, to help laryngectomees speak louder with their pseudo-voices. These patients, whose voice boxes have been removed because of cancer, learn to speak in a highly controlled form of burping. Studies at the Royal Victorian Eye and Ear Hospital at Melbourne indicate that when such patients learn to speak against a loud background noise their loudness and intelligibility are improved.

One researcher claims that shouting was discovered by

Adam as a way to outtalk Eve. Thus, John C. Webster, Ph.D., of the U.S. Navy Electronics Laboratory at San Diego, pointed out, the effect of noise on speech is not a new problem. "Deafening effects of noise probably started with the discovery of gun powder, or at least with the Industrial Revolution, and are only now starting to get out of hand with the invention of the electric guitar," he said. "Speech communication in noise started becoming a problem when Henry Ford and the Wright Brothers invented our most insidious sources of noise, and De Forest invented the means to give speech a fighting chance against noise."

To be intelligible, speech must be of proper sound frequencies and loudness. Also, a certain percentage of the spoken syllables, words, phrases, or sentences must be heard correctly. One measure of the effect of noise on speech intelligibility is the Articulation Index, or A. I. Another is the Speech Interference Level, or S. I. L. Even easier (if not as accurate) is measuring the level of background noise with the A scale of a noise meter.

One principle of speech-and-noise is: as the noise gets louder, or as the speech task becomes more demanding, low speech frequencies become relatively more important. These low frequencies of sound are the ones we don't normally pay much attention to. Thus, to have 90 percent speech intelligibility between two people standing a meter (39 inches) apart, the background "white" noise (of mixed frequencies) cannot exceed 95 dB and low-frequency background noise cannot exceed 105 dB. When conversationalists are not face-to-face but are speaking by way of electronic equipment, the intelligibility/noise ratio worsens. For one thing, they can't see each other's lips; for another, each is immersed in his own noise environment. Dr. Webster is interested in this problem because of the intense noise level of ship decks, especially of aircraft carriers, where the din frequently exceeds 100 dB-A.

A similar problem in the effects of noise on speech com-
munication occurs at big fires. This is one reason the New
York City Fire Department asked for the help of Thomas H.
Fay, Jr., Ph.D., associate professor of Audiology and Speech
Pathology, and associate director of New York University
Center for Research and Advanced Training in Deafness
Rehabilitation. Dr. Fay's preliminary report noted that environmental "noises have a highly destructive effect on
speech formulation and reception" so that "during extreme
fire-fighting activities . . . in the very situations where
communication efficiency should be maximum, it, more
often than not, becomes minimal. The messages become less
routine and, therefore, less predictable. The Lombard Effect
becomes a critical factor, wherein the talker raises the intensity level of his own voice in response to an increase in
the level of environmental noise . . . but at the expense of
intelligibility loss due to the shouting." As to the fire department's radio system, "Even the finest transmission system
cannot create an intelligible output from an unintelligible
input. Furthermore, a system may impose distortions of its
own upon shouted speech input." And, if the listener has
impaired hearing (from noise or other sources), he may
guess wrongly at what he thinks he has heard. "A situation
of this type is a disturbing prospect," Dr. Fay wrote.

It can be a dangerous prospect not only at the scene of a
devastating fire, but on the location of the construction of a
building, or in a factory or on a busy street. Misunderstand-
ing a shouted warning can be more dangerous than not
hearing it.

Technically speaking, what you hear one moment decides
what you'll hear the next. A. R. D. (Roger) Thornton, a
young researcher at the Institute of Sound and Vibration
Research at Southampton University, England, has studied
the hearing nerves of cockroaches as a model for this post-
auditory masking. Bits of sound lasting longer than 200

milliseconds are heard as a continuous sound. The human ear, he explained, in 20 to 30 milliseconds makes the decision about masking the next sound or not. So there are some sounds you never hear, although your ear senses them. Remember this. It will be particularly ominous when you read in a later chapter about the experiments with sleeping subjects performed by Dr. Gerd Jansen in Germany. Dr. Jansen found that bursts of noise of 300 milliseconds had definite effects on the cardiovascular system, from which the body took *minutes* to recover. This may mean that even while we are awake, but in noisy environments, we are bombarded by sound which our hearing sense won't perceive but to which our bodies, and perhaps even our emotions, will react!

Interference with speech has serious long-range social, as well as individual psychological, results. This was revealed in the study of the effect of aircraft noises on the communities around Heathrow Airport, west of London. "The noise interferes with work by disrupting conversation, disturbs the patients and staff of local hospitals, and disrupts teaching in schools," stated the Wilson report. "Enquiries by Her Majesty's Inspectors of Schools confirmed the serious effects of the noise on some schools in the area. One Inspector, while doubting whether it was possible to prove what effect the frequent interruptions have on children's attainments over their seven years primary schooling, pointed out that the standards of work in one school were in many ways below average, although the staff were certainly not below average in teaching ability. On a previous visit by the Inspector to this school, the half hour assembly had been interrupted ten times and on the following day it had to be abandoned."

English schools are far from unique in this respect. Even in America, reported Dr. Alexander Cohen of the U.S. Public Health Service, "The penetration of outdoor noises into school buildings and churches have created serious disturb-ances and annoyance reactions, again owing largely to problems of speech interference. In describing such problems caused by aircraft noise in his school district, one school superintendent reported 40 to 60 interruptions per day in the classroom listening activities of three schools lying within 1½ miles of a major commercial airport. From 10 to 20 minutes per day were lost in each classroom because of this aircraft noise intrusion. Summing this time for the total number of affected classes yielded a cumulative loss of from 700 to 1,400 minutes per day of instruction time."

Even more annoying than its imposition into lectures and conversations is noise's interference with our sleep. No one knows why we need sleep, but we do. It seems to give us certain recuperative abilities, both psychologically and physiologically. When we are sick we sleep longer; conversely, we need our daily (nightly) rations of sleep to stay well. One of the world's leading sleep researchers, Nathaniel Kleitman, Ph.D., of the University of Chicago, found that everyone has "an obligatory need for sleep, which varies with the physical, mental and temperamental characteristics of the individual, and an accessory indulgence in sleep, influenced by age, sex and day-to-day fluctuating environmental factors. A person's irreducible sleep fraction is best expressed by its complement, the maximum sustainable duration of wakefulness."

Sleep, of course, can create its own noise, as those muscles that normally keep the jaw closed relax and let the mouth droop open, especially when the sleeper is supine. As the sleeper inhales, the soft palate and its appendage (the uvula) vibrate, producing the only too well-known noise known as snoring. Snoring has interfered with many a romance and marriage. "Laugh and the world laughs with you, snore and you sleep alone" is more than a saying. Yet according to estimates, one of every eight persons snores.

That means there are 400 million snorers spread across the face of the globe—half producing noise at once; the other half, on the other side of the world, being awake at the time.

The noise that impinges on our sleep need not be so obvious nor from so close a source as snoring. H. R. Richter of Basel, Switzerland, studied the brain waves (electroencephalograms or EEG) of sleepers and concluded that "noise associated with modern civilization (automobiles, trucks, elevated and underground railways, jets) and even natural sounds (birds, etc.) frequently disturb the rest of sleepers" without their usually being aware of this. This finding agrees with that of Dr. Gerd Jansen in Germany, who found that similarly moderate noises had their definite effects on sleepers' physiology. "All sounds audible at night impair the quality of sleep," in his view.

Research indicates that even very low noises can interfere with sleep. George J. Thiessen, Ph.D., head of the Acoustics Section, Division of Applied Physics, National Research Council of Canada, Ottawa, took the brain waves of sleepers who were exposed to sounds that most of us would hardly consider noise—those in the range of a quiet radio or passing truck, technically about 50 dB. What the low noise does, Dr. Thiessen found, is lift the sleeper from a deeper phase of sleep to a shallower phase, from a very shallow phase to awakening.

Our night's sleep is divided into phases, each clearly distinguishable by different heart and respiration rates, body temperature, and brain activity. We sink from drowsiness to light sleep to heavier sleep to deep sleep, which rises again, only to fall later. A night's sleep thus is a cyclic sequence of lighter sleep and deeper sleep. During the lighter phases we dream. It was Dr. Kleitman who discovered this by watching the eyes of sleepers in his laboratory. Rapid Eye Movements (REM), representing the scene being scanned in

the dream, are easily measured and are now a positive way
of assessing how long dreams last. Our dreams last from 5 to
50 minutes, and we total about two hours' worth of dreaming per night. Dr. Thiessen's findings indicate that even the
sound of a low-playing radio or far-away traffic can raise a
person's stage of sleeping from dreaming to mere drowsiness.

What about the effect of more startling noises, such as
those of jet airplanes, or even a supersonic plane? Preliminary studies at Stanford Research Institute in California
indicate that sonic booms indeed awaken people, or, at least,
disturb their sleep. What was surprising in these studies was
that overhead jets flying slower than the speed of sound
were even more disruptive of sleep than sonic booms.

That there is a difference between the sexes as to wakefulness due to noise was found by researchers at Duke University in 1965. Drs. William P. Wilson and William W. K.
Zung reported that women were three times more likely to
be roused from sleep by noise than men. The scientists
reasoned that the female nervous system is probably primed
by female hormones so as to be sensitive to noise. This
would be natural, since mothers must be alert to their
babies' needs. This would also explain why husbands can
sleep through the babies' cries, which so easily awaken their
wives. The Duke doctors said this could also explain why
depressive disorders are twice as frequent among women as
among men. Interrupted sleep had been identified as a
significant condition which accompanies depressive disorders. Their earlier studies had shown that depressed patients were more easily awakened by noises than were
emotionally healthy people.

Russian investigators blame sounds of the same level as
that used by Canadian researchers (about 50 dB) for making falling asleep a lengthy process, of about an hour and a
half. Deep sleep which followed lasted only an hour; this
was followed, on wakening, by "a sense of fatigue accom-

panied by palpitations." (Noise hangover?) The fairly quiet level of 35 dB, the Russians found, was the threshold for optimum sleeping conditions.

Many things happen to persons deprived of sleep. Dr. Kleitman found that the most prominent effect is extreme muscular weariness. He wrote, "Among other features of behavior in sleep deprivation are irritability to the point of irascibility in normally even-tempered subjects, and a mental disorganization, leading to dreaming while awake, hallucinations and automatic behavior, occasionally bordering on temporary insanity. It is easy to understand why the third-degree method of continuous interrogation for many hours will make a person sign a 'confession,' even if he is innocent of the crime he is accused of having committed. He wants to be permitted to sleep, and he fails to realize the seriousness of his self-incrimination."

England's Wilson Report stated, "Of all noise's effects, repeated interference with sleep is least to be tolerated because prolonged loss of sleep is known to be injurious to health."

Two New Yorkers, one a psychiatrist, the other a psychologist, told the New York State Assembly's Mental Hygiene Committee in 1966 what can happen to people noisily deprived of sleep. According to accounts of testimony which were reported in *The New York Times* and the St. Louis *Post-Dispatch* (confirmed to be accurate), Julius Buchwald, M.D., psychiatrist with the Downstate Division of the New York State Medical Center, said that interruption of dreams can lead to psychotic symptoms ranging from mild to severe. Among these are nightmarish memories, paranoidal delusions, hallucinations, and suicidal and homicidal tendencies (viz., the three noise-instigated crimes cited in the previous chapter). Noise, further, can reduce one's sense of humor and ability to handle ordinary, everyday frustrations. Dr. Buchwald's comments helped explain the behavior of residents living near Kennedy International Airport on Long Island, New York, who threatened armed violence if jet noise was not reduced.

Howard M. Bogard, Ph.D., Chief Psychologist at Queens Hospital Center, told the committee that he agreed about the effect of noise on dreams and that interruption can lead to psychoses. "The tolerance threshold of each human being to noise is a subjective and individual matter. What only mildly annoys many well-adjusted can acutely threaten the emotional stability of those who are making borderline psychological adjustments and barely holding onto reality," he said. He added, "I have heard of several instances of children running into houses absolutely terrified" by overhead jetliners. "People should not be subjected to intimidation by outside forces over which they have no control."

Former Princeton University psychology professor Silvan S. Tomkins, Ph.D., wrote that "anything which disturbs the requisite number of hours of sleep indirectly increases fatigue and pain and therefore distress. Frequently psychological problems become more distressing than they need be, because they interfere with sleep. This then increases the distress of the individual, and summates with the original problem to magnify it in a spiraling build-up. In a few cases I have observed this spiral terminated in a psychotic episode."

Further, said this expert on emotional responses, "since a high level of noise arouses in us either distress or anger—you can see the distress response in children; make a loud enough noise, and they will begin to cry—we're paying a very high price for the noise that surrounds us in that we are all much more ready to cry or become angry than we need to be."

Vern O. Knudsen, Ph.D., the Los Angeles physicist whose views on hospital noises were quoted earlier, put it plainly: "If noise does nothing more than interfere with sleep—and this it does on a gigantic scale—it is a menace to good health."

The most primitive emotion that noise touches in man is fear. This may be the ominous feeling that a siren in the night conveys, or the near-certainty that an airplane flying low overhead is going to crash. Take the latter: while America is a nation on the move, looking with reference and reverence to the Jet Set, two-thirds of the American people still have not set foot in an airplane! To find out why, eight airlines, *Life* and *Reader's Digest* magazines, and the Canadian Travel Bureau sponsored an in-depth study. Funded by $100,000 and conducted by Behavior Science Corp. of California, the survey's results had not been revealed as of this writing. However, we need only turn back to the C.H.A.B.A. Report of 1954 which stated that "80 percent of the people who are greatly annoyed by aircraft noise have a certain amount of fear of the aircraft." There is but little doubt that the answer to the airlines' survey is that people are afraid of airplanes because they crash. And when people are suddenly and unexpectedly reminded of this by loud jet noises, they are afraid anew. With the sound and shock of sonic booms, perhaps they imagine they hear the thunder of the crash they so dread.

The phenomenon of the sonic boom has given researchers an excellent discrete model for appraising the fear effects of noise. The sonic boom (called "bang" in England) is the thunderlike explosive sound produced by overpressures or shock waves which trail behind objects flying through air at speeds exceeding the speed of sound. It is the bang or "crack" you hear when a bullet is fired: the explosive discharge of the cartridge is less noisy than the shock wave of the bullet after it emerges from the muzzle. And supersonic planes (examples are the SR-71, B-58, B-70, in the United States; the Lightning fighter in England; and the Supersonic

Transport or S. S. T.) go faster than a speeding bullet. Sonic booms occur suddenly and without warning; they are startling and difficult to identify immediately. It is the unexpected suddenness of the boom that leads to fright, just as does an unexpected truck backfire, thunder, or a slammed door.

A U.S. Air Force scientist, Henning E. von Gierke, Dr. Eng., noted at the Sonic Boom Symposium held in St. Louis in 1965 that "the fact that sonic booms come without warning, unlike most equally loud intruding noises from other sources, can make them more startling than most of these. . . . such sonic booms can hardly be considered different from or more dangerous than other minor stresses of daily living."

Karl D. Kryter, Ph.D., of Stanford Research Institute, tested the effects of real sonic booms on people placed in homes near Edwards Air Force Base, California, and of simulated sonic booms on people in his laboratory. He concluded that "with the advent of the supersonic transport many more people, of the order of tens of millions, will be exposed to a sound that is as noisy or as objectionable as that now experienced under the flight path of jet aircraft within about 1½ miles from an airport." He also found that booms are more likely to awaken older people than younger, and that "there appeared to be little adaptation to the booms."

And the Human Responses Subcommittee of the National Academy of Sciences said in a 1968 report, "A review of field studies of the psychological impact of the sonic boom shows a growing concensus that is discouraging for the use of the current version of the commercial supersonic transport over populated areas at speeds at which it will be generating a sonic boom."

A point was made well in a letter published in *The New England Journal of Medicine* in 1967 by William A. Shurcliff, Ph.D., a physicist who is director of the Citizens League Against the Sonic Boom. Tests conducted thus far on populations, he asserted, "violated the principles of objective medical investigation." The subjects who were used all knew about the tests, and were all adults, wide awake, and in good health and relaxed. "There was little recognition of the fact that far greater distress might be experienced by infants, the aged, the very ill, highly nervous persons or mental patients," Dr. Shurcliff wrote. The tests "provide no indications of the effects of sonic boom on persons who are trying to sleep and are having difficulty doing so, on those who are resentful at finding themselves captive victims of uncontrolled and unnecessary noise, on persons concentrating deeply on exacting tasks (a surgeon performing a delicate operation, for example), on persons already under great strain or on persons in despair at the prospect that the booms will continue day and night, weekdays and holidays, for the remainder of their lives."

Finally, an editorial in the distinguished English medical journal, *The Lancet*, noted that "sudden loud noises, when they are entirely unexpected, startle and frighten those who hear them. Babies scream: adults often react aggressively. Many a child has, to its astonishment, been cuffed by a normally good-tempered and phlegmatic parent who has been startled out of his wits by the game of shouting 'Boo!' behind father."

The fright which sudden and loud noises provoke should not be dismissed lightly. They should be considered ways of warning, a sort of biological protective mechanism which induces or compels us to separate ourselves from the noise and thus be able to recover. Fear and annoyance are akin to fatigue, hunger, chill, and flushes as feelings of discomfort which have bodily meanings. They are psychological protectors of our physical beings.

Noise can literally provoke some persons into fits. I won't belabor the point, since the phenomenon is considerably rare. But you should know that there is such a thing as the *audiogenic seizure.* About a decade ago it was discovered that certain strains of laboratory mice would have serious seizures, often resulting in death, when a loud enough noise—such as a doorbell in the cage—was sounded. Loud enough means about 100 dB. Because this predisposition is such a strongly inherited trait, scientists have used it more for research in genetics than for research in effects of noise on the nervous system.

The audiogenic seizure would be a laboratory curiosity if it weren't for the fact that people with certain forms of epilepsy can have a seizure at the sound of certain music, a radio announcer's voice, or a startling doorbell. Dr. Francis M. Forster of the University of Wisconsin Medical Center, Madison, has demonstrated that such seizures, which occur in one percent of epileptics, are caused by the brain's reaction to noise. Such brains have been damaged or suffer from some sort of chemical or electrical abnormality.

Noise annoys us; frightens us; makes our working conditions dangerous; wakens us; imposes on our secret dreams at night; and interferes with our speech, our appreciation of music, our viewing of television at home, our whisperings in what we take for granted to be the privacy of our homes. All of these invasions and violations of our persons have effects on our efficiency and on our sanity. However, it is rather surprising that as well defined as are the effects of noise on our emotions, their influence on behavior is not as definitely pinned down. This is probably because behavior is such a vastly complex subject, one which is only now beginning to be studied with any fine organization. The complaint is an example of behavior and, as explained earlier, is dependent on many things besides the physical values of noise.

One factor is personality, which was studied by Professor Salvatore Maugeri, director of the Industrial Health Clinic at the University of Pavia, Italy. Dr. Maugeri and his colleagues tested 80 of the university's top students, first for personality characteristics; then, for performance under factory noise conditions, under milder noise conditions, and under quiet. His most interesting finding was that subjects with stable, introverted personalities gave more answers on the tests under noisy conditions but also scored higher percentages of errors. Their errors increased the longer they were in the noisy environment. Unstable, outgoing personalities did better in noise, probably, in Dr. Maugeri's view, because they were able to learn, were able to become a bit more organized in the disturbing environment. Because they were less likely to be precise to begin with, their work reflected that they were less disturbed by noise than were the stable, introverted students. Dr. Maugeri's results have been confirmed in studies conducted by Dr. Alexander Cohen of U.S. Public Health Service.

Another factor affecting behavior is the nature of the noise. Dr. Broadbent, one of the world's authorities on noise-and-work, has found that different pitches of noise have different effects on work behavior. High frequencies provoke more mistakes than do low frequencies. Also, unusual noises, when first heard, reduce working efficiency.

A third factor is the nature of the task itself. The Wilson Report stated, "If people are doing work which, by its nature, already maintains a state of alertness, a loud noise may cause them to become jittery and make more errors. This result supports the general experience that routine work is less affected by a loud noise environment than is work of an exacting kind."

Noise has been around to distract us from our tasks as long as we have had such tasks. In 1953, W. R. Miles of the Department of Psychology, Yale University, pointed out, "Man had to learn to labor while the elements were in a state of storm. It isn't easy to shave or get a meal in the presence of a lustily crying baby. Factories are often of necessity too hard on the ears for working comfort. The problem has a very long past but a brief scientific history."

Tests of the effects of noise on work generally go back to the 1930's:

> —D. A. Laird in 1933 found that pure tones affected production less than did mixed noises, and that mixed noises had their worst effects on production when they were unsteady and varied.
> —H. C. Weston and S. Adams about the same time showed that British weavers increased their efficiency by 12 percent when they wore earplugs.
> —S. S. Stevens, in experiments conducted at Harvard University in 1940, using simulated noise of bomber airplanes, showed that noise was uncomfortable, but influenced work output but little when the crew's motivation and health were normal and their work consisted of well-practiced routines.

If the results of this sample of studies seem inconsistent, that is the nature of this field of industrial hygiene research. That noise affects us as we work is an obvious enough statement; to prove that noise does, and to show how, are far from obvious and far from easy.

One reason that early investigations were later invalidated was what has come to be known as the Hawthorne Effect (named thus because it was discovered at the Hawthorne plant of Western Electric in Chicago in 1947). This effect operates when some part of a worker's environment is changed experimentally to see if it will affect his output. It always does, not because of the change in environment per se, but because the change is a sign that management is concerned with him and his problems.

For example, an office in which typists worked was made quieter to see what effect this would have on their speed. They typed faster, but their speed remained faster than before even when the noise was restored. A group of perforating-machine operators improved their production when the noise in their section of the plant was lowered 10 dB with acoustic treatment. But their production also improved in another room with the same noise level as their original room.

The best documented effect of noise on performance is that on intellectual tasks: noise stimulates us to a nervous peak. Dr. Broadbent said that noise "is over-arousing because it represents too high a level of stimulation." Arousal means one is "ready to make a response." Too much arousal means a person is too ready. As a result he may make errors. This is, in fact, what happened in Dr. Broadbent's experiments with British sailors. He found that "laboratory experiments have now established that an effect of high-intensity, meaningless, and continuous noise may appear on working efficiency in laboratory tasks which are long and require continuous attention. The effect of noise is to increase the frequency of momentary lapses in efficiency rather than to produce decline in rate of work, gross failures of coordination, or similar inefficiency." The experiments then were duplicated in work situations with machine operators, with the same results. Concluded Dr. Broadbent, "Noise does produce human error in a real-life situation, even amongst people who are used to it."

This is as true of children in school as it is of adults at work. In 1964, when the Japanese National Railways wanted to put train tracks only 40 meters (120 feet) from an elementary school, concern was expressed that the noise of trains running on those tracks would harm the children and their education. So experiments with children and noise in classroom situations were conducted by the Nimura Research Group of Tohoku University in Sendai. One set of experiments, conducted with second, fourth, and sixth graders by Yasuhiro Nagatsuka, revealed that "the working efficiency under noisy circumstances [74 phons] was inferior to that under the conditions of low level of noise. That is, the scores of the experimental children was lower than those of the control children. This tendency was remarkable especially among the lower grades." The effect of noise on interfering with learning was continued in a 1969 study of the London Institute of Psychiatry.

There seems to be an important exception to the effect on intellectual tasks of noise—and that's when the noise is popular music, the task is homework, and the listener is a teen-ager. Joyce Brothers, Ph.D., the syndicated psychologist, answering a query from a high school senior, wrote, "Various studies have been made of the effects of music on mental performance. With few exceptions, they almost all indicate that music tends to increase concentration especially among people of high intelligence. At least none of the researchers have found that music is detrimental except among people of low ability. . . . The reason for most music helping study for many people is that music increases mental energy and concentration which transfers over to the work being done." A study she may have had in mind was one conducted by John E. Hoffman as research for his Ph.D. degree at the University of Southern California. Dr. Hoffman gave 281 eleventh graders a verbal reasoning test for 30 minutes while recorded music blared at them at 85 dB intensity. Some other students were exposed to playground noise, for comparison. A third group took the test in quiet. Students in all three categories scored about the same. Although the noise would bother an adult, it didn't at all bother the junior high students, Dr. Hoffman explained. The loud music, in his view, "puts them in a good mood and they are more receptive."

But the noise they study by can have secret and not beneficial effects. This was indicated in experiments in subliminal perception performed in 1960 by Dr. Fred Pine of New York University. He had twelve college students each read a paragraph about a cow. Simultaneously, a voice reading a completely different paragraph, about a hook, in the next room, could be heard. The cow paragraph was written softly, containing such sentences as: "Lands where grass is lush and plentiful are the special home of the cow." The hook paragraph was hard, with sentences like this: "Coldness, hardness, silvery steel: These are the qualities of the hook." Another twelve students read about the hook as they heard about the cow.

Each student Dr. Pine questioned was proud of his concentrative ability, told about the paragraph he had read and said he remembered nothing about the noise. Then the psychologist asked each student to invent a story and tell it to him. Surprisingly, elements of the noise, not the silently read paragraph, entered these tales. Students who had heard the hook paragraph told about negative and clashing relationships, usually about adults, and usually around such themes as death and aggression. Those who heard (not read) the cow paragraph, by contrast, told stories about children in warm, positive relationships amid themes of sympathy, welfare, and mother love.

Apparently, the noise these students heard—but were not paying attention to—had more effect on their unconscious minds than did the paragraphs they quietly, consciously, and determinedly read. In psychoanalytic terms, the noise cues had become part of their primary process thinking.

Noise can also have its subtle and secret effects at manual work, as well as at intellectual tasks. After Dr. Jansen of West Germany received his doctorate degrees in medicine and in psychology in 1956, he received a commission from the government of Luxemburg to study the psychological effects of noise on more than a thousand workers in sixteen German steel factories. During the next two years each worker received a comprehensive physical examination, then was interviewed about his health and his life. The two-thirds

of the workers who earned their livings in very noisy circumstances (more than 90 dB-A) were compared with a
third who worked in somewhat noisy circumstances (less
than 90 dB-A). Statistically, the average worker in the study
was 41 years old and had been at his job eleven years. (None
of the subjects was younger than 23 years nor at his job less
than three years.) The workers in both groups were matched
as closely as possible socially, economically, ethnically, and
occupationally.

Dr. Jansen found that there was little difference between
the two groups as to their consumption of tobacco, coffee,
and alcohol. He found the quieter workers easier to interview, the noisier workers more aggressive, distrustful, and
even paranoic. He attributed part of the noisier workers' behavior to their noise-induced hearing losses. These workers
were far more likely to quarrel constantly with their foremen
than were the quieter workers.

Thus noise had its effects on the men's personalities and
on their jobs. It also affected their home life. Higher-noise
workers had more than twice as many family problems as
did lower-noise workers—12 percent versus 5 percent.

What about the ultimate psychological-psychiatric effect
of noise? Can it, indeed, drive you crazy? Is it detrimental to
mental health?

The Wilson Committee wasn't convinced it could. It
wrote, "We found very little specific evidence to support this
view. In talking, for example, to medical practitioners with
practices in the vicinity of a major airport, we heard of only
one patient whose mental illness was attributed by his doctor to the noise to which he was exposed, and these practitioners had no evidence that the consumption of sedatives
and hypnotics was greater in their areas than in other areas
where they had practiced."

Dr. Broadbent wrote, "One allegation often made is that
noise produces mental illness . . . if there is any effect of

noise upon mental health it must be so small that present methods of psychiatric diagnosis cannot find it. That doesn't prove that it doesn't exist; but it does mean that noise is less dangerous than, say, being brought up in an orphanage—which really is a mental health hazard."

Still, a later English study, reported in *The Lancet* in December 1969, found a significantly higher incidence of mental illness requiring treatment among people most exposed to the noise of aircraft operating near Heathrow Airport. They were compared with people who lived outside their area, farther from the airport, who were less likely to require psychiatric treatment.

There are also those comments quoted earlier by the New York psychiatrist and psychologist of the mental whirlwinds which may be reaped by noise that continually interrupts sleep and dreams. Dr. Bogard pointed out that noise can be especially harmful to persons already under other kinds of stress by lowering their ability to cope with their emotional problems. "The noise could trigger this person into a neurosis. Without noise, he might be able to deal adequately with his problem. . . . When a person hears an unwanted noise, the person has a massive feeling of impotence and frustration. He thinks, what can I do? About many things, he can do something. About unwanted noise, he cannot." Noise to Dr. Bogard is the uninvited guest at the party, an intruder.

U.S. News and World Report in 1963 quoted an unnamed "medical expert" as saying, "It is not an exaggeration to say that quite a few cases of insanity are caused by nervous systems that cannot adjust to the constant bombardment of noise."

Von K. Bättig, an associate of Dr. E. Grandjean at the Swiss Federal Institute of Technology in Zurich, found that "frequent subjective discomfort due to noise can eventually disturb the emotional balance."

Dr. Fabian Rouke of Manhattan College said, "One of the

insidious aspects of sound is the fact that an individual may be unconsciously building up nervous tension due to noise exposures. This may cause a person thus exposed suddenly to be precipitated into an act of violence, or mental collapse, by some seemingly minor sounds which drive him beyond the point of endurance."

Bruce L. Welch, Ph.D., a noise-weary Baltimore psychologist, has conducted much research on how the brain and body adapt to environments. He finds that "it is bad for the nervous system and for the rest of the body, in many ways, to be overactivated much of the time. This is, of course, exactly the situation with which we are faced in many modern environments. Noise—like it or not—is one of the major contributing factors to harmful overactivation. The worst possible situation is that in which the nervous system is frequently surprised by very loud noises. For such noises, in a real sense, catch the brain by surprise. They hit it all at once while its protective inhibitions are not in action and, by so doing, they deliver a devastating shock not only to the nervous system but also to the endocrines and the cardiovascular system. . . . We require a reasonable level and variety of stimulation to maintain our mental and physical health. But it is also true that stimulus overloading can cause breakdowns of both our mental and our physical health."

Noise may not, by itself, cause mental illness, as such distinguished authorities as the Wilson Committee and Dr. Broadbent believe. But a considerable weight of learned opinion, if not objective data, bears down on the probability that noise, as unwanted but additional stress in our modern lives, can provide the leverage to precipitate emotional crises—or psychoses—that may already be teetering on nervous brinks. That probability alone makes noise a dangerous threat to the mental well-being of millions.

6

WHAT NOISE
DOES TO YOUR BODY

((((((((((•))))))))))

It begins before life itself, that cacophony of the world which imposes itself upon our beings and adds yet another stress to the ever-present struggle for existence. It is, in a sense, a first greeting from the world, a sonic jarring that, could any fetus realize it at the time, would forewarn it of the din which after birth and for all of its days will assault its body.

The inner sea of fluid in which the unborn floats protects as it cushions him from major physical trauma such as light and shock. But from noise it protects little, as it transmits sounds from within and without—the incessant pounding of his mother's heart, the swishing of air into her lungs, the very sound of her voice. In effect, the unborn child has a biological stethoscope on his mother's body, an ear to her insides.

Dr. Margaret Liley of New Zealand and writer Beth Day of New York City expressed it well:

> The womb, we have found, is an extremely noisy place. The unborn is exposed to a multiplicity of sounds that range from his mother's heartbeat and her voice to outside street noises. Especially if his mother has not gotten too plump, a great many outside noises come through to the unborn baby quite clearly: auto crashes, sonic booms, music. And the rumblings of the mother's bowel and her intestines are constantly with him. If she should drink a glass of champagne or a bottle of beer, the sounds, to her unborn baby, would be something akin to rockets being shot off all around.

This all begins for the unborn about the sixth month after conception, when the hearing mechanism has reached normal development. One month later, in the seventh month of pregnancy, the fetus's body responds to noise by changes in his little heart's fast rate of beat.

Lester W. Sontag, M.D., Director of Fels Research Institute, Yellow Springs, Ohio, explained that,

> In the 1920's a German investigator reported a number of cases of expectant mothers who complained that they could not go to symphony concerts because of the greatly intensified activity level of the babies they were carrying. Another reported a case of an expectant mother who found that the applause of the audience at the symphony caused such extreme fetal activity that it was painful. When a small block of wood is placed over the abdomen of a woman eight months pregnant and a doorbell clapper is permitted to strike at the rate of 120 vibrations per second, there is, in about 90 percent of cases, an immediate and convulsive response on the part of the fetus. The response is in the form of violent kicking and moving. There is also an increase in heart rate. This increased heart rate occurs even

when, in a small percentage of cases, there is no movement response. This startle reflex is, we believe, the
same response as the Moro reflex* after birth.

Exactly how the unborn child's heart responds to specific
noise has been studied in Stockholm, Sweden, by Dr. Bertil
Johansson and his colleagues at the world-famous Karolinska
Institute. They first beamed sound into the still-swollen
abdomens of women who had just given birth to babies at
Sabbatsberg Hospital. They found in measurements with a
vaginal microphone that about half of the sound energy was
absorbed by the mother's body, by the placenta, and by the
organs. Then they successfully studied the fetuses of ten
pregnant volunteers. They aimed a pleasant 3,000 Hz tone of
110 dB loudness for one second at a time into the belly of
each woman, knowing that the fetus would get about 50
dB.

That the fetuses heard and reacted even to this low
(about the sound level of a quiet office) sound was apparent
in their heart rate: in a typical case, the rate momentarily
climbed from about 130 beats per minute to 150. In some
fetuses, it zoomed to as high as 170 beats per minute.

(By showing how unborn babies respond physiologically
to noise, these Swedish experiments hold promise of a new
test for checking for congenital deafness, especially when
the mothers-to-be have contracted German measles. With
such a test, doctors could tell months before the baby was
born whether or not it had any ear damage. Unfortunately,
Dr. Johansson explained, the test won't be an indication for
abortion. At least, not in Sweden. The limit of pregnancy for
abortion there is 24 weeks, one month before the test can be
given.)

* Behavior of an infant when he feels he is falling, or there is a loud
noise. He throws out his arms, then brings them together in a jerky
movement.

Dr. Sontag feels that the effects of noise on the fetus may be even more dire. His experiments indicate that prenatal noise can cause predisposition to audiogenic seizures after birth. Citing this, and the results of other research as evidence, he believes that loud noises, and especially the sonic boom, can be as much a teratogen—an instigator of congenital malformations—as can such drugs as thalidomide and such viruses as German measles. Some of these effects of prenatal noise may be so subtle as to be responsible decades later in the behavior of the person then grown into an adult. Dr. Sontag concluded, "I believe I have mustered enough evidence of the vulnerability of the mammalian fetus to environmental stress and the child-adult consequence of such stress to justify our concern about the possibility of fetal damage from such violent sounds as sonic booms. It seems not unlikely that adults are not alone in their objection to such noxious stresses. The fetus, while he cannot speak for himself, may have equal or greater reason to object to them."

Everyone has experienced the startle reflex, provoked by a sudden and unexpected tap on the shoulder, or by the sight of something dangerous heading his way, or of a sudden loud sound, as a dropped book. Outwardly, he jumps and raises his arms defensively. Internally, other things occur, as explained by Dr. John Anthony Parr to British radio listeners. He explained that a sudden and loud noise sets off our inborn alarm system. When this happens, he said, "We automatically get ready either to defend ourselves or for fight. Our muscles tense and we jerk, our abdominal blood vessels contract to drive extra blood to our muscles and this produces that feeling of the stomach turning over, and in an instant the liver releases stores of glucose to provide fuel for the muscles which may have to fight or run. This internal upheaval if repeated again and again is exhausting physically and mentally, and ultimately can cause a nervous breakdown and then it is but a step to contracting one of the stress diseases."

England's Broadbent agreed: "However desirable in emergencies, this kind of change is obviously not wanted for long periods."

Although noise has been with us since the beginning of time and has annoyed man since his emergence from lower forms on this planet several million years ago, it was not until about 1930 that there was any serious medical awareness of noise. It was about then that auto horns started making our streets noisier than ever. It was in 1929 that New York City was first surveyed for noise. (That was even before decibels were used as a measurement.) Bell Telephone Laboratory sound men measured the noise of autos, steel mills, elevated trains, etc., and tried to compare their loudnesses with that of a standard reference sound. The first sound-level meter, made by Western Electric Co., a Bell subsidiary, appeared in 1932.

Most medical investigations of the effects of noise then were on hearing. Of necessity they lagged the development of the understanding of how the ear handles sound and works as a transducer, and of how sound and noise affect and damage the ear.

One of the earliest studies of the biological effects of noise was the BENOX report, funded by the office of Naval Research, conducted by the University of Chicago, and published on December 1, 1953. BENOX was the acronym for the mission of the study: Biological Effects of Noise. The Navy was primarily interested in the effects of noise of aircraft carrier decks on their crews. The report noted that "excessive fatigue, occasional nausea, and loss of libido are common complaints of men working in noise."

Discussing effects of jet noise on the central nervous system in that report, Arthur A. Ward, M.D., a neurosurgeon then with the University of Washington, noted that intense noise causes changes in brain waves (EEG, or electroencephalogram), in vision, and in deep-tendon reflexes. It also causes the body to react as it does in adrenal stress.

The late University of Chicago medical psychologist, Ward C. Halstead, Ph.D., found:

"1. Complaints of tiredness, irritability, insomnia, and possibly some reduction in libido, have been encountered in civilian maintenance workers who are intermittently exposed to the noise levels close to jet aircraft. . . .

"2. Evidence was obtained which may indicate the existence of marginal 'stress' syndrome in some civilians who work without ear protection and who have the responsibility for executing critical maintenance operations in jet aircraft. This syndrome is reflected in certain tests of higher brain functions. The impairment of function detected thus far includes loss of information through the tactual [touch] route."

Since the BENOX report, several American researchers have tested in their laboratories the physiological effects of noise on animals under controlled circumstances.

Here is a sampling.

A. F. Rasmussen of the University of California at Los Angeles Medical School, found that exposing laboratory mice to loud noises made them especially susceptible to infection by viruses.

Mary F. Lockett, M.D., of the University of Western Australia, found that noise affects experimental animals by interfering with kidney function and by stimulating changes in hormone output, a fact that has also been confirmed by Amilcar E. Arguelles of Hospital Aeronautico, Buenos Aires, Argentina.

Two Boston University psychologists, Leo J. Reyna, Ph.D., and Alberto Di Mascia, Ph.D., and a dentist, Norman Berezin, D.D.M., beamed loud, white noise (a hissing mixture of sound frequencies) of 115 dB at rats and found that they were more likely to develop tooth decay than were rats living at normal sound levels. The experimental rats were subjected to ten-second bursts, five times per hour, 16 hours a day for four months.

Dr. Claude Fortier of the University of Montreal subjected rats to the noise of a siren. They suffered, he found,
thymus gland atrophy, overstimulation of the adrenal
glands, and gastric ulcers.

Physiologists Meyer Friedman, Sanford O. Byers, and
Alvin E. Brown of Mount Zion Hospital and Medical Center,
San Francisco, and Lockheed Research Laboratories, Palo
Alto, California, studied the effects of noise on the plasma
lipids (blood fats, such as cholesterol and triglyceride) of
both rats and rabbits. The animals were exposed night and
day to both a white-noise background of 102 dB and to
intermittent random one-second noises of 114 dB. Depending on the experiment, the noise exposures lasted one, two,
three, four, and eight weeks. The triglyceride (a blood
lipid) concentration in test rats' blood was double that of
control rats and, once high, stayed high for three weeks after
the experiments ended. Tests indicated the rise in this fat in
the blood, which is believed heavily responsible for clogging
up blood vessels and producing heart attacks and stroke, is
tied to noise-induced overproduction of corticosteroid hormones by the adrenal glands.

The blood of rabbits exposed to the noise for four weeks
showed significant rises in cholesterol content. Cholesterol is
another fatty substance which clogs blood vessels. And,
interestingly enough, autopsies showed that the insides of
aortas of noise-subjected rabbits were far more heavily
coated with accumulations of this arterial "rust" than were
control rabbits that had been exposed to normal noise. Even
before death, the effects of noise on cholesterol could be
seen. Cholesterol was deposited in a snowflake pattern more
heavily in the eyes of test-rabbits than in the eyes of normal
rabbits.

A set of experiments conducted at Galesburg State Research Hospital, Galesburg, Illinois, correlated the brain
waves of rabbits with their blood pressure. The researchers,
J. W. Kakolewski (later at Fels Research Institute, Yellow

Springs, Ohio) and Y. Takeo (later with the Takeda Chemical Industry, Ltd., Osaka, Japan) subjected the animals to the noise of either a buzzer or an audiometer's tone of 2,500, or 3,500 Hz for three to five seconds at a time. They found two kinds of EEG patterns—a short one, which lasted about five seconds after the noise stopped; and a long one, which lasted more than ten seconds. Rabbits that reacted with the short EEG pattern showed no significant blood pressure rise in the arteries. But in those with the longer pattern, the arterial pressure was significantly elevated.

Experiments at the University of South Dakota Medical School produced similar results—and then some. In a set of experiments on rats, Pharmacologist William F. Geber, Ph.D. (later at the Medical College of Georgia) and Biochemist Thomas A. Anderson, Ph.D. (later with the H. J. Heinz Co., Pittsburgh) found that "serum cholesterol levels remained essentially unchanged through the first 24 hours, but rose markedly at the end of 24 hours and remained elevated at the end of 21 days of the audiogenic stress."

Compared to human standards, the "audiogenic stress" wasn't very harsh. The rats heard a mixture of ringing and buzzing, and of screeching white noise for six minutes out of every hour; the noise averaged 83 dB.

The results showed that "noise level can be an immediate and effective factor in producing a stress reaction in the animal body." Serum cholesterol went up and stayed up. Ascorbic acid (Vitamin C, which protects against scurvy) concentrations fell in the adrenal glands, and climbed in the brain. And there was a dramatic decrease—50 percent—in the number of eosinophil white cells circulating in the blood. Both the Vitamin C and eosinophil reductions were clear signs that the test animals' adrenal glands were responding to stress. And the stress was noise, since the control animals which lived in normal laboratory noise (about 70 dB) showed no similar physiological changes.

In another set of experiments, Drs. Geber and Anderson found additional evidence that noise acts to stress the body physiologically. The hearts of rats and rabbits, which had been exposed to the same noise level as the animals in the first experiments, increased significantly in weight. At the same time, the rest of the animals' bodies lost weight and their adrenals, ovaries, and kidneys shrunk. "Thus," concluded the researchers, "it is evident that the body responds to this type of stress [noise] in such a manner as to alter significantly both the biochemistry and the anatomy."

There was this item on the lethality of noise in a special issue (July, 1967) of the *UNESCO Courier:*

> *Noise a Killer*
> Laboratory experiments have demonstrated that sound with an intensity of 150 to 160 decibels is fatal to certain animals. The animals suffered from burns, spasms and paralysis before dying.

Curt Wiederhielm, Ph.D., a Seattle physiologist, uses a rather unique experimental animal. His physiology laboratory at the University of Washington School of Medicine concentrates on bats. He implants a small plastic window into the very thin skin of the bat's wing through which, with a microscope, he can see and photograph the tiniest of blood vessels. He has recorded on color film the actions of these vessels and of the blood cells which course through them. Noise is only of incidental interest to him. Nevertheless, in a 1968 report of his studies he said, "In cases where the animal was startled, for instance by tapping on the box [in which the bat was held], a profound vasoconstriction could be induced in the arteriole. . . ."

Basic studies with animals have paralleled research on the effects of noise on the body. In Europe—essentially in West

Germany and in Italy—physiological research on noise
(*Lärm*, in German; *rumore*, in Italian) has been done in
human volunteers. Not too surprisingly, perhaps, people's
bodies react to noise pretty much the same as do animals'.
The combination of data adds up to a solid if alarming
biological case against the noise in our environment.

The original investigations of the effects of noise on the
human body were started at the Max Planck Institute of
Occupational Physiology in Dortmund, an industrial city in
the rolling Ruhr area of West Germany. The noise research
pioneer there was Dr. Gunther Lehmann, director of the
institute. In the mid-1950's he and his colleagues performed
the first controlled studies in men of what they termed the
"vegetative" reactions to noise. These are involuntary bodily
reactions (as opposed to voluntary or willful reactions).

In 1956 Dr. Lehmann published the first comprehensive
report of his work in a German physiology journal. He and
his collaborator, J. Tamm, had found that noise has a profound effect on blood vessels, particularly on the tiny ones
called precapillaries. It makes them constrict, or narrow.
These tiny streams of blood are far from the rush and beat of
the heart, but not so small as capillaries.

That same year, when 27-year-old Gerd Jansen received
both his M.D. and a Ph.D. in psychology, he won a research
commission from Luxembourg to study the neurotic behavior of 1,000 steel workers. He tended to his main charge,
described previously, but became fascinated by these men
who worked every day in loud noises. As Dr. Jansen explained it, "Their skin was pale, the mucosa of their mouths
were pale and dry, their hearts had extra systoles. Their
peripheral circulatory systems were apparently under high
tension."

At Max Planck Institute he turned to the laboratory and
did some experiments on the effects of noise on animals. But,
as he expressed it, "It was not so important to make more

and more experiments in animals, but to see what noise does to man. Is it possible, for instance, for noise to cause hypertension in men?"

Dr. Jansen looked around for techniques to detect and measure those subtle changes which occur involuntarily in man's body, without his being aware of them. He followed the lead of Dr. Lehmann and subjected volunteers to 90 dB of white noise from loudspeakers in the laboratory. Under the guidance of Dr. Lehmann (with whom he collaborated until 1966), Dr. Jansen looked for an effect of noise on blood pressure, because the results of animal experiments had been so positive. Of course, he explained years later, the animals had been subjected to the terrible noise level of 150 dB. He couldn't possibly do that to people, as noise produces pain in the ears at 120 dB. The effects of 90 dB on his human volunteers were minimal, but consistent. A change was detected in the diastolic pressure, the background pressure of blood measured when the heart relaxes between beats. A man with a normal blood pressure of 80 mm Hg (for millimeters of mercury) in a normal sound environment would have 83 to 85 mm Hg when the noise was turned on—and then only for a few seconds. Dr. Jansen could measure no effect of noise on the systolic pressure which surges through the arteries as the heart beats.

He also tried to assess the effect of noise on the rate of beat of the heart. Again, his finding was mostly negative. For a few seconds after noise began, the pulse rate would quicken, then slow down, then return to what it had been. This result was extremely disappointing, since pulse rate is so important a measurement in determining how hard a man is working.

Dr. Jansen qualified his pulse and blood pressure findings by saying, "If noise has some communication for you, if it makes you angry, or you are in opposition to the noise source, or if it frightens you, pulse and pressure will go up."

But these would be psychological reactions, not physiological.

Dr. Jansen next checked to see if noise affected blood
supply at all. And this led to his most important findings. His
first test in this area used transillumination. It was based on
the technique of shining a light inside the mouth and measuring the amount of redness of the cheeks as seen from
outside. The redder the cheek, the more blood was there; the
paler, the less blood. When noise was turned on, the subject's cheeks became paler, indicating significant reductions
in blood supply.

He also measured skin temperatures (under conditions of
no wind and controlled humidity and room temperature).
When noise was on, there was a 1° to 2° C. cooling—another indication of lessened blood supply.

He refined this experiment and used two electrical contacts placed on the skin of an arm, about two inches apart.
One contact provided a constant amount of gentle warmth.
The other measured the temperature of the area. Heat loss
between the points would be proportional to the amount of
blood flowing through the area and carrying the heat away.
Sure enough, when noise was up, so was warmth, indicating
a decrease in blood flow.

Dr. Jansen also placed subjects in a unique device called
the ballistocardiogram. They merely lay there quietly on a
suspended platform to which was attached a gauge for
measuring the recoil of the heart with each beat. This indication of the stroke volume of the heart is often seen by thin
people standing on a bathroom scale: the weight needle
jerks rhythmically in concert with the heart. When noise
was on, the ballistocardiographs showed a decrease in the
stroke volume of the subjects' hearts.

Another test performed used the ancient principle of the
plethysmograph, to measure the small changes in volume of
the tip of a finger. This volume fluctuates in rhythm with the

volume of blood sent through on heart beats. Under noisy conditions, the volume dropped, indicating lessened blood supply.

All of Dr. Jansen's results add up to one finding: noise, at even relatively low levels, causes the tiny peripheral blood vessels in fingers, toes, abdominal organs, and skin to constrict, cutting down the supply of blood there. Vasoconstriction—the closing of small blood vessels—is a reflex action produced by signals from the sympathetic nervous system. It can be triggered by the production of certain body chemicals, especially adrenaline (epinephrine), the hormone secreted by the adrenal gland in stress situations.

Vasoconstriction, he believes, is the body's reflex reaction to the stress of noise. With less blood in the vessels to pump, the heart reacts involuntarily by reducing its stroke somewhat. The blood that is removed from circulation, believes Dr. Jansen, is probably stored in the spleen. One of the projects he began when he moved to Essen to become Head of the Department of Noise Research at Ruhr University Hospital in 1968 was to find out.

There he also continued his studies which showed the range of noise exposure that are needed to invoke a reflex reaction in the body. At Dortmund, for instance, he had found that the body responds in a direct mathematical way to both the intensity and the duration of noise—how loud and how long. In one report, he wrote,

> In further experiments it was possible to demonstrate a mathematical relationship between the duration of brief sound stimuli and the duration of the response to them. The response persists for a relatively long time after the end of the stimulus. When the sound stimulus lasts several minutes the total response time is about four times as long as the duration of the stimulus. In addition to duration, the intensity of the sound stimulus is of importance in determining both the occur-

rence and the degree of the autonomic reaction. Below
60 dB there is no peripheral vasoconstriction in experimental subjects in the waking state, while vasoconstriction proportional to the increasing sound intensity
begins at about 75 dB. . . . the frequency range of a
noise exerts a powerful influence; the broader the
spectrum of the noise the greater is the autonomic reaction.

And his experiments showed that white noise produced the
same results as recordings of industrial noise.

How sensitive the human body is to noise was best shown
in his experiments with sleeping subjects. To the volunteers'
heads were attached the leads to brain-wave recorders
(EEG). On their fingers were placed detectors for measuring vasoconstriction. In the room were loudspeakers which
delivered noise of moderate intensity. By the EEG's flat
tracings, Dr. Jansen could tell when the person being tested
was in deep sleep. Then he would turn on the sound, for
anywhere from six seconds to small fractions of a second,
and measure the small blood vessels' response.

The results are frighteningly ominous, he believes, for
people who live and sleep near airports or highways. He
reported: "We gave sound stimuli of the low intensity of 55
dB during the different stages and were able to produce
vasoconstriction in all. The level of 55 dB corresponds approximately to the noise made by heavy lorries on main
roads at night" as measured in bedrooms in nearby homes.

He even found that 70 dB noise lasting but a third of a
second caused vasoconstriction. And the blood vessels did
not immediately recover. Recovery took minutes even at the
fraction-of-a-second exposure!

"This means," wrote Dr. Jansen, "that all sounds audible
at night impair the quality of sleep . . . there would seem
to be some evidence here that noise can endanger health."

Dr. Jansen's studies were performed with three kinds of volunteers. First were the steel workers. Then he worked with students at Dortmund (some of whom worked their way through school on their earnings from experiments). Of interest is the fact that the students exposed to loud noises for the first time exhibited the same bodily responses to noise as did the steel workers who had worked in the same level of noise for ten years. And from first experiment to the last, each student's involuntary reflexes were of the same degree of reaction. This led Dr. Jansen to the conclusion that "an adaption made by a person to noise is done at the intellectual, not physiological, level. You can become accustomed to noise, but your body can never adapt to noise." Adaption, he explained, is the loss of reaction to a stimulus.

A third group of subjects were the members of the Mabaan tribe whom Dr. Samuel Rosen visited in 1960, as we saw in Chapter 2. Besides finding their hearing phenomenally acute, Dr. Rosen found little evidence of atherosclerosis (hardening of the arteries of the heart) or of high blood pressure, and discovered that heart attacks were practically unknown there. Particularly interesting to Dr. Rosen had been the discovery that even aged Mabaans had "young" ears and "young" arteries. He felt that there surely must be some connection, that perhaps the healthy capillaries in the inner ear provided a full supply of blood, contributing greatly to the normal functioning of the organ of hearing, the snaillike cochlea, even in advanced age. Drs. Lehmann and Jansen had shown that noise constricted small blood vessels. Perhaps absence of noise would keep small vessels, especially those in the ear, open. So Dr. Rosen invited scientists from Dortmund to come with him to Sudan in 1963. Dr. Jansen and J. Schulze, M.D., accepted. In Africa they duplicated the tests for vasoconstriction they had performed in Dortmund. They found that, in general, the physiological responses of the Mabaans to noise of 90 dB

was stronger than that of Dortmunders. Mabaan children
aged 8 to 11 responded with far greater vasoconstriction to
noise than did Dortmund children. Old Mabaan men, aged
60 to 85, showed less vasoconstriction to noise than did 20-
to 35-year-old Mabaan men. In his report to the American
Academy of Ophthalmology and Otolaryngology in October,
1963, in New York City, Dr. Jansen concluded that his
findings "may indicate a greater elasticity of the precapillary
vessels and possibly a slower aging process among the
Mabaans." Perhaps the quiet in which they lived was partly
responsible.

Following the lead of Drs. Jansen and Rosen were Y. P.
Kapur, M.D., and A. J. Patt, M.D., of Vellore, India. They
studied the Todas, a buffalo-herding tribe which lives in the
pastoral Nilgiri plateau. Tests showed the Todas have more
acute hearing throughout their lives than do Americans or
Englishmen. Furthermore, despite their high saturated-fat
diet of milk and milk products, they have no high blood
pressure and heart attacks are unknown among them.

All of the evidence points to the inescapable conclusion
that the human cardiovascular system thrives in quiet, and
that in modern civilized countries it reacts reflexly to the
punishing noise that impinges on it. Said Dr. Jansen: "Loud
noises once in a while probably cause no harm. But chronic
noise situations must be pathological. Constant exposure to
noise is negative to your health. Except for hearing loss,
there is no noise illness, *per se*. But noise has to be a compli-
cating factor. It is a stress applied to your body without your
being aware of it. It can be, for instance, superimposed as an
additional and subtle destructive factor on the diabetic's
already impaired blood circulation."

This same reaction to noise was noted by Dr. Kylin of
Stockholm. He explained that woodmen, who work with
extremely noisy (125 dB-C) motor saws, frequently complain that after they go home their fingers turn first blue

then white. This is the symptom of vasospastic disease, caused when small blood vessels in the hand constrict so as to cut off the blood supply. It is much like Raynaud's Disease, otherwise known as "dead fingers," because that's how they feel to the victim. Since 1811 it has been known that Raynaud's Disease occurs in men who handle vibrating machinery. Raynaud's Disease occurs in both hands, since both are used to grasp the air hammer, or whatever it is that is vibrating. But in the case of the woodmen, Dr. Kylin found "dead" fingers on only one hand, even though both hands grasp the motor saws. His guess is that the vasospasm is a bodily reaction to noise. The vasoconstriction effects of noise have also been confirmed by Dr. Etienne Grandjean of Zurich, Switzerland.

The other major center of research into the general physiological effects of noise is the Institute of Occupational Medicine at the University of Pavia. It is in northern Italy, just below Milano, at the 1,100-year-old center of learning where Christopher Columbus had been a student. Modern medical researchers became interested in noise's effects logically: the area is very industrial and metropolitan, so millions of Lombardians there are exposed to heavy concentrations of noise, at their work and in their cities.

There the effects of noise on the blood vessels have been mainly studied by Professor Dott. Giovanni Straneo, M.D., who takes time off regularly from his cardiology practice in the town of Tirano at the foot of the Alps to conduct research in the laboratories of Pavia, about 100 miles southwest. He is of the same age as Dr. Jansen (and, coincidentally, me) with whom he has frequently matched results. He became interested in noise in 1956, when he noted what he thought was a high incidence of high blood pressure among men who worked in metal fabrication plants in the area. Interested in the causes of hypertension, and suspecting that the din of the factories was one such cause, he began studying the effects of noise under controlled conditions.

The noise laboratories at Pavia are a hi-fi enthusiast's dream. The system reproduces factory, city, and musical sounds from magnetic tape with crisp reality and great power. Dr. Straneo's experiments on finger pulse amplitude confirmed the findings of Dr. Jansen, that noise of even a mild degree causes vasoconstriction. Exactly three seconds after noise of 87 dB starts, arterioles contracted, cutting the volume of blood within them by half. When the noise stopped, it took these small blood vessels about five minutes to recover. But they stayed constricted as long as the noise was on, and whether the subject was awake or sleeping. This was true whether factory noises were reproduced or a 3,000 Hz tone was played.

Dr. Straneo then did a few things that Dr. Jansen didn't do. He looked for vasoconstriction with a camera as well as the plethysmograph. He found that the capillaries of the conjunctiva (the whites of the eyes) respond to noise exactly as do the capillaries in the fingers: they tighten. His photographs of these tiny but very visible blood vessels are dramatic proof of noise's profound but unperceived effect on the human body's cardiovascular system. In a parallel series of experiments, his photographs showed how the administration of the powerful drug, digitalis, which is used to stimulate the heart, produces the same kind of vasoconstriction.

But the blood vessels on the retina of the eye, which can be seen with a strong beam of light, did the opposite. They dilated, or opened. Dr. Straneo pointed out that they are anatomically different from peripheral vessels.

The eye vessels findings led Dr. Straneo to study the effects of noise on the blood vessels in the brain itself. He used a device called a reograph, which uses electrical current to measure the flow of blood through vessels that serve the brain. He found that they, like the retinal vessels, dilate when noise is on. There is, he pointed out, the danger that these brain vessels could overdilate and this could cause headache. This could be the mechanism by which noise produces headache in some people.

Changes in the vascular system are bound to affect the heart. In fact, Dr. Jansen had shown this with his ballisto-cardiogram. So Dr. Straneo tried another approach to test noise's effect on the heart. He used the electrocardiograph, or ECG, to measure the electrical signals of the hearts of cardiac patients whom he exposed to pure tones of 8,000 Hz. In some of these patients who previously had had infarcts, or heart attacks, he noted significant deterioration of their ECG tracings. In medical terms, what were affected were de-formation time, true isometric contraction, and isotonic systole. In his report (written with A. Taccola and G. C. Bobbio), Dr. Straneo said he believed "that the observed changes may represent the resultant of a double stimulation due to noise: one neuro-vegetative, the other constituted by the repercussions on the heart of the peripheral changes of hemodynamics." Noise, in other words, can affect the heart directly through some nervous system stimulation, and indi-rectly by changing the dynamics of the vascular system.

Another finding at Pavia was also related to the possibility that noise can bring on heart attacks. This involves what has been called "blood sludge." Stated more medically by Dr. Straneo, this is the aggregation of erythrocytes (red blood cells) in the tiny vessels which contract in spasm under noise. More work needs to be done in this area, but if noise causes the blood to thicken or to clot, the implications in terms of heart attack and stroke are ominous indeed.

The total results of the Italian cardiovascular research, taken together with the German results, lead to the conclu-sion that the general effects of noise on the body occur through the sympathetic division of the autonomic nervous system.

This aspect has been more thoroughly explored by Dr. Straneo's chief, Salvatore Maugeri, M.D., who is director of Pavia's Institute of Occupational Medicine. Dr. Maugeri found that 30 patients suffering from arteritis (Raynaud's or Buerger's diseases) whose sympathetic nerves had been cut surgically had no vasoconstriction in noise experiments.

He has other evidence which shows that noise stimulates the sympathetic section of the autonomic nervous system into exerting subtle, but inappropriate, influences on the body. One is the electrodermal response, known in the United States as the galvanic skin response. It is one of the tests used in the polygraph or lie detector. Two electrodes are placed on the skin of the palm. When mind and body are calm, the galvanometer, a sensitive meter which measures low voltages, is calm. But when something nervously exciting happens—an inner stimulus like an emotion or an outer stimulus like noise—the electrical conduction of the skin increases within two seconds and the galvanometer needle is deflected. Between the stimulus and the galvanic skin response is the sympathetic nervous system. (The galvanometer, incidentally, was named after Luigi Galvani, an eighteenth century Italian physiologist.)

Dr. Maugeri has found that when noise is turned on, his subjects show a positive galvanic skin response and, at the same time, the tiny blood vessels contract. If the noise continues, the galvanic response disappears and returns to normal, but vasoconstriction remains. But if the quality of the noise changes, if it gets louder or the tones are altered, there is another galvanic response.

His son, Dr. U. Maugeri, has performed noise experiments at Pavia with a "radio pill." This is a tiny electronic device which is the size and shape of a capsule of medicine. At one end is a transducer which measures acidity (pH) and produces a corresponding electrical signal. The other end of the capsule is a radio transmitter which broadcasts this signal.

The younger Maugeri had volunteers swallow the radio pill, and when it was in their stomachs he turned on the noise. A sensitive radio receiver detected the pill's acidity measurement broadcasts. Dr. Maugeri found that in people with healthy stomachs, noise had the effect of stimulating mild gastric secretion, much the same as an aperitif does. But people whose stomachs usually secrete too much acid, such as ulcer patients, react exactly oppositely: the secretion lessens with noise.

7

HOW NOISE CAN KILL

$$((((((((((\cdot))))))))))$$

Russian architect Constantin Stramentov, a specialist in noise control, wrote in the *UNESCO Courier* in its July, 1967 issue:

> So harmful is noise that it can sometimes kill. The hooting of a car symbolizes this mortal danger. The noise made by a motor horn two yards away is estimated at 85–100 phons. It has been established that man's visual reaction drops by 25% when the noise level rises to 90 phons. The possible consequences of this need no elaboration.*

And English radio audiences in 1966 heard Dr. John Anthony Parr say in an interview:

---

* Phon is a measure of loudness; while decibel is a measure of sound pressure. At 1,000 Hz, 100 phons equal 100 dB; at 3,500 Hz, 100 phons equal 89 dB; and, at 50 Hz, 100 phons equal 110 dB.

One experiment conducted in France submitted a group of soldiers to a loud noise for 15 minutes. They were then tested and to everybody's surprise it was discovered they were color blind for over an hour.

Dr. Jansen in Germany, whose vasoconstriction studies were described earlier, also performed experiments to assess the influence of noise on the eyes. Since the size of the pupils are controlled by sympathetic nerves, as are blood vessels, the connection seemed quite logical. He focused the lens of his camera on the eyes of volunteers and turned on the noise. His first photographs were made in infrared light, because he felt then that any visible light source would produce a pupillary reaction of its own, the usual one which is responsible for light adaption. In the darkness, the pupils of the eye, he found, start opening or dilating slightly when noise reaches 70 dB, and fully at 75 dB. (Vasoconstriction in fingertips occurred simultaneously, incidentally.) His measurements showed that the diameter of the pupil increases linearly as the decibels increase, until a maximum is reached.

Dr. Jansen reasoned that if the pupil stays open when there is noise, the lens has to be affected and the convergence of the eyes must therefore change. Using an instrument called a horopter, he found that this, indeed, does occur. In a noisy environment, test objects were not where the subjects thought they were! In one report Dr. Jansen wrote, "In occupations requiring fine precision work under visual control, noise may have such a powerful influence that the worker is forced constantly to readjust his depth of focus. Some of the occupational groups in which noise might influence performance are lathe operatives, drivers, surgeons, and watchmakers." That may also be why, he explained in an interview, surgeons and watchmakers demand quiet. It could also explain another source of headache—caused by eyestrain—that noise provokes in some people.

Miss Moyra Patrick at the Institute of Sound and Vibra-

tion Research of the University of Southampton, England,
studied the effects of noise on the pupils of the eye in
controlled task conditions. She operated an elaborate television monitoring system which focused on the subject's eye.
During experiments, her TV screen was filled by one eye and
she took her measurement of pupil area directly from this
set. She explained that Daniel Kahneman of Harvard University and Jackson Beatty of the University of Michigan
discovered that the human eye pupil gets bigger when one is
trying to memorize something, and smaller when one reports
what was remembered. Her subjects tried a variety of tasks,
including the memorizing and repeating of random telephone numbers, sets of letters, and simple mathematical
problems. All of these tasks, she found, were accompanied
by increases in pupil size. She tried noise levels of 73, 93,
and 96 dB-A. The two higher levels of noise, she found,
impose a secondary pupil-opening effect on the primary one,
which was induced by the mental concentration on the task.

All of these effects of noise—on pupil size, gastric secretion,
galvanic skin response, vasoconstriction, and heartbeat are
controlled by the sympathetic nerves. Others are the ear, the
brain, and the self-regulating autonomic nervous system
(especially its sympathetic division).

The effects of noise on the body are mediated in the brain,
as are so many other stimuli. Professor Maugeri, the elder,
explained this lucidly:

> Light causes small vasospasm reactions and a galvanic
> response. Taste does this, too. When these senses are
> stimulated, the duration of reaction is only a matter of
> seconds, whereas with noise, the reaction lasts as long
> as the noise does. With light, for instance, there is
> recovery; not so with noise. This is explained by the
> anatomical formation of the brain itself and of the
> sensory organs. All sensations but hearing are differ-

entiated by a sensory organ. In taste, for example, the papillae of the tongue tell whether a food is sweet or sour. The brain only localizes such sensations, deciding whether the food is on the right or the left side of the mouth. Thus, there is a sensory organ between stimulus and the brain. The brain only gets a sensation which has already been analyzed by a peripheral sensory organ. But after the frequencies of sound are sensed by the Organ of Corti (in the inner ear), these data are sent to the brain, where different areas of the cortex distinguish the different characteristics of the noise.

Thus, it is the brain not the ear which determines the nature of noise. This can be shown in patients with head injuries. If they have lesions in the sound-sensing part of the brain, their hearing can be impaired. In fact, this gets specific. Discrete lesions prevent the perception of specific frequencies. A lesion, for instance, can prevent a patient's hearing a 4,000 Hz tone. So noise affects not only a peripheral sense organ, but the brain itself.

While noise is being perceived by the cortex, which is the highest functional area of the brain, it is also stimulating lower brain functions, specifically what is known as the *reticular formation*. This is a mass of cells at the center of the brain stem, located at the base of the brain. The reticular formation has direct connections to higher levels of the brain, to the cortex. It also has connections with the spinal cord, where it works its unperceived effects.

Dr. Maugeri showed that inhibiting the action of the reticular formation cut out the effect of noise on the sympathetic nervous system. He did this with the tranquilizer mebutamate. When this drug was given, he reported, "noise did not cause any spasm of the peripheral vessels, nor any galvanic skin response. The action of noise disappeared even at 90 and 95 dB." He also tested the reverse process and gave subjects substances to increase reticular sensitivity. Then, he said, "under the noise stimulus the reaction of spasm heightened and the galvanic response continued." All of this showed, in his opinion, that the physiological trigger of noise is the reticular formation of the brain.

Etienne Grandjean, M.D., professor and director of the Department of Hygiene and Work Physiology of the Swiss Federal Institute in Zurich, agrees in the main. He differs only in believing that nerve impulses from the inner ear can go directly and simultaneously to both the cortex and to the reticular formation. According to him, "The reticular formation is somehow a central alerting or activating system which enables the whole organism to react in an adequate way to the given outworld situation. The stimulation of the reticular formation by noise . . . will arouse the animal or human being in order to enable it to focus its attention to the external acoustical information. Therefore, the ability of paying attention depends on the reticular formation."

The autonomic nervous system is the body's self-regulating communications network. It works without conscious direction to help the body respond to variations in its internal and external environments, to maintain its status quo. In modern biological terms this is called *homeostasis*. The task of the sympathetic division of this network is to strengthen the body's defenses against the dangers it senses. Its signals branch out from the spinal cord and prepare the body for danger, from head to foot—dilating the eyes for the dark; opening up the sweat glands and gastric acid glands for future use; constricting the peripheral vessels so that blood can pool in the abdomen, where it is safer; increasing the amount of red cells in the blood to prepare for blood loss; reducing the stroke of the heart to make it more efficient; and signaling the adrenal and other glands to get ready for "fight or flight."

These signals noise provokes. Thus noise means "danger" to the most primitive pith of our beings. Without any thinking being necessary, the human body prepares itself for danger; it gears up for imminent attack. It seems like an evolutionary vestige of what would be life-saving readiness from the roar of a saber-toothed tiger, a mastadon, or a volcano. And the "roar" does not need to be so loud to arouse this animal reaction within us. Most researchers agree that levels of only 70 dB-A can do this, while 85 dB-A certainly can. The latter is generally used as the threshold of reaction, the line between response and no response. The trouble comes in today's modern world, where bodily responses to noise are too many and too often. Thus what developed over millions of years as protective physiological responses now only serve to deteriorate the body.

Princeton University psychology professor Silvan S. Tomkins said it well:

> When life and death hang in the balance, most animals have been endowed with the capacity for terror. This is appropriate if life is to be surrendered only very dearly. The cost of terror is so great that the body was not designed for chronic activation of this effect. A human being who responds as if he had reason to be chronically terrorized is properly diagnosed as ill. This is as unnatural a state as perpetual hunger would be, since both of these are incompatible with optimal existence.

A generation before, Lord Horder had said: "Doctors are definitely convinced that noise wears down the human nervous system, so that both the natural resistance to disease and the natural recovery from disease are lowered. In this way noise puts health in jeopardy, and most intelligent folk can understand this from its effect upon themselves."

One treatment of "noise sickness" would be to remove the sympathetic nervous system. Experiments with animals indicate that this nervous network is not necessary to life—so long as the body is kept warm and is otherwise well-tended.

But, of course, there are things the sympathectomized body cannot do. One of these is labor, since the body's automatic "coal-stoking," its mobilization of sugar from the liver, is impaired. And, even if such an operation were justified in man, it would be far easier instead to merely excise, or to significantly reduce, the noise itself.

The effect of noise on the body already described were produced by audible sounds—those that human beings can and so often do hear. There are also profound effects on the body which are produced by noise that cannot be heard, noise either in the *infrasonic* or *ultrasonic** frequencies.

Ultrasound is more familiar to most people. These frequencies range from about 20,000 Hz (the upper limit of hearing) to 1,000 mega Hz, and even higher, and have been used medically for years.

Feeble bursts of ultrasound are beamed into eyes, brains, fingers, uteri, and other parts of the body, and their echo-time measured by sophisticated electronic instruments and displayed on glowing screens to produce X-ray-like images. Unlike X-ray, however, these bursts of weak ultrasound cause no damage to cells. Ultrasonography, as this medical extension of sonar (the technique for detecting submarines) is called, provides a sophisticated, harmless new way to look inside the body for slivers of wood or brain tumors, and to measure the flow of blood through vessels and the beat of an unborn child's heart.

More powerful beams of ultrasound are used to create dense cold fog for the treatment of asthma, cystic fibrosis, and other severe respiratory ailments. Ultrasound is used by dentists to dislodge tartar (calculus) from teeth. Ultrasonic cleaners are used in hospitals to strip blood and other debris off of surgical instruments prior to their steam-sterilization,

---

* *Supersonic* is an aviation term and applies to speeds, not frequencies.

and are being used in homes to clean jewelry, tools, and dentures.

Even more powerful ultrasound has been used as medical therapy since it was introduced in Germany before World War II. In the first wave of enthusiasm, doctors aimed ultrasound beams at thousands of patients in an attempt to cure them of a wide assortment of ailments ranging from sinus infection to plantar warts, and including slipped disc, rheumatism, and stiff neck.

Medical authorities today know ultrasound is not to be treated lightly. Like X-ray, it can cause irreparable harm if improperly applied. The American Medical Association's Council on Physical Medicine and Rehabilitation warns that therapeutic ultrasound (not weak diagnostic ultrasound) should not be directed at the brain, spinal cord, or vital nerve centers; or at the eyes, ears, heart, or reproductive organs; or at areas of inadequate blood circulation; or at cancers or infections—unless surgical destruction is intended. The bone-growth centers of children, in wrists, ankles, and other bones, are especially sensitive to ultrasound.

Therapeutic ultrasound is generally used in physical therapy. No one knows precisely how it works, but in certain conditions it does. One of its effects is to produce heat. This makes ultrasound a good source of deep heat for muscle relaxation and blood vessel dilation. This also gives therapeutic ultrasound a built-in safety factor. If the ultrasound is incorrectly applied, the area focused on feels uncomfortably hot. When the patient complains, the physician or therapist can reduce the power of the beam or move it around more quickly so that all of the energy is not concentrated on one area at one time. This is one reason ethical and careful operators of therapeutic ultrasound devices never apply it to diseased limbs or to areas of the body that have no feeling.

Ultrasound's medical benefits may come from an action that has been called "micromassage." David I. Abramson,

M.D., an internist who is professor and head of physical medicine at the University of Illinois Medical Center in Chicago, explained that ultrasound literally shakes living tissue so as to stimulate its blood flow and to loosen harmful or foreign substances. This, believes Dr. Abramson, is why ultrasound is often effective in treating bursitis: it loosens and mobilizes the tiny, jagged deposits of calcium in bone joints (usually the shoulder) which cause the pain and limit motion. This ultrasonic vibration is also what makes this form of physical therapy useful in softening scar tissue and in reducing nerve-tissue growths which cause pain after amputation of a limb or other extremity.

The most powerful beams of ultrasound are used surgically as a sort of bloodless scalpel to destroy tissue without cutting it away. Ultrasound can be focused on very small areas so that the beam's destruction can be precisely pinpointed. Used this way, ultrasound has been developed, in a joint University of Illinois/University of Iowa effort, to destroy bits of tissue in those areas of the brain—usually the globus pallidus—which are sending out erroneous nerve signals that result in Parkinson's Disease (shaking palsy). Beams of ultrasound have also been used to successfully treat Ménière's Disease, an affliction of recurrent dizziness, buzzing in the ear, and creeping deafness. The treatment, originated in Padua, Italy, consists of destroying the vestibular labyrinth in the affected inner ear with a tiny ultrasonic beam. Equally exact in its surgical application is the destruction with ultrasonic waves of the pituitary gland at the base of the brain, via a sinus cavity reached through the nose. Destruction of the pituitary is useful in treating Cushing's Syndrome. The destructive effects of ultrasound have also been used to treat bone cancer.

At the other end of the sound spectrum are frequencies below those which can be heard. This is the world of infrasonics. The noise here ranges from about 20 Hz downward to 1 Hz. Among the scientists who have been most concerned with infrasonics are an American with a German name and a Frenchman with a Russian name. The first is Henning E. von Gierke, Dr. Eng., of the Aerospace Medical Research Laboratories at Wright Patterson Air Force Base, Ohio. His main concern is the effect of aerospace environments on pilots and astronauts. One aspect of these environments is noise. It starts at launch time, as rocket engines blast back their tremendously powerful fires of propulsion. With this rapid expenditure of energy come high intensities of noise. Most of it is noise that can be heard—at the site of blast-off, beneath the path of the rocket during the first minutes of flight, and in the space capsule itself. Much of the noise, though, is infrasonic and unheard.

Dr. von Gierke and his colleagues, Capt. George C. Mohr, M.D., John N. Cole, and Lt. Col. Elizabeth Guild, tested the effects of 1 to 100 Hz noise on five "noise-experienced" officers. As they pointed out, ". . . the upper limits of human tolerance and performance in such noise environments are not known. In view of the virtual certainty that increasingly high levels of low sonic and infrasonic noise will be generated [in aerospace systems], it is essential that these limits be defined . . . each additional pound or cubic inch of acoustical isolation material means deletion of valuable payload."

The subjects—"four males, one female, aged 24 to 46"—were subjected to infrasonic noise in four situations. Two used large and powerful electrodynamic loudspeaker systems; one used a J57 jet engine afterburner which closely simulated the noise in a Saturn-boosted space compartment; the fourth was a high-velocity hot-air tunnel. All of the subjects wore ear protectors against the noise, which ranged from 85 to 150 dB.

The Air Force researchers found that "In the very low

sonic frequency range, chest wall vibration, gag sensations, and respiratory rhythm changes were regularly observed." In the 50–100 Hz range, "responses including headaches, choking, coughing, visual blurring and fatigue were sufficiently alarming to preclude undergoing higher level exposures without more precise control of the noise environment and definition of the physiologic effects elicited."

Electronic Engineer Vladimir Gavreau of the French National Center for Scientific Research at Marseilles became interested in infrasonics as a result of what happened when his electro-acoustical research group moved into a new building in 1964. The staff started to complain of headaches and nausea. Work was stopped and everyone left the vicinity. Stray electromagnetic waves—radar perhaps—were suspected. But detection instruments could find no such waves. Then ultrasonic noise, the laboratory's main interest for eighteen years, was suspected. But none of these sounds could be detected either. Then one of the technicians thought of low frequencies and brought out an old infrasonic detector. His hunch proved correct. Some scientific sleuthing led them to a giant industrial ventilator in an adjoining building. Their discovery led to a modification of the ventilator so as to change its harmful noise downward in intensity from 120 dB and upward in frequency to the audible range.

It also led Professor Gavreau and his researchers to find out more about the properties and propagation of infrasound. The first infrasonic generator they built was a giant whistle powered by compressed air. It is officially called the Lavavasseur Whistle, after the engineer who designed and built it, but was nicknamed "The Little Monster" by his colleagues. The first test of it was almost catastrophic.

A London *Sunday Times* account quoted Professor Gavreau as saying, "Luckily we were able to turn it off fast.

All of us were sick for hours. Everything in us was vibrating—stomach, heart, lungs. All the people in the other laboratories were sick too. They were very angry with us."

Its output was 300 acoustical watts, or 300 times that of an ear-piercing policeman's whistle (which has an intensity of only one acoustical watt). Small wonder that Professor Gavreau couldn't work for a couple of days after that first test! In spite of the fact that he had been wearing ear protection, he suffered from ringing in his head for 24 hours.

Professor Gavreau and his research team persisted with their infrasonic experiments and as a result have developed a family of devilish devices which generate sounds of disruptive and destructive force.

More Lavavasseur Whistles were built. The largest was 60 inches in diameter. It reportedly produced such severe vibration in the walls of the building that it was never operated at full power. Professor Gavreau conceived of building one 18 feet in diameter which would be mounted on a truck and powered by the blast of a small airplane engine. He believes it could kill at a five-mile distance. The effect of powerful infrasound on the body, he believes, is centered on the viscera. "It works directly on the internal organs. There is a rubbing between the various organs because of a sort of resonance. It provokes an irritation so intense that for hours afterwards any low-pitched sound seems to echo through one's body."

The team at Marseilles found that the frequency of 7 Hz is fatal. They believe this is related to the frequencies of the rhythm of the brain. Brain waves or electroencephalograms, show three frequency bands: alpha, 8 to 10 per second; beta, 15 to 60; and, delta, 1 to 5 per second. The alpha waves disappear when the eyes are open—but a flickering light can cause the waves to assume its very own frequency. Perhaps infrasound has the same effect of making the brain fall into step. A person exposed to infrasound of 7 Hz has a vague impression of sound and a feeling of general discomfort but is totally unable to perform mental work, even simple arithmetic. As the intensity of the unheard sound increases, dizziness sets in, then nervous fatigue and seasickness. (Notice that these findings are somewhat similar to those of von Gierke.) At still higher intensity, the internal organs vibrate and the resulting friction produces quiek but painful death.

Thus, Professor Gavreau's most fiendish research instruments are in effect infrasonic weapons. One is a 24-meter (78-foot) organ pipe which weighs over 2,000 pounds because, to keep it rigid, it is cast in concrete. In fact, it rather looks like a sewer pipe. For comparison, a 32-foot organ stop produces the lowest note likely to be encountered in music, the low C of 16 Hz. This is the C below the lowest C on a piano keyboard and is felt rather than heard. Theoretically, the second C below the lowest C on a piano (8 Hz) would be produced by a 64-foot pipe. The 78-foot French pipe is actuated by one of three mechanisms—a large loudspeaker diaphragm, a mechanically driven piston, or a jet of air. It can produce not only a note of 7 Hz, but one of 3½ Hz as well. The latter, which, of course, cannot itself be heard, has an interesting incidental effect: it attaches itself to other sounds, so that everything else that is audible seems to undulate rhythmically. In time, the effect of 3½ Hz is to fix its rhythm on the senses in a most irritating way.

Professor Gavreau's ultimate infrasonic weapon is what he calls his "acoustic beacon" or "acoustic laser." It is a weird-looking bouquet of 60 tubes, each of which leads from a forced-air source, and all of which are of the same precise low frequency. The free ends of the tubes are sound emitters held in a plane by a metal framework and spaced precisely one-quarter of a wave length apart into a square pattern with rounded corners. The device projects a narrow beam of sound, an acoustic beacon, which reportedly can be aimed with great precision. A battery of these devices focused on a platoon of men or a structure could destroy them. Because it is deadly yet inexpensive, it has been turned over to weapons technicians of the French army for testing.

Professor Gavreau's devices are admittedly exotic. They do not produce infrasound of the intensities one is liable to be exposed to in everyday life. Still, sounds of these frequencies are components of everyday noise. Unheard and unknown, they may well be taking their toll. Ultrasonic frequencies, as is discussed in a later chapter, are indeed commonly emitted by the countless turbines which have become so omnipresent in modern civilization. Infrasonic frequencies, too, are present everyday, as Professor Gavreau discovered when he moved into his new laboratory. It may well be the reason airplane passengers, pilots, and astronauts sometimes have vague feelings of malaise and discomfort. The National Bureau of Standards actually measured infrasounds below 15 Hz in Washington, D.C., and found far more than they expected. Some of the sources of the infrasound were identified as tornadoes in Oklahoma, a thousand miles away; an earthquake in Montana, halfway across the continent; and magnetic storms at the upper limits of the atmosphere. About a dozen sources of infrasound measured by the Bureau were unidentified. Some may even have come from other parts of earth. The Bureau studies were an outgrowth of an observation made in 1883, when Volcano Krakatoa, in East India, produced a sound heard 'round the world. The noise was recorded by pressure barographs not once but several times as the sound repeatedly circled the globe before dying out.

This has particular significance since such global infrasound waves can also be propagated by man-made sources, specifically sonic booms. Early in the 1950's explosive sources in the lower atmosphere were found to produce seismic waves. In 1968 three scientists recorded the first well-developed seismic waves generated from sonic booms of jet fighter planes at high altitudes. The strength of these waves, as measured at Cape Kennedy, Florida, was comparable to that generated by a large pile driver about 200 feet away! In some cases, sound can have the *effect* of a pile driver, as we will see in the next chapter.

8

HOW NOISE DESTROYS

$$((((((((((\cdot))))))))))$$

Besides the toll which noise imposes on our bodies, our emotions, and our hearing, there is the physical mayhem and destruction it wreaks. For noise not only shocks us, maddens us, distresses us, and deafens us, it physically wrecks our surroundings as well.

Legend has it that the walls of Jericho crumbled from the intense sound made by the horns of Joshua's army. That an operatic singer can, by holding a note, cause a crystal goblet to shatter is well known. Perhaps the most spectacular recent destructive effect of noise was what it did to Great Britain's civil aviation post-war pride, the de Havilland Comet. The first of the world's jet airliners, it began service with British Overseas Airways Corp. in 1952—four years ahead of Russian, and six years ahead of American jet airliners. Compared to the slower propeller airplanes of the

119

day, its 475 mph performance and its smooth ride were spectacular. The Comet's first route was from London to South Africa, initiated on May 2, 1952.

Besides having great speed, the jet was more comfortable to ride in: it was bigger and roomier than the prop planes; the ride was smoother because the plane flew at higher and more meteorologically stable altitudes; and, the passengers weren't shaken as much by any piston-engine vibrations.

The Comet was the transportation wonder of the world, flying closer to the speed of sound than any previous airliner. It was a prediction come true of How Things Will Be After the Long War. But along with the clanging fall of the Iron Curtain and other post-war disappointments, the Comet soon disillusioned everyone, after three of them fell from the skies. The first was a rather unpublicized crash at Calcutta on May 2, 1953. The second was a Comet code-named Yoke Peter, which had taken off from Rome at 9:30 A.M. on January 10, 1954. Twenty minutes later, when it was at 26,000 feet, Yoke Peter exploded, carrying 29 lives to their ends near Elba, Napoleon's island of exile. Thus ended Yoke Peter's 10 million miles of pioneer jet transport. Three months later, on April 8, 1954, another Comet, code-named Yoke Yoke, exploded south of Naples on a run from Rome to Cairo.

B.O.A.C. grounded the rest of its Comets and began one of history's most intensive and detailed studies of the cause of air crashes. Each bit of Yoke Peter and Yoke Yoke that could be recovered was examined. In addition, existing Comets were subjected to extensive testing, especially since in both crashes the fuselages had exploded when the higher pressure inside the cabins was suddenly released to the rarefied outside atmosphere of the high altitudes at which the planes were flying.

The lines of study converged on a navigation window on top of the fuselage. A tiny crack had started at the edge of the window frame and widened, finally ending in the fatal explosive decompression. But what had caused the crack? One theory blamed the many cycles of heating and cooling—the heating occurring from friction through the air at high speeds, the cooling from the plane's sitting on the ground between flights. Another theory blamed the noise and vibration of the jet engines which were tucked in trim pods at the intersection of the wing and fuselage. A facility which became The Institute for Sound and Vibration Research was started at Southampton University to look into the noise theory.

Although the Final Report of the Royal Aircraft Establishment in February, 1955, merely listed "metal fatigue" as the cause of the Comet's calamity, Southampton researchers had indeed found that the metal fatigue was of the kind known as acoustic fatigue (not to be confused with the old term for temporary loss of hearing mentioned in a previous chapter). High-pitched noise from the jet's own engines had caused its destruction.

Researchers at Southampton, such as Robert Crawford, now have rigs for studying the acoustical fatigue of metals and can very graphically demonstrate how broad-band sound at, say, 150 dB can start a crack in a metal part and make it propagate until the metal part fails. Often in such experiments they use the maddening noise of giant sirens that are reminiscent of Professor Gavreau's noise-weapon studies in France.

Auditory fatigue in metals is of serious concern not only in aviation. The 180 to 200 dB noise of cooling fluids which circulate under high pressure around nuclear reactors have been known to cause cracks in the piping. This phenomenon, too, has been under study at Southampton.

Noise works to fatigue metals and other materials by its incessant repetition of cycles of overpressure and underpressure. What happens is that the sound waves work first the molecules, then the crystals of metal away from each other. As the material's cohesion is destroyed, the faults or cracks widen.

The opera singer's voice works in a slightly different way to shatter a glass. If the glass is properly made, it has a natural resonance frequency which is identical to some pure musical note which the singer can sing and hold. The glass tries to duplicate the vibrations of the air, much as a still tuning fork does to an identical one which is vibrating, or a still violin does to one which is played nearby. But the glass lacks the elasticity necessary to vibrate more as the intensity of sound increases, so as it enlarges its sympathetic vibration, it shatters under its own brittleness.

The Comet case opened the eyes of aeronautical engineers to the tremendous importance of acoustic fatigue. It tragically demonstrated that noise must be included among the tests that structures need to undergo. It helped launch the beginning of a modern surge in environmental testing which blossomed later with the design and building of rockets and missiles. In 1958 Werner Fricke, Ph.D., of Bell Aircraft Corp., told the Acoustical Society of America, "In the last three years, airborne noise has become an important new environment in the test program for aircraft and missile components. Intense airborne noise can produce a surprising number and variety of component failures." Dr. Fricke then put the structural noise problem in perspective: "The overall noise levels increase toward the rear of the fuselage and can reach 145 dB in airplanes and missiles of the low- and middle-thrust class. Levels of 160 dB exist in missiles of the high-thrust class during the boost phase. . . . Examples of components which are likely to be 'sound-sensitive' are electron tubes, relays, microwave equipment, baroswitches, and accelerometers." Failures because of noise also exist, he said, in "gyros, electronic systems, resistors, capicitors, and semiconductors."

Dr. Fricke has been a strong advocate of the importance of considering noise when designing and testing airborne and spaceborne equipment and structures. In 1962, for instance, he reported to fellow environmental engineers the results of his laboratory tests on the "arm-safe" component of a guided missile, which showed that "the noise environment produced an output signal which, under actual flight conditions, would have caused destruction of the missile before reaching its intended target."

In 1967 he and a colleague at Bell Aerosystems Co. (the new name of the company) reported to the Acoustical Society of America about their sonic concerns in the design of ducted propellers for Bell's experimental V.T.O.L. (Vertical Take-Off and Landing) aircraft. The three-bladed propellers rotate inside a cylinder-shaped duct. The ducted-propeller design gives more thrust at low speeds than does a free propeller. And, in fact, the closer the tips of the propeller are to the inner wall of the duct, the more thrust it can deliver. But the closer this tolerance is, the more intense is the noise field it creates in the duct. This sound, explained Dr. Fricke, "may reach values that can cause acoustical fatigue of the duct structure. To prevent such damage, a duct must be designed capable of resisting the acoustical loads. This task, in turn, requires knowledge of the sound field inside the duct." Noise levels measured in the duct in fact reached almost 170 dB.

If the tragedy of the Comet made engineers and physicists such as Dr. Fricke acutely aware of the acoustic fatigue problem, it also frustrated them. Not all aerospace noise problems are as readily predictable as is the noise generated by a ducted prop. But they do yield in time if the pressures of research are incessant enough. This happened in the case of combustion instability in rockets. The problem was that the noise produced by the rocket engine formed sound waves which interacted with spent gases in the combustion chamber, there to form hot and cool spots on the metal wall. The result was intense heat localization, which could cause a rocket to blow itself up or to veer off its course.

Only trial-and-error experimentation was available to correct the problem until two Tennessee Technicological University engineers, Drs. Allan E. Hribar and Kenneth R. Purdy, worked out mathematical models for predicting combustion instability with a view toward correcting the design of rocket combustion chambers to withstand the appropriate noise level and kind.

The beneficial physical effects on the body of ultrasound—sound of frequencies that are beyond the range of hearing—were described in the previous chapter. Ultrasound can achieve powerful proportions and, when it does, can be used as an industrial tool.

Ultrasound is used by dentists to clean the tartar (calculus) from patients' teeth and by the edentulous to clean their artificial dentures at home. Sinks that use ultrasound instead of soap in the cleaning water are used in hospitals. At home, ultrasonic cleaners are especially good for cleaning jewelry and fine china. Ultrasound is also used in heavy industry to machine very hard materials, to solder metals, to produce metal alloys and glass; in chemical processes to break up long-chain polymers; in metal rolling; and in the detection of cracks and other faults in aircraft frames and in automobile parts. In light of the Comet story, it is ironic that one supersonic transport design called for small ultrasonic transducers built into the air frame at critical points to give data during flight about any metal fatigue that might develop.

Ultrasound, in other words, is becoming ubiquitous, just like the kind of sound we can hear. But while what we hear can serve as a warning, what we can't hear can still hurt us. One of ultrasound's negative effects is that it can harm living tissue by heating it from within. It is used, in fact, to destroy bacteria and other microorganisms. Ultrasound can be safely used when it is well-contained. But if it follows the general rising trend of heard sound in our society, we are perhaps only a decade away from the time when our sensitive germ cells (ova and sperm) will be in far more danger of mutation than they ever were from atomic fallout. And beyond that is the time when our body cells may be endangered; and, beyond that time, if the ultrasonic decibel background rises still further, to the era when our homes and possessions will be endangered by ultrasound in the unheard background.

If the dangers of ultrasound are still largely conjectural, the dangers of the sonic boom, which is produced by supersonic aircraft, are real. In 1968 three farm workers at Cannes, France died when a sonic boom sent a loft of barley down upon their heads. A hard $1,460,000 was paid by the U.S. Air Force for sonic-boom glass and plaster damage claims between 1956 and 1968. Documented, too, was the fragmentation of red-walled prehistoric Indian dwellings at the de Chelley National Monument in northeastern Arizona; the damage to red sandstone columns in Bryce Canyon, Utah; and the damage of Indian dwellings at Mesa Verda, Colorado—all by sonic booms. In a report to the U.S Secretary of the Interior dated January 10, 1967, George B. Hartzog, Jr., National Park Director, gave this example: "On October 12, shortly after three exceptionally short booms, approximately 10 to 15 tons of dirt and rock was found to have fallen from one of the formations. . . ." He and other National Park Service officials expressed the dark possibility that new collapses caused by sonic booms could destroy ancient artifacts and structures yet unexcavated by archeologists and quietly obliterate important records of human history—ironically with one of the latest instruments of human technology.

Great Britain is also concerned about the possible damage to its ancient architecture and late in 1968 began studies to

see what effects sonic booms would have on such great
structures as Westminster Abbey, Winchester Cathedral,
and Canterbury Cathedral. The study was being conducted
by, among others, researchers from the University of Southampton's Institute of Sound and Vibration Research.

Sonic booms, it turns out, affects more than merely the
glass of buildings, despite the reluctance of the U.S. Air
Force and supersonic transport (S.S.T.) advocates to admit
it. But Harvey H. Hubbard, head of the Acoustics Branch of
the National Aeronautic and Space Administration's Langley
Research Center, pointed out that "a building is subjected to
a variety of loading events as the [N] wave pattern sweeps
over it." First it is "forced laterally as a result of the initial
positive loading on the front surface. Then it would be
forced inward from all directions, then forced outward and
finally forced laterally again because of the negative pressures acting on the back surface. This loading sequence,
which would be applied within a time period of about 0.3
seconds can result in complex transient vibrations of the
building."

Superficial damage which has been reported as a result of
sonic boom tests, or because of random sonic booms, has
been associated with what Hubbard called stress concentrations. "Stress concentrations in buildings may be due to
factors such as curing of green lumber, dehydration, setting,
poor workmanship, etc. Such factors exist in varying degrees
in all carpentered structures and could contribute to failures
when a triggering load is applied. The overpressure of a
sonic boom has this triggering capability."

Sonic-boom experiments conducted at Edwards Air Force
Base, California, in 1966 and 1967 concentrated, in part, on
two test houses built on the base, plus the existing bowling
alley and an existing two-story house in nearby Lancaster,
California. According to the report of Karl D. Kryter, Ph.D.,
of Stanford Research Institute, who directed the study, "No

damage that could be attributed to sonic booms was observed in the test structures during these experiments. However, some damage was alleged to have been caused by sonic booms in the vicinity of Edwards Air Force Base during these tests. Fifty-seven complaints were received."

Dr. Kryter also noted, despite that disqualifier, that "sonic booms from large aircraft such as the XB-70 and the future Supersonic Transport will affect a greater range of structural elements . . . than will sonic booms from smaller aircraft such as the B-58 and F-104" used in the tests.

One of the 367 test booms caused a complaint which was more than merely alleged. It occurred in the U.S. Post Office at Tehachapi, a tiny desert town, on June 20, 1966. At exactly 10:43 A.M. a B-58 Hustler bomber had just completed its turn on the easterly leg of its run over Edwards. Its position was fixed later by a review of the radar plot of its run. The time was exactly known because, by coincidence, the postmistress just happened at that instant to be looking at a clock opposite her desk. The boom generated by the bomber broke the post office window and, in the adjoining department store, broke a window and extended cracks in the plaster walls.

Here are summaries of the results of other sonic boom damage tests.

During November 6–12, 1961, and January 3–6, 1962, B-58 supersonic bombers and F-106 supersonic fighters flew seventeen flights over St. Louis, Missouri, to see what kind of damage to structures the sonic booms would cause. An architect-engineer team provided under contract to N.A.S.A. by the firm of Clark, Buhr & Nexsen, of Norfolk, Virginia, investigated 84 reports of sonic boom damage and concluded that:

—"Overpressures have the capability of triggering cracking or complete failure at a stressed portion of plaster and/or causing an existing crack to become more extensive.

—"Overpressures have the capability of triggering cracking or breaking of glass that was stressed by improper installation, building settlement, previous damage or poor quality [but not] good quality, properly installed glass.

—"Some persons claimed broken vases, fallen pictures, and fallen wall racks. In observing the above claimed damage, it was noticed that in most cases the fallen objects were insecurely attached to the wall.

—"On several occasions television sets were claimed to have failed as a result of sonic boom. Upon investigating, it was learned that antennae, both 'rabbit ears' and roof top type, had fallen from their normal position.

—"The overpressures could possibly have triggered cracking at a stressed condition in a structure and/or caused an existing crack to open up or grow longer."

In 1964 Oklahoma City, Oklahoma, was subjected to eight daily sonic booms for 26 weeks (for a total of 208 booms), to see, again, what the effects on structures might be. According to one report, there was a significant increase in the occurrence of minor cracks in the paint over nailheads and in the corners of the wallboard interiors of two test structures. These small but significant clues pointed to the fact that the walls of the homes received rather severe jolts from the boom noise.

Two back-to-back 1964 reports of sonic-boom effects on buildings added further explosive data. One concluded that "there was evidence of resonant vibration of parts of the buildings under suitable incident shock conditions, and it appears that such resonant vibration could be harmful at certain discrete points within a boom area should a boom fall on an extensive built-up area."

The other report concerned damage to a nearly completed terminal building caused by the boom of an F-104 fighter. The glass wall of the terminal was shattered, and building roofing, curtain wall, doorways, and interior ceilings were damaged.

The physical effects of the sonic boom were explored in a report (by that name) issued in February, 1968, by the National Academy of Sciences' Committee on S.S.T. Sonic Boom. While, the report said, "the probability of material damage being caused by a sonic boom generated by an aircraft operating in a safe, normal manner is very small," there has been "lack of attention heretofore given to that aspect of the materials response problem which involves incipient and progressive failures." The committee called for extensive testing in engineering colleges of materials susceptible to damage by sonic booms. First on the list was glass: what it takes in a boom to break glass, how the urban environment affects such glass breakage, and how glass might be made to withstand the overpressures of the boom. Second on the list was plaster, including basecoats, finish coats, stucco, and wallboard. Also needing study, said the sonic-boom research group, was the effect of the boom on masonry such as interior tiles, brick, concrete blocks and stone; organic adhesives; roofing materials and roof construction; thermoplastic building materials; wallpaper; and such assorted structural components as:

—Deteriorated caulking, adhesive gaskets, and sealants.
—Deteriorated fasteners for building materials and systems.
—Plaster with weakened bond.
—Deteriorated brick courses, particularly at roof lines.
—Cornices and copings in weakened conditions.
—Lay-in acoustical ceiling panels.
—Lay-in lighting units.
—Incipient nail popping.
—Partitions under thin flat-slabs subject to creep.
—Partitions framed into exposed structural columns.

The committee also suggested research into the effect of sonic booms on earth structures. "There are indications that there are some earth structures that may be susceptible to failure under dynamic loadings such as sonic booms, namely (a) slopes, either cuts or fills, which have critical or small factors of safety and (b) foundations on unstable sand strata or 'quick' clays."

Explaining (b) further, it said, "There are known examples of failures of foundations under structures where either sand strata or 'quick' clays become unstable under certain conditions as a result of loadings. For example, a large structure above ground may receive either an impact loading from a wind gust or sudden pressure wave or from an earth tremor which may, in turn, be transmitted to an unstable strata and thus trigger the material into instability."

The committee noted, too, that "some natural formations, notably those at a point of incipient failure, may be potentially susceptible to sonic boom damage."

Cautioned the committee, "Future claims of damage to materials in the foregoing list will be difficult to evaluate unless definitive statistical information is developed."

Dr. Cyril Stanley Smith, an eminent physicist and materials researcher, noted about the S.S.T.'s booms: "In a city with a million housing units there will therefore be a hundred of them damaged—approximately one for every passenger on the plane, who will save less time than it takes to repair the damage produced. This is in addition to the discomfort, the disturbance of normal activity, and the interruption of conversation or of thought of hundreds of thousands of individuals."

Even more dire in predicting boom damage was one of the world's foremost aeronautical engineers, Dr. Bo K. O. Lundberg, former director general of Sweden's Flygtekniska Försöksanstalten (Aeronautical Research Institute), who advocated jet airliners in 1943, and who designed Sweden's successful J-22 fighter for World War II. He said "boom carpets" would crisscross the civilized world under the flight paths of the S.S.T.'s, when—and if—they are operated commercially. He told the Fourth International Congress for Noise Abatement in 1966:

"Surely, most of the hundreds of millions of buildings all over the world that will be covered by the boom carpets have numerous sensitive areas or 'weak spots,' in the sense quoted [in the U.S. Federal Aviation Agency's report on the Oklahoma City boom tests]. The number of such spots is probably even greater than the number of people. This means that there will be many thousands of millions of 'weak spot' boom exposures per year on typical S.S.T. routes, of which many millions will be greatly magnified. The enormous numbers of such exposures will inevitably result in uncountable cases of 'minor' damage and numerous cases of serious structural damage. There will probably be a hundredfold or a thousandfold more damage than has been caused by military supersonic activity.

"According to estimates in the U.S.A. the cost of structural damage in North America due to the booms will amount to some 50 million dollars per year."

Most of this damage, Dr. Lundberg said, will not occur at the beginning of S.S.T. operation, but later, as the effects of sonic booms accumulate, and as new weak spots are hit, especially by "magnified" booms, which occur under certain atmospheric conditions when the supersonic plane turns or accelerates. Also, shock waves from two or more supersonic planes can meet on the ground and cause superbooms.

The Citizens League Against the Sonic Boom (headquartered at 19 Appleton St., Cambridge, Massachusetts, 02138, and directed by physicist William A. Shurcliff, Ph.D.) in its Fact Sheet 15 (May, 1968) estimated an even greater toll in dollars which would be caused by the destructive results of a single S.S.T. flight across the United States:

> The U.S. has a population of about 200 million and an area of 3,615,211 square miles; thus the average population density is about 55 individuals per square mile.

A transcontinental supersonic flight 2,000 miles long and with a bang-zone 50 miles wide could then result in 5.5 million boom exposures. A larger number of exposures may result unless the S.S.T. flightpath is deliberately routed away from heavily populated areas. . . . a single transcontinental supersonic flight could result in:

> 219 complaints
> 75 damage claims
> 44 paid-out damage claims, and
> $3,322 actual payment

If the average S.S.T. carries 200 passengers, the latter figure suggests that a ticket surcharge of at least $16.60 per ticket may be necessary in order to pay for the sonic boom damage. The cost of processing and handling claims would, of course, increase the figure.

The implications . . . are even more disturbing if one looks at the yearly totals for a time when a total of, say, 150 S.S.T.s might make 5 transcontinental trips daily, 365 days a year. This would amount to about 274,000 flights per year, and accordingly one might expect 21 million damage claims per year. The processing of these claims would require an effort comparable to the existing Income Tax Bureau. In a full year, the 274,000 flights would result in about $910 million in damage claims.

Noise destroyed the first generation of Comets by starting small cracks in the walls and making them grow until the metal failed. The next generation of jetliner may destroy our homes by starting small cracks and hitting them again and again until the walls fail. Thus does noise, in the form of the sonic boom especially, hang over our heads threatening to attack our health (both emotional and bodily), our hearing, and even our houses.

2

WHERE NOISE
COMES FROM

$(((((((((\cdot)))))))))$

9

OUR NOISY WORLD

$$(((((((((\cdot)))))))))$$

There are few spots in the world where it is really quiet, and there have been few times in the history of the civilized world when it wasn't noisy. There are caverns such as those in Mammoth Cave, Kentucky, which are walled by many feet of solid rock and are naturally so still that you can hear the quiet hum of blood coursing through your middle ears. There are also such isolated places as the Antarctic, during those rare times when the wind is not howling and the seals are not barking, when it becomes so quiet that you get the feeling that the world has stopped. In these particular circumstances one finds the silence eerie indeed, but then so is the total sensory experience. In the cave the quiet is joined by profound subterannean darkness; in Antarctica it is accompanied by the sight of the overhead sun, pale behind a white overcast hanging over a white landscape—inappropriately at midnight.

Although the creation of the earth and the solar system
may have been physically cataclysmic, the chances are that
over the eons, this slow accumulation of swirls of dust and
gases created little noise. Only as the hot, dense stuff became
the burning sun and its satellites may noise have begun. But
there was no air to carry any sound—nor any ear to hear it,
save that of God. Later, the creation of the earth's continents
and the formation of its mountain ranges must have been
noisy indeed. Today's reverberations of this geophysical
history so testify: earthquakes, volcanic eruptions, and land-
slides. And what of the other natural phenomena that are so
noisy: waterfalls, thunder, tornadoes, roaring, bellowing
animal herds, and flights of screaming birds?

The seas are filled with the clatter of underwater life
which chirps, grunts, pops, clicks, croaks, and moos. According to a British naturalist, the 15,000 species of fish in the
ocean make more noise than all the animals on land, man
included. The jungle is a particularly noisy place, as naturalist Ronald McKie found in Malaya. There, he wrote, "the
noise, the endless noise, came so close at times to pain." He
first noticed the noise of the jungle when awakened by a
cicada, likened to "the jangle of your alarm clock amplified
many times." But, let McKie tell it:

> About 140 different species of cicadas live in Malaya
> and there are thousands of creeping, crawling, hop-
> ping things. All have voices and all use them at the
> same time. The noise of a metropolis is a murmur be-
> side the din of the jungle, especially during the day.
>   When one first registers the jungle clamour it seems
> to be, like jungle perfume, a solid lump. But gradually
> one learns to penetrate the lump and distinguish, first
> groups of noises then individual sounds. The jungle
> sings, whistles, rings bells, squeaks, squeals, buzzes.
> It plays scales, pipes, hoots, howls, scrapes in a dry
> sandpaper way.
>   . . . black gibbons, with faces like great-grand-

mother, whoop-whooped from their tree beds, and on
the canopy the first hornbill sounded off like a frontier
railway engine, a prolonged steam-driven hoot that
ended in a terrible laughter. . . .

Among all this noise there was still space for other
sounds—steam presses, grinders, squeaking wheels—
an entire foundry collection, metallic and harsh.

One wag, cartoonist Johnny Hart, in his *B.C.* strip of
Sunday, April 2, 1967, said, "It is written that he [Adam]
cast his rib upon the ground and said, 'Let there be noise.'"
The Old Testament mentions the clatter of stone hand-
mills. Eyewitnesses in ancient Rome wrote that even before
sunrise, the hammering of metal workers and the yelling of
children were deafeningly combined with the cries of bakers
and cowherds hawking their bread and milk. Silence was
held off throughout the day by cattle herded through the
streets, peddlers crying their wares, mountebanks singing
and strumming, town criers giving loud oral notice that
some jewelry or slave was lost, that a shop was for sale, that
dwellings were available for rent. Punctuating the voices of
animals and man were the musical instrument-makers' off-
notes, the clatter of wagon and chariot wheels on the cob-
blestones, the staccato of smiths and carpenters. At night,
free-roaming dogs howled. It is small wonder that Roman
satirist Juvenal wrote,

> Because they get no sleep,
> Many of the sick perish in Rome . . .
> And even a prince of sleepers like Claudius
> Awakens with the din.

During the Dark Ages, things didn't quiet down too much.
Wagons still rattled through city streets and hawkers still
cried their wares. In Paris, Berlin, and Vienna, street criers
persisted for centuries. "Some 300 years ago people in London were complaining about the cries of street hawkers, and

the clanging of muffinmen, and so on, in our streets," recently observed a British government official. A vendor of
hotcakes in London in 1833 learned how to turn silence into
a profit. A nervous lady who was particularly disturbed by
his cries offered to pay him regularly if he would simply
avoid her street every day on his route. He agreed, then
cleverly thought that there might be other streets which
would similarly pay such noise-protection money. There
were! He did so well getting money for *not* crying aloud that
he gave up his cake trade and lived on the proceeds of his
noise-control measure!

To German philosopher Arthur Schopenhauer (1788–
1860), "Hammering, the barking of dogs, and the crying of
children are horrible sounds; but your only assassin of
thought is the crack of a whip. . . . The most inexcusable
and disgraceful of all noises. . . . In Germany it seems as
though care were taken that no one should ever think for
mere noise." He quoted Thomas Hood as saying of Germans,
"For a musical nation, they are the most noisy I ever met
with."

In noise as with every other aspect of human life, history
has shown that nothing changes but time and techniques.
Noise, for instance, is still a problem in the Germany of
today. A 1968 public opinion survey found that every other
West German feels harassed by noise. The main causes of
noise annoyance are still related to the streets, to transportation, and to work. Thus, the survey found this order of hated
sounds by frequency of complaint: motor vehicles, aircraft,
builders' machines. The reasons for the annoyance are clear,
according to a report by the *London Economist:* "The number of private cars alone rose from 4 million in 1960 to 10
million in 1966, and is expected to reach about 20 million by
1980. Over roughly the same period the number of aircraft
calling at West German airports has doubled. The renascent
Luftwaffe is more often heard than seen. New roads and

buildings proliferate seemingly overnight, but never silently."

Rome's noise problems, too, have only a new coat of modernity. Julius Caesar banned chariots from the city during daylight hours because they clogged the streets and assaulted the ears and nerves. Modern Rome contains a million registered cars, all of which, at one time or another, create such traffic jams as, to quote a dispatch in *The New York Times*, "make Midtown Manhattan streets look like thruways." As a move to reduce its traffic and traffic noises 2,012 years after the death of Caesar, Rome bans the parking of cars in its central areas during weekdays. Professor Maugeri of Pavia measured the ancient and modern fountains of six cities in Northern Italy (Milano, Brescia, Varese, Cremona, Bergamo, and Sondrio, each a capital of its own province in Lombardy) and found that these romantically described cascades of water seriously increased the noise levels of the city squares. "The noise produced by these fountains," Dr. Maugeri said, "was found to be of almost lethal proportions in intensity and frequency."

Owing to our modern and mechanized ways, the noise of our world increases. "In all probability, the noise level will grow not only in urban centers, but, with increasing population and the proliferation of machines, noise will invade the few remaining havens of silence in the world," said noise control expert Leo L. Beranek of Boston. "A century from now, when a man wants to escape to a quiet spot, there may be no place left to go."

Drs. Doughtery and Welsh, also of Boston, pointed out that "in the community, the noise-pollution problem is just beginning, for noise in any machine is related to power output, a quantity that is growing as rapidly in the home as in industry or on the street corner. . . . To gain an estimate of growth of sound sources in the home, it might be interesting for the reader to count the electric motors in the average home. . . . Community noise exposure is often above maximum standards for industry. The saving quality heretofore has been that community noise has been a short-term exposure as compared to an eight-hour period in industry."

The problem, pointed out Canadian noise researcher Tony Embleton, chairman of the Noise Committee of the Acoustical Society of America, "is that noise pollution has crept up on us. Ten years ago someone said it was climbing at the rate of one decibel a year. That's still true."

Dr. Beranek added, "For man in the present 'advanced' stage of civilization noise is no longer a trivial problem. It is ironic that the United States, with its genius for creating technical marvels and solving technological problems, allows this most unpleasant affliction to debase its culture." The United States is not alone. Said *The London Times* of July 3, 1963, "Britain should be considerably quieter than it is . . . unless something is done the situation will soon become intolerable." Senior noise scientist Vern Knudsen of Los Angeles was even more pessimistic when he said, "Noise, like smog, is a slow agent of death. If it continues to increase for the next 30 years as it has for the last 30 it could become lethal."

Perhaps Dr. Knudsen was right. We may be all very much like the British counterintelligence agent who, in the book *The Ipcress File*, was strapped to a chair and bombarded with agonizing noise. We may all be trapped in our seats of civilization, doomed not by The Bomb but by The Boom, or perhaps by the Sonic Flood. The end of our world (in the next century?) promises to be far more noisy than was its beginning five or so billion years ago.

One decibel is about the level of the weakest sound that can be heard in an extremely quiet location by a person with very good hearing. It is, in other words, the optimum threshold of human hearing. A soft whisper 5 feet away registers about 30 dB. The human voice in normal conversation is about 70 dB; a blaring radio nearby, 110 dB; a 75-piece orchestra in crescendo, 130 dB; a turbojet with afterburner blasting, 160 dB; a Saturn rocket, 195 dB. Ear discomfort usually occurs at about 120 dB, ear pain at about 140 dB.

The Saturn rocket, designed to take men to the moon, produces some of the loudest noises in history when it blasts off. The only louder man-made noises have been American and Russian nuclear explosions in the atmosphere; the only louder natural noises have been the eruption of the Krakatoa Volcano in the East Indies in 1883, and the crash of a great meteorite in Siberia in 1908.

Supposedly the noisiest place in the world on a regular basis is the landing deck of an aircraft carrier. Bendix Corp. researchers measured 150 to 155 dB in the catapult launch area and the catwalks.

Noise surveys, where noise levels are measured and recorded at specific locations and at specific times, are not new, especially in industry. When noise-level meters were first available, the noisiest cities were, as you might expect, the first surveyed. New York City thus was measured by Dr. E. E. Free, science editor of *Forum* magazine, during 1925–1926, shortly after the Bell Telephone Laboratories 3-A Audiometer became available. Noise surveys of the Chicago Loop, Washington, D.C., St. Louis, and other American cities quickly followed. The method involved listening with a telephone receiver at one ear to a buzzer-produced standard noise, while the other ear heard the noise outside, then subjectively matching the electronic noise to the real-world noise and reading the dial. A second noise survey in New York City by *Forum* showed that in the skyscrapers which form the canyons of Midtown Manhattan the noise of the streets reverberated all the way up to the 12th floor without much diminution, and then only gradually lessened to the 20th or 25th floor. Noise surveys of New York were also taken during 1929–1930 by the city's Department of Public Health, as a preamble to the establishment that year of the New York Noise Abatement Commission.

Another early way of measuring noise, also subjective, was to strike a tuning fork, which hummed at 90 dB and decayed at the rate of one and a half decibels a second. By striking the 640 Hz fork, then measuring the time it took for it to fall to the same noise level as that of the background heard in the other ear, A. H. Davis surveyed the noise of London and New York, while another investigator used it in Newport News, Virginia.

The direct forerunner of present noise level meters was the "noisemeter" or "acoustimeter," which used a different reference sound pressure (0.001 dyne/sq. cm., rather than today's 0.0002 dyne/sq. cm.). It was used in the 1929 New York survey. More modern instruments were used in a survey made in 1952 and duplicated in 1959 by the New York *Journal-American*. That comparison, incidentally, showed that perhaps some progress was being made at the time to hold back the flood of urban noise. Readings taken at the same places at the same times of day showed 5 dB to 11 dB reductions. Here are some of the data:

	1952	1959
Times Square	81 dB	76 dB
7th Ave. & 38th St.	80 dB	74 dB
5th Ave. & 72nd St.	69 dB	62 dB
Columbus Circle	75 dB	68 dB

Community noise surveys have also been made in Germany—of Charlottenburg in 1938, of Dusseldorf since 1951, and of Dortmund. London has been surveyed many times, as have been Manchester and its environs. Tokyo has also been noise surveyed. In the United States, surveys have been made of University Park, Pennsylvania, and of three residential suburbs in New Jersey, to name just a few.

The suburban surveyers compared the New Jersey ambient, or general background, noise-level measurements of 1963 with ambient noise levels measured in Chicago in 1951 by G. L. Bonvallet of Armour Research Foundation, and with ambient measurements made in rural France. The Chicago noise then was greatest, the mean average being about 40 dB. The New Jersey average was about 35 dB. But the provincial French background noise was lowest, averaging about 28 dB! The New Jersey researchers, Paul B. Ostergaard and Ray Donley, commented that the French measurements "are of somewhat more than passing interest in that the areas in which they were made do not have electrical noise from oil furnaces or similar equipment, a situation which is nearly impossible to duplicate in the United States of America. These [French] measurements are believed to be nearly the upper limit of ambient noise in nature."

During the research phase of writing this book, I made use of a sound-level meter kindly lent for this purpose by the General Radio Co. of West Concord, Massachusetts. This highly portable Type 1565-A was carried at the end of a nylon cord which remained around my neck for three weeks while I traveled from my home in Chicago to visit noise researchers and noise controllers in seven European countries. It also accompanied me on a trip to Berkeley, California, to see Dr. Lee E. Farr, and to Washington, D.C., to attend the two-day National Conference on Noise as a Public Health Hazard.

The result was that I constantly recorded noise levels wherever I went, just as tourists record the images of what they see photographically. The record of my noise exposures forms the diary of noise exposure which is printed as Appendix B.

I think of Paris (where noise is *bruit*) as the noisiest of the cities on my European odyssey. Examples are its noisy Metro, the 75 to 86 dB (with frequent peaks of 94 dB) rush-hour noises along the otherwise romantic Champs Élysées, and the general din one hears sitting and trying to relax at one of the open-air sidewalk cafes for which that city is famous. Neither was London quiet, with its 86 dB noisy omnibuses (measured from the curb) and its 80 dB traffic sounds at 2:30 A.M. on Sunday on Oxford Street. I understand that there are Oriental cities whose din exceeds any in the Western Hemisphere. Particularly noisy are Calcutta, Bangkok, Hong Kong, and Tokyo. I must admit that omitting these areas is a shortcoming in my research, caused by a shortage of funds to support such a world-wide noise-measuring effort.

Experts might also argue that my measurements were made casually and momentarily, in comparison to the way noise levels are measured in industrial situations, as described elsewhere in this book. They would be correct. I could not have ranged so widely, however, had I had the cumbersome equipment they use; also, in most instances no one but myself knew what I was doing so there was no opportunity for contrivance. It was interesting to find that measuring the sound levels of their own offices was something that the noise experts I interviewed had never gotten around to doing! These measurements reflect readings that lasted only a few seconds or a minute—they do not tell how long I endured each noise level. In some cases—such as the pilot talking on the public address system of an overseas jetliner—I was exposed to 106 dB-A as long as he continued talking, perhaps a couple of minutes. In other cases—such as drinking Dutch beer while listening to an electrically amplified band at Bird's Place in Amsterdam—I was exposed to 102–106 dB-A for an hour or two. This question of duration is one reason why the Average Decibel Figure I derived is not quite accurate. Also, you cannot really average decibels, since as explained before, they are logarithmic, not linear measurements. But as I am not a mathematician, I simply added up the total decibel readings in given categories and divided by the number of readings, to arrive at what I consider to be a mean measurement.

Over the 21 days on my trip, I recorded 224 kinds of noise exposures on the A-weighted scale and found that the average exposure was 73.45 dB-A. But the exposures ranged from the very nice quiet of a few offices—at 40 dB and even 35 dB—to the 103 dB I heard in my seat on a DC-9 jet as it landed at Copenhagen, the 102 dB of a Trident jet passing obliquely overhead as I stood waiting to board a bus at Milan airport, and the 99 dB experienced in a Paris subway train. At home, there was the 96 dB I suffered for a half hour twice every week as I pushed my power mower over the grass of my front and rear lawns, the 92 dB of my 4-year-old son's screaming, the ear-shattering (115 dB) band at a friend's birthday party, and the 109 dB of the Chicago subway. The heliport at Berkeley, California, gave me a screaming 104 dB kick in the ear as I left it.

Also not recorded in the diary were my feelings about various noises, irrespective of their sound levels. The British Museum background noises for instance, were a rather diffused 50 to 60 dB most of the busy Sunday afternoon I spent there. In that setting, the 68 dB clatter of a group walking through the King's Library as I was studying that near-holy document, the Magna Carta, was as disturbing as the Trident jet at Milan. Too, the 52 dB noise of a car passing in the street below recorded in my room in the Royal Hotel in Copenhagen at 3:00 A.M., as I was trying to sleep, was more disturbing—because it was more unexpected— than the 102-109 dB noise of the Chicago subway as I was riding it underground.

Thanks to interstate highways, railroads, airplanes, industry, mechanized farm equipment, and snowmobiles man has banished forever the rural areas as refuges from the noise he makes. Even the quiet of the rivers and lakes of the world is shattered all too often by speedboats racing, and roaring through the water as they do so. "There is no doubt that the countryside is getting noisier," stated the Wilson report. "In fact most of the noises that occur in towns also occur in the country, but to different degrees. It must be remembered, however, that the same noise may give rise to greater annoyance in the country on account of the lower background noise, and for the same reason a lesser noise may still cause significant annoyance. . . . We hope that in such places as National Parks and National Trust properties, endeavours will be made to preserve, or create, havens of quiet where those who wish to can escape from noise for a time."

The sources of country noises are all those mentioned earlier. Among them are mining noises such as those of blasting and pneumatic drilling; such forestry sounds as those of chain saws; such gardening noises as those of power mowers; agricultural noises such as those of tractors.

A newer source of noise in the country, especially in Europe, is the sonic bird scarer—the sound of which is said to be far more effective than the sight of an old-fashioned scarecrow. Unfortunately, the sound frequencies to which birds react are similar to those to which men react, and at the same sound levels, above 85 dB. So the sonic scarers scare both birds and people with their blasts of birds' distress calls.

In the winter, the countryside, usually stilled by the acoustically deadening effects of snow, is disturbed by that earsplitting menace which has grown so popular: the snowmobile. Then, the north woods and the hillsides and mountains are no longer still. In the United States alone, there are almost three-quarters of a million of these vehicles, which skim over the whiteness at speeds up to 85 mph (or even faster) while they tear the ears with noises equal to those of chain saws.

My noise diary in its entirety shows that we all exist in a din that is not over the recommended maximum of 85 dB, which is the highest considered to be safe for our ears, and may be the maximum noise which the rest of the body can safely take. But the average noise that pollutes our environment is very close to that level. If, as the experts say, our world is getting noisier by an average of one decibel a year, then we of the Western world have until about 1979 to stem the tide of noise or we will be at the threshold of 85 dB, which can mark permanent hearing loss. Until then, however, many people (who knows how many?) with more sensitive ears than average, will lose their hearing, first temporarily and then permanently. In the meantime, too, the general damage inflicted on our bodies and to our emotions can only worsen. We face the prospect of being, in that magic year of Orwell's 1984, a shouting civilization that is hard-of-hearing, jumpy and nervous, and suffering from premature heart disease. The last quarter of this century promises to be a far cry from the Golden Age which statesmen and uninformed politicians paint for us. For every material, but noisy, advance we make, the quality of our living recedes another mark.

10

AT HOME AND AT WORK

(((((((((((•)))))))))))

As the next chapters will detail and document, noise is with us from the moment we arise in the morning, following us around our homes to our work, bombarding us as we work, as we play, and even as we sleep, or try to. It has become "a new form of trespass, a new invasion of privacy," to quote Charles Abrams, Columbia University urban planner. Australian Alan Bell in his report on noise for the World Health Organization said, "Before the Industrial Revolution, comparatively few people were exposed to excessive noise. The position changed rapidly with the advent of power-driven machinery."

"The public today is an unwilling guinea pig being exposed to types of noises and noise levels that did not exist 30 to 40 years ago," said Robert Alex Baron, executive vice-

148

president of Citizens for a Quieter City, Inc., of New York City. "Air pollution kills us slowly but silently; noise makes each day a torment."

You need not go farther than your home to realize how noisy our world is. In New York City, for instance, the Daily Decibel Diet starts at 7:00 A.M., the legal time for socially useful noise-making. New Yorkers are most often awakened by jackhammer and garbage truck reveilles.

Wrote Baron (in the *American Journal of Public Health*), "[at home our urban early riser] is bombarded by noise from within his building and from without. He probably is forced to listen to his family's TV set, his neighbors' TV sets, and details of his neighbors' personal lives, as well as to the air conditioners in his own quarters. Any time during the night his sleep may be disturbed by many noise sources: buses, trucks, motorcycles; the sirens of fire engines, police cars, and ambulances; auto horns, barking dogs, planes—and his neighbors' air conditioners."

Architectural consultant Paul Dunham Close pointed out that wherever there is a motor-driven appliance in the home, there is a source of noise. This includes, he said, "garbage disposals, dishwashers, mixers and blenders, refrigerators, vacuum cleaners, exhaust fans, oil burners, forced air heating systems, upward acting garage doors and air-conditioning compressors." There are many sources of noise in the home which are not related to motors. Examples are "singing" toilets, showers, water hammer noise in pipes, radios, TV's, stereos and hi-fi's, and the neighbors' children. There are also the noises of other homes which intrude into yours. "Poorly designed ventilating and air-conditioning systems make excellent speaking tubes between apartments or offices. When casement windows swing open facing each other in adjoining apartments, they may provide a sound-reflecting system for the transmission of a neighbor's radio, television, hi-fi, or family confidences," Close said.

Lee E. Farr, M.D., a noted California public health physician, was a pioneer in America in calling attention to the din of our dens. He said that kitchens, the noisiest rooms in our homes, have been inadvertently turned "into miniature transient simulators of old-fashioned boiler factories by introducing a variety of sound-producing mechanical devices." Besides the makers of noise in the kitchen there are also "the steel cabinets or hard plastic covered surfaces [which] reflect, augment, and cause [noise] to reverberate." The noise levels in a kitchen can run from 56 dB to more than 100 dB. In a speech to the American Medical Association in 1963, Dr. Farr explained one such kitchen noise survey:

> The vent fan over the stove, a single speed unit mounted in a metal canopy on the wall and ceiling, operated to produce a sound level of 84 decibels. When the dishwasher was run simultaneously the level rose to 88 decibels, and if at the same time, the sink garbage disposal unit was turned on, sound production rose to 91 decibels measured at the lower and steady level of sound effects of the disposal unit. At peak noise levels for the garbage disposal unit the total sound production was over 100 decibels. Thus we see that in the kitchen we can produce sound at such a level of intensity that if one were exposed to it for a full working day over an interval of time acoustic damage would result.

In a 1967 report in the *Journal of the A. M. A.*, Dr. Farr said he was no longer just concerned with the threat of home noises to hearing, but wanted his fellow physicians to be aware that "home sounds can threaten the health and well-being of one's emotional state as well. . . . It is his emotional status rather than his hearing acuity that is in the greater danger."

The living room is not very quiet either. First of all, the sounds of the kitchen often make conversation in the living room impossible. This is especially true in most modern apartments. There are also the television sounds (68 dB-C at average volume) and hi-fi sounds (80 dB 16 feet away, on loud setting). And there is the vacuum cleaner, which makes 73 dB-C of noise 6 feet away, when the nozzle is fully engaged on the rug, but 81 dB when the nozzle is lifted from the rug.

Bedrooms are usually quieter, in the range of 55 dB-C, but many now have incessant air-conditioning sounds. Bathrooms are noisier. Dr. Farr measured 72 dB-C with the toilet and ventilating fan running.

It is indeed interesting, in Dr. Farr's view, that "increasingly, thought has been given to temperature and humidity control within the home, as well as light, color, and ventilation. It is time that man realizes that his home can be designed to acoustic criteria."

Anne Kelley, a writer for the Chicago Daily News, took a General Radio 1565-A sound-level meter around her home and recorded (on the C-weighted scale, as did Dr. Farr) conversations between children in the 80's dB, a screaming subteen at 112 dB, a slammed door 4 feet away at 116 dB, and a cocktail party late in the evening at better than 100 dB. "I can conclude that any housewife who is offered a sound-level meter for keeps and chooses an economy mink instead is making a big mistake," she wrote. "Mere possession of a meter could do more to reduce her household noise level than all the acoustical tile and 'QUIET' signs in North America." It was very interesting, she found, to see how "the very presence of a meter in the home tends to make the little family unit self-conscious" and softer spoken.

Another danger around the home which is even more dire is that of cap pistols and firecrackers. Joseph Sataloff, M.D., of Philadelphia, a renowned noise researcher, has seen many children with noise deafness so induced. He told of the case of a boy who came to him at the age of 16 years complaining of ringing in the ears and difficulty in understanding people speak. Careful questioning by Doctor Sataloff revealed that a cap pistol had gone off right beside the boy's ear when he was 6 years old; when he was 10, he had fired a .22 pistol. "If permanent hearing damage can be produced so readily by apparently innocuous cap pistols and firecrackers, then preventative measures should be instituted," he said.

As will be seen in the third section of this book, one way to keep noise away is with some solid barrier: the best of these absorb the total energies of all sounds and prevent them from going any farther; in other words, they prevent their transmission. Masonry walls 8 or 12 feet thick did this nicely, and that is one reason why tall office and apartment buildings built before this century of steel were relatively quiet compared with today's. The walls were so thick and heavy that sound simply dissipated and died rather than being transmitted between rooms.

If the barrier does not have enough mass and enough dead space to absorb noise, it will simply transmit it. This is what happens in so many of the buildings that were erected in the 1950's and 1960's. Solid, thick load-bearing masonry walls became too expensive to build and were replaced by lighter and more flexible steel frames. Inner walls are now made of 2 x 4 studs spaced (usually) on 16-inch centers. To each edge of these vertical studs are nailed sheets of lath, over which plaster is applied, or to which plasterboard is nailed. As a result the wall is, in effect, a drum. Noise that imposes on one side of the wall makes it vibrate sympathetically and transmit the noise directly through steel nails and wooden studs to the other side, where the plaster vibrates almost like a loudspeaker.

To make matters worse, in a further move to save money through lowered labor time, the electrical outlets are installed back-to-back, connected by a conduit for wires which acts like a small sound tunnel. Plumbing is also installed back-to-back; so are ventilating ducts.

Private homes are little different. We've returned to noisy

wooden-frame construction after a couple of generations of quieter brick homes. While frame homes cost fewer dollars, they cost more in shattered nerves.

Another concept the homeowner should understand is reverberation. In effect, this is the noise that remains in a room after the sound has stopped at the source. It's analogous to the smoke that hangs in the air after a match or a cigarette has been put out. What you hear is a diminishing echo still being reflected from one wall to ceiling to wall and back, etc. To describe this, acoustical engineers use the term *reverberation time*, which depends on the frequency of the sound as well as on acoustic features of the room. Technically, reverberation time, or decay rate, is the time it takes sound in a room to decay by 60 dB (10^{-6} of its original value). A room with a short reverberation time is "dead" because the sound in the room stops almost as soon as the sound source is turned off. Such rooms are seldom "filled" with sound. A room with a long reverberation time is "live" because the sound stays in the room so long.

Since sound travels slowly, about 1,100 feet per second in air, sound that bounces for 100 feet, for example, is heard at the time it's issued and again one-eleventh of a second later. Reverberation time should match the use of the room: in church, a short reverberation time would emasculate the sound of an organ; in a too-live assembly hall, a speaker is very difficult to understand because the syllables of his last word is still bouncing off the walls as he is speaking the next one and the audience can hear them both.

Noise produced in the air—such as the blaring sound of your neighbor's television set—can travel on every possible air pathway between his apartment and yours, including not only such direct pathways as exhaust air ducts, but also the many hidden pathways of air and sound, such as small openings in floors, and the space around I-beam supports and pipes, spaces left open in suspended ceilings and via open windows.

In addition, the structure of a building itself transmits and radiates, and at a different speed than air, impact noises such as footsteps, slammed doors, water hammer in pipes, motors that start and stop, those caused by heavy vehicles passing nearby, and sonic booms. Many vibratory noises are also transmitted such as those from fluorescent lights and motors, air conditioners, washing machines, and dryers.

There is too much noise in apartments, homes, and offices simply because of bad planning or bad design, or lack of planning and lack of design. Architectural Consultant Paul Dunham Close put it mildly when he wrote, "Many unfortunate noise problems have occurred as the result of failure to consider noise control in the design and layout of new buildings intended for residential occupancies, particularly multifamily dwellings [apartments]. Most of the problems could have been avoided by proper design and arrangement of rooms or apartments and recognition of fundamental acoustic principles. . . . Usually it is much easier and far less costly to design a building in advance, so that it will have the proper acoustical environment when completed, than to attempt to correct unsatisfactory acoustical conditions. . . ."

One's job can be the noisiest experience of the day. If you're a rock-driller at a quarry, you may be experiencing more than 100 dB noise all day. At this level, only about five minutes' worth of the noise is the safe daily dose. If you work in the wood products industry (as almost 800,000 American men do) you are also immersed in a sea of noise all day. A 1956 survey by the U.S. Public Health Service found that "operators of saws, planers, routers, molding machines, shapers, jointers, and sanders are exposed to average overall sound-pressure levels which exceed 95 dB. For several of these operations, the average level may be as high as 115 dB." A survey of Swedish foresters by Doctor Kylin found that the average noise (C scale) to which they were exposed was in the range of 90–95 dB, but that the motor saws which many of the foresters operated had loudnesses of 80–90 dB when idling, 99–105 dB when stems were being trimmed, 110–112 dB when cutting branches, and up to 125 dB at other times. These were not momentary noises, he pointed out, since it took 27 minutes of sawing (on the average) to fell a tree, 200 minutes to strip its branches, 23 minutes to cut up the trunk; and the saw was left idling for 83 minutes, on the average, between trees.

Construction and demolition sites are also particularly noisy. The Wilson Committee in England noted, "Quietness has not been a factor to which much attention has been given by most manufacturers or users of contractors' plant, so that unless the need for effective noise control is recognised, further increases of mechanisation in the construction and demolition industries will inevitably result." Pneumatic tools, the committee found, were among the noisiest machines in this industry: "A typical noise level produced by a pneumatic drill is about 85 dB-A at 50 feet. With several operating at once under practical conditions, with some sound reflection, the level may well exceed 90 dB-A at nearby buildings." In other words, construction and demolition workers are not the only ones exposed to the noise. Midtown Manhattaners well know this; nor are they alone. All the big cities of the world have been tearing themselves down and rebuilding themselves incessantly since World War II. Everyone for blocks around each building that is being torn down or is being constructed is exposed to many decibels each workday for the long months it takes to get the job done.

Factories, as detailed earlier, can be very noisy working places. North Fleming of Eastbourne, Sussex, measured various kinds of factory noises in England and gathered these data:

Boiler works	118 dB-A
Metal powder works	114
Steel works, fettling	114
Metal saw	110
Wood planing machine	108
Metal working shop, grinder	106
Weaving shed	104
Sweet-coating machine	102
Screw-heading machine	101
Casting falling into bin	97
Envelope machine	99
Diesel-electric generator house	96
Printing works	96
Automatic lathes	87

What was perhaps the most thorough decibel survey of American occupations, which correlated quality of noise exposure with the quantity of workers exposed, was performed by Carnegie-Mellon University researchers under contract with Resources for the Future, Inc. Among their findings were that 20,000 blacksmiths were regularly exposed to noise of 100 dB in their daily jobs, while 24,000 boilermakers were occupationally exposed to 110 dB; 199,000 excavation machine operators to 110 dB; more than a million foremen to better than 80 dB; more than 2 million mechanics to more than 80 dB; 270,000 stationary engineers to 116 dB; 290,000 mine workers to 100 dB; a million and a half truck drivers to 95 dB; 162,000 taxicab drivers to 85 dB; 63,000 weavers to 102 dB; and 182,000 bus drivers to 90 dB.

Stated categorically below are the number of American workers exposed to noise levels above 80 dB, in the estimation of the Carnegie-Mellon researchers:

Professional, technical, etc.	865,000
Farming	3,000,000
Clerical and kindred	4,265,000
Sales	249,000
Managerial and official	2,200,000

Crafts and skilled labor	8,042,000
Operative and kindred	10,953,000
Household and service	2,401,000
Labor	2,102,000
TOTAL	34,077,000

Herbert Jones of the U.S. Public Health Service measured various industrial sounds: wood planer making furniture parts, 108 dB; test of a 150-hp internal combustion engine, 102 dB; inside a power house, 116 dB; control room of a jet engine test cell, 107 dB; cold-fog aerosol generator, 101 dB.

The noise of industry spills over onto the streets frequently—all too frequently, in the opinion of residents of many communities. Said Alan Bell of WHO, "Some industries, by their very nature, are noisy. Yet industry cannot exist without the community where it is sited, and the community cannot be economically healthy without industry." The Wilson Committee found that "people living in the old established industrial areas of the country are more tolerant of industrial noise than those who live in areas in which noisy industry is not so well established. The simplest explanation of this difference is, of course, that people get used to noise. We think, however, that this explanation may be an oversimplification and that the answer is a more complex one reflecting different social and economic attitudes towards industry. We consider it likely that, as economic standards of living rise, the public's tolerance of noise, as of other discomfort, will fall."

In a brief tabulation of city noises, Industrial Acoustics Co. of New York City found that, at 100-foot distances, transformer stations gave out 55–65 dB of noise; generating plants, 100–120 dB; air-conditioning cooling towers, 85–95 dB; light manufacturing plants, 50–90 dB; and heavy manufacturing plants, 50–100 dB.

Perhaps the best solution is to copy the example of Congo

natives put to work on construction projects. Reared in the relative quiet of the wild bush, they were not used to the terrible noises of the strange machinery and simply walked away from the work. They came back again when adequate mufflers were put on the machines, a technique which will be discussed later, along with other kinds of noise control techniques.

White-collar job environments are substantially quieter, but the noise levels are not always exactly in the safe or the sanity-promoting ranges. Thus a secretary sitting near a Xerox machine may hear 75 dB-A all day; an accounting office din is about 79 dB-A; a keypunch room, 84 dB-A; a computer operations room, 85 dB-A. Dr. Maugeri recorded 103 dB on the floor of the Milan, Italy, stock exchange.

Often, too, there is the Muzak or other kind of piped-in music which is beamed to the sonically captive workers.

That music can affect your psychological state has been known, perhaps, since the first note was played. Nicolas Slonimsky, a composer and noted lexicographer of music, pointed out that "since ancient times the function of music has been to impress, inspire, or alter the psychological state of the listener. The affective spectrum of music ranges from the deepest gloom to the highest state of exaltation." He pointed out, as examples, that Ravel's *Bolero* "is decidedly psychedelic," as is Shostakovich's *Fifth Symphony;* Chopin's funeral march is depressing; Beethoven's *Kreutzer Sonata* for violin and piano is supposed to be possessed of aphrodisiac power which is depicted in a Tolstoy tale, a painting, and an ad for perfume. Music therapists well know of music's effect on emotions. Two such Massachusetts music therapists analyzed Gershwin's *Rhapsody in Blue* and found it to be "a startling example" of sexual expression, "suggesting not only erection but ejaculation." The researchers, Dr. Harold Lee and Myrna Rybczyk, also found *Bolero* to be "frankly erotic." Music, they believe, helps us discharge our anxieties and has certain similarities to dreams in providing "regressive transformations."

Perhaps this is why we need music. Perhaps we dream too little. And perhaps this is because of the noise in our lives that keeps us from sleeping soundly enough. In any case, some personnel directors attribute our generation's need for music and Muzak to our addiction to background music. Music is everywhere these days. It has been since radios became popular and, especially, since transistor radios were placed into every youngster's hand.

The Muzak programing of musical selections is done very carefully, designed to pace the workers at their work. Slow, low-key musical numbers are played in the morning when they arrive on the job. Then the tempo gradually increases as monotony sets in and energy diminishes. The music reaches its emotional peak between 10:00 and 11:00 A.M., when employee efficiency is said to be at its lowest level. Then the music-designed-to-pick-you-up may likely be some sprightly number like "The Naughty Lady of Shady Lane." All of the music consists of standard, well-known numbers and is played by woodwinds and strings—a mild musical medium halfway between a string quartet and a brass band.

According to a Muzak maestro, the recordings beamed at workers are aimed at combating the tension caused by the monotony of their work, by fatigue, boredom, anxiety—and noise. "We have been able to prove that Muzak results in increased efficiency, fewer errors, and happier employees and customers," stated Olan Chan, Midwest regional manager of the company.

Public address systems have invaded retail stores, airplanes, rest rooms, and even elevators. This last invasion of privacy by unwanted music (and therefore noise) almost cost one New York landlord the lease of a rather large magazine's operations. The editor of The New Yorker, according to writer Sam Blum, threatened to move the publication's entire operations to another building if the management didn't turn off the music in the elevators. It did and saved a lease.

Dr. Farr deplored what he called "the constant bombardment of messages we are subjected to." He stated, "You have music wherever you go—but it is not the music you yourself select to take you out of a mood or put you into a mood which you want to get into. In cocktail lounges and restaurants, even at small tables, you have to bend over to be heard. Yet people patronize only noisy restaurants. Maybe those who turn up their radios and TV's are used to having loud noises in the background. But we older persons are used to quieter backgrounds. One of the results of all this noise is that we don't hear the important messages, such as a speech by the President, or instructions from your wife."

Dr. Farr's office in Berkeley overlooked a park called Provost Square, which is a rallying point on the University of California campus for students, especially students bent on demonstrating their dissent over one thing or another. He sighed as he looked out his window one sunny day and quietly said, "It gets pretty noisy down there sometimes."

11

ON THE ROADS AND RAILS

$(((((((((\cdot)))))))))$

The sounds you hear in the street which offend your ear, your emotions, or your general physiology come only partly from industry. Much of the noise comes from traffic—the various kinds of transportation we moderns use in place of our feet in response to our urgent personal and business needs. Dr. Leo L. Beranek said, "Today's urban noise is largely the result of people's insatiable desire to reach distant places ever more rapidly and comfortably. As we have developed faster ways to transport ourselves and our commercial goods, we have created a noise nuisance that is becoming increasingly difficult to live with. Cars, buses, trains, trucks, and airplanes are a necessary part of our lives. It does not follow, however, that all the noise created by these machines must also be a part."

In the United States in 1968, 101 million motor vehicles

were operated by 105 million licensed drivers. America's 84 million private automobiles account for about 93 percent of its passenger travel. And the four-wheeled population keeps increasing exponentially. So do the numbers of those raucous two-wheeled ear-splitters and bone-breakers known as motorcycles. In Chicago, for instance, the number of licensed motorcycles almost doubled from 5,533 in 1965 to 9,403 in 1966 and proliferated to 12,500 in 1968. In the Chicago suburbs the motorcycle population tripled between 1965 and 1968.

"The noise of vehicular traffic is the most important of our common noises because of its prevalence and its intensity or loudness," said a researcher who extensively surveyed city noises in the 1950's. Heavy traffic noise, found G. L. Bonvallet of Illinois Institute of Technology, often reached close to 80 dB and exceeded industrial noises. "Apparently the public condones this noise more than others because it depends upon motor vehicles as a means of convenient transportation. Such noises have enjoyed a certain degree of 'acceptance,' although there is no good reason for it."

The most obvious and alarming noise from motor vehicles is that caused intentionally by their horns. Laymon Miller of Bolt Beranek and Newman, Inc., explained to science writers at a special 1967 symposium in New York City that horns are designed to blare in the frequencies that are most easily heard, in order to get our attention. The horn produces, he said, "a raucous, demanding sound. It projects anger and impatience and ill will. No wonder it is so annoying." David C. Apps, General Motors' noise expert, pointed out that auto horns must get louder and louder in order to pierce through the accumulating noises which drivers hear at increasing highway speeds. Besides the noisiness of their cars produced by speed, there are also the new noises inside the car, specifically the air-conditioning system, and the stereo speaker system which blasts music from radio and magnetic tape recordings. "The passenger-car 'horn' is actually a pair of horns having a fundamental musical interval of 5/4—a major third. A typical frequency combination is 310 and 390 cps [Hz]," Apps explained in his well-detailed chapter on automobile noise in the *Handbook of Noise Control,* edited by Professor Cyril M. Harris of Columbia University. "Apparently a raucous sounding horn has better penetration than the melodious sounding horn, according to the audibility curves. Since the spectra of the two horns have about the same density and arrangement below 2,000 cps, it appears that the better penetration may be attributed to the dense grouping of frequencies in the 2,000 to 3,000 cps range." His discussion sounds much like that of a weapon and is reminiscent of Professor Gavreau's work. The horn is certainly a weapon against the ear, no doubt of that. Sound level measurements made by Apps at 25-foot distances showed that auto horns produced close to 90 dB.

To get the sum total of noises which the driver of a car is exposed to, Apps placed the microphone of a sound-level meter on the right front seats of two kinds of 1955 G.M. sedans and drove the cars over level concrete. At 20 mph, the noise in Car A was 73 dB-B; Car B, 71 dB-B. At 40 mph, Car A was 84 dB; Car B, 73 dB. At 60 mph, Car A's noise was 83 dB; Car B, 77 dB. At 70 mph, Car A was 84 dB inside and Car B 80 dB. (It's even noisier in a sports car.)

Apps has done perhaps the most complete analysis of auto noise sources in print. These sources are many and are not surprising when you consider that the automobile is a box made of metal components (which rub and squeak against one another), which whips through the air as it runs on the ground under the propulsion of its engine powered by well-timed and well-contained sequential explosions of gasoline-air vapor. The number of parts that whirl and reciprocate is on the order of thousands. On the one hand, it seems a modern wonder that automobiles are not noisier; on the other, it seems more wondrous that cars are so noisy considering all of the engineering that goes into them.

Much of an automobile's noises come from its engine, where there are unbalances due to acceleration of the reciprocating parts of the engines—essentially the pistons and connecting rods which travel up and back at high speeds. There are also unbalances in the various rotating parts, such as the crankshaft, flywheel, cooling fan, electrical generator, and alternator. In one case, Apps found that a generator rotated at exactly twice engine speed, producing a very audible and disturbing beat. There are also various gas noises caused by the explosive nature of the cylinder gas pressures. As he explained, "Each time a charge explodes, the cylinder distorts in a sort of breathing fashion; and this distortion, transmitted to the exterior surfaces, radiates noise not only locally but throughout the entire exterior surfaces of the engine as these distortions are propagated along the engine structure. This situation is exaggerated in modern engines, in which the trend is toward higher compression ratios and higher peak combustion pressures." Noise expert Lewis Goodfriend of New Jersey pointed out another engine noise—"a rushing, hissing sound which sometimes contains the mechanical sounds of valving."

He and Apps agree that the most offensive and disturbing noise (besides that of the horn) is produced at the waste end of the engine: the exhaust. This is the gases produced by the explosions that make auto engines internal combustion engines. These gases literally blast out of one cylinder after another. Civilized mufflers are designed so that the energy of these gases is spent safely and quietly in a set of baffles. Less civilized mufflers, such as those of sports cars and motorcycles, let much of the explosive sounds out—and even treasure them somewhat in devices called resonators. The idea, say racing drivers, is to not impose on the engine the back pressures caused by the muffler's impeding the fast exit of the exhausted gases. But engineers say they are wrong in this conception. Apps measured the exhaust noise of a 1954 sedan at three-fourths throttle and found that at a distance of one foot behind the tailpipe and one foot to the left the noise reached 100 dB, with the emphasis at the low frequencies around 100 Hz.

The noise of cooling fans are also annoyingly loud, especially at high speeds. There may not only be rotational imbalances, but the fan is a propeller that sucks air in from the front to flow through the radiator. In fact, it is much like the VTOL ducted-propeller problem discussed earlier. "The adoption of air conditioning has heightened the cooling-fan-noise problem," Apps wrote, "because higher capacity fans are required."

Gear noise is also important, especially with automatic transmissions and their planetary gear arrangements. The noise is characterized by the whine of the gear teeth meshing at high speeds of rotation. In sports cars, with their high-speed engines, this is especially troublesome.

Brake squeal, at frequencies ranging from 2,000 to 50,000 Hz, but especially strong at the irritating frequencies between 10,000 and 15,000 Hz, is very annoying, too.

Noted the Wilson Committee, "There is evidence of a great deal of annoyance from the noise of car doors being slammed." Too many people, it noted, ironically "use unnecessary force and, in doing so, cause permanent distortion of the vehicle body and make subsequent closing a still more noisy operation."

Perhaps the most irritating source of noise which is unrecognized by the public is tires. This "hidden source" is responsible not only for the noise it conveys directly to the ear but the noise which it transmits throughout the automobile via the suspension and steering systems. Francis M. Weiner of Bolt Beranek and Newman, Inc., measured the noise at the outside of a fully loaded medium-heavy American passenger car equipped with 8.00 x 15 four-ply tires. He found that the tire noise was composed of sounds which included all the audible frequencies. The tires were noisier on rough roads and reached levels of 100 dB during his measurements. Smoother roads made for less tire noise, about 10 dB less. The speed of the car over the road (and, hence, the speed of rotation of the tires) was also an important factor: the faster the car, the more noise its tires created. Again, this was about a 10 dB difference—so that at 30 mph, over a smooth road, tires made just about 80 dB of noise, whereas at 50 mph over a rough road they made the 100 dB noise.

Weiner also found in his tests that the construction of the tires made little difference in the noise levels they generated. There was, he said, "a remarkable constancy of the noise spectrum with respect to changes in the fiber material of the tire reinforcing fabric and the tread rubber composition for a given set of operating conditions."

So insidious is tire noise that the manufacturers of expensive English automobiles turned to researchers at Southampton for help. They managed, they said, to make their cars very quiet, so quiet that all that could be heard on the road at high speeds was the whine of its tires! The reason for tire noise is rather basic, as explained by acoustician Christopher G. Rice of Southampton: the tire treads act as a sort of siren. Treads represent a regular pattern and can be likened to the regular pattern of the blades of a siren. Every tire tread has a speed at which it begins to produce noise—a function of the effect of speed of rotation on the tread pattern. As the tire's speed increases, its noise level increases, and so does the power of the higher frequencies, which produce the whine of high speed.

Tires produce other kinds of noise, due to their lifting off the road and then being slapped down again. This is the thump you hear over pavement joints and brick roads.

Finally, the faster a car moves, the more air it has to move out of its way. This causes wind noises that can resonate throughout the various hollows of the car and also causes squeals as wind is forced through narrow crevices in windows or doors.

Trucks are even noisier than cars. Goodfriend considers these monsters of the motorways "the most notorious of the highway-noise sources. . . . At high speeds on modern highways the exhaust and tire noise predominate. However, at low speeds and under acceleration conditions, engine and transmission noise can be the loudest sounds. . . . Even when stationary, a truck can be noisy. The noise in this case is usually generated by a refrigeration compressor, or by a materials-handling compressor used to load and unload dry materials and fluids from or into tank trucks." (Or, we add, by attending garbage men.)

More fuel for such feelings came in 1967 when Jerome K. Brasch of the University of Michigan School of Public Health at Ann Arbor published the results of his survey of the noise of a busy highway. A unique combination of engineer and industrial hygienist, Brasch set up his recording and measuring instruments just north of Interstate Highway I-94 about five miles west of the Detroit city limit. He installed a microphone 4 feet above the ground at a distance of 100 feet from the edge of the highway pavement. He recorded the noises of perhaps 460 vehicles in a series of twelve ten-minute periods. His conclusion: "Overall sound-pressure levels ranged from 63 dB (minimum background noise) to 100 dB. . . . with few exceptions, all peaks of traffic noise with overall level of 80 dB or greater were due to trucks, singly or in combination. It can only be concluded that the noise problem near high-speed highways is largely a matter of truck noise."

Buses can also be noisy (as I found in Chicago and London). Said Goodfriend, "Plenty of horsepower, little space for adequate mufflers, and rapid acceleration can make these very undesirable noise sources. When buses have been in service for some time they become far noisier. This is because of damage to engine compartment seals. Diesel engines, such as those used on buses, radiate almost as much power from the engine casings as they radiate through the exhaust system. . . . In some cases the engine housings are so badly distorted that the sound radiates almost as freely as if there were no engine compartment."

This is one reason motorcycles are so noisy: the engines are fully exposed, so that noise radiates directly from the engine cylinders. The other reason is that they are operated with no mufflers or with inadequate mufflers for pretended reasons of power and real reasons of sounding powerful. Apps measured the sound levels of motorcycles at points 18 inches above their tailpipes and recorded as high as 122 dB (at 45 mph on a two-cylinder, four-cycle, 45° V engine). The lowest he recorded was 110 dB (at 20 mph on a single cyclinder, two-cycle motorcycle engine). Motorcycles are purposely made noisy, says the Council of Europe, and the industry which makes them devotes much attention to acoustic performance. The reason, they say, is that purchasers demand loud 'cycles!

Aging *per se* makes motor vehicles neither noisier nor quieter. Kajland of Stockholm and a colleague, P. Hammarfors, studied the noise of 60 new and 105 used vehicles (autos, buses, trucks, motorcycles, and powered bicycles) and found that, except for the last category, "age had very little influence on the noise emitted." Maintenance, or the lack of it, made the noise difference in time. The loudest kind of vehicle was the motorcycle, with trucks and powered bicycles tying for second, and private cars a close third.

A Stockholm survey by Kajland's colleagues, Erland Jonsson and Stefan Sörenson, found that of all disturbing noises, traffic and especially that of motorcycles and motor bicycles was considered by the public to be the worst.

In terms of their sound levels, I found some of the worst noises were those associated with air and rail travel. As calculated from my noise diary (Appendix B), the noise to which I was exposed while riding in airplanes was an average of 82.80 dB (mean for 67 exposures recorded). If you think rail travel is any quieter, look at my average of 83.8 dB for 21 exposures. Of course, rail travel includes subway trains which, though probably not any noisier *per se,* travel in tubes whose walls are about a yard away and are shaped concavely to better reflect the sound waves back to the passengers. When a train is out in the open, much of the noise is lost to the rural air. Thus, as a passenger in a Paris Metro subway train, I was assaulted by noise of 96 to 99 dB, and in London's Underground subway train, of 90 dB. The wonderful train to Southampton only subjected me to 75 dB, and the noisier train to Manchester was an 86 dB experience.

William A. Jack of the Johns-Manville Research Center in New Jersey explained that "a large tractive force is required to pull these relatively heavy cars on steel wheels over steel rails. As a result of this tractive force on the train-track system considerable noise is produced—a noise level which is increased by the auxiliary equipment. A passenger within the car will feel the vibration of the seat, floor, and portion of the wall he may lean against. He will hear noise inside the car." Just how much noise? He found that it depends, for one thing, on speed. At a "typical passenger location near center of car," it can range from 70 to 85 dB at 30 to 90 mph speeds—and more, if the windows are opened. Trains also generate lots of noise to the rest of the world. The noise comes primarily from the steel wheels on steel tracks and from the engine. Diesels are noisier than steam engines and electric trains are the quietest of the three. Noise levels frequently exceed 90 dB. The engine noise sources are almost identical with those of automotive, truck, and bus diesel engines. Trains are noisiest when they round curves.

"Wheel squeal" occurs because each axle is a solid rod with wheels attached at each end. The outer wheel has to rotate faster than the inner wheel, causing the inner wheel to skid on the rail and producing friction noise between the two steel surfaces. Trains also have clarion-call horns which they sound as they approach crossings—no longer required in the United States because there are few busy crossings left exposed without a crossing gate.

During 1945–1946, 2.8 billion passengers were carried by rail rapid transit systems in the United States. Twenty years later, in 1966, the annual total number of such travelers had dropped a billion to 1.8 billion. The difference is explained by the fact that while our population grew, so did our reliance on our own wheels, hence there was an increase in automobiles. Now, strangled by auto congestion, big cities are turning again to rail systems to transport people. Chicago is expanding its subway and rapid rail system; so are Toronto and Cleveland. San Francisco's BART system, although beset by financial troubles during construction, is another. Montreal opened three new such lines in time for its Expo '67 fair. Monorail systems in Germany and in Japan, and high-speed rail systems between cities such as Washington and New York and Boston promised to increase rail passenger travel again and to bring even more noises to the countryside and to the city. Jet engine-propelled trains and air-cushioned trains were planned; while faster, they are also noisier. At the same time, the long-distance rail haulers are moving more freight and fewer passengers. American railroads have about 9,000 passenger coach cars, contrasted with a million and a half freight cars—all pulled by more than 30,000 locomotives. "To achieve increased productivity, the railroads are moving toward higher-speed operation of freight trains and toward longer trains," noted Professor William A. Seifert of M.I.T. Given existing technology, this combination can only add up to more noise for our already sonically saturated society.

12

IN THE AIR

((((((((((•))))))))))

In the annals of racket, airplanes have a chapter all to themselves. "Air transportation," pointed out Professor Seifert, "has demonstrated a sustained growth rate matched by few industries. Today, the scheduled airlines of the United States account for approximately two-thirds of all passenger-miles attributed to the common carriers. Although air cargo still accounts for a minor fraction of the goods transportation in this country, it too is growing very fast. Air transportation has, thus, moved from the status of a struggling fledgling to that of an industry of major importance. However, this development has brought not only great opportunities, but increasing problems."

Total passenger traffic handled by scheduled airlines grew 22 percent between 1966 and 1967 and is expected to grow at an annual rate of 15 percent until 1975, when the total revenue passenger-miles should be 300 billion. By 1980, total

171

world traffic is expected to reach beyond 600 billion revenue passenger-miles. Perhaps more meaningful is the fact that American scheduled airlines carried 70,000 more passengers a day than they did the year before. Internationally, more than half a million passengers are airborne every day. Private planes (company, business, and personal) are also growing rapidly in America—from 95,442 in 1966 to an anticipated 210,000 in 1980.

The kinds of planes being added most quickly to the nation's and the world's airborne population are those which make the most noise: jet-props, jets (including supersonic craft), rotating wing (helicopters), and V.T.O.L. (vertical take-off and landing).

The growth of air travel is a boon not only to the carriers and to the aircraft manufacturers and suppliers, but also to the cities served. Said Professor Seifert: "Cities like airports because they facilitate the flow of passengers and goods to and from the area and thus represent an important source of income. On the other hand, residents who are or might be affected by the noise of aircraft landing and take-off are becoming more and more vocal in their opposition to building and expanding airports. Unfortunately, the possibility for major noise quieting is one area in which no technical breakthrough appears imminent. . . . How strongly the public will react against sonic booms remains to be seen."

This view was also expressed by John O. Powers of the Federal Aviation Administration's Office of Noise Abatement. He told a 1967 meeting of the Acoustical Society of America: "Noise now threatens to choke the orderly development of commercial air transportation and if the increase in noise is permitted to continue unabated the air transportation system will not realize its full potential. . . . there will not be in the foreseeable future a simple, single solution by which the noise problem can be reduced to acceptable dimensions."

Business Week on March 16, 1968, also concurred: "Jet noise . . . will get a lot worse before it gets better. Nothing now in the works will make planes substantially quieter before the mid-1970's. By that time the number of take-offs and landings will triple. The problem is not confined to the big cities. New, short-range jets are bringing high decibel counts to an increasing number of smaller communities. Within a few years, jets will be operating out of more than 400 airports—more than double the number handling them today."

To give you some idea of what the magazine was talking about, here are two statistics gleaned from *Air Transport World:* During the twelve months ending June 30, 1968, airlines in the United States flew short-runway, two-engine DC-9 jet airliners for a total of 344,044 hours, and B-737's for a total of 4,404 hours. Other jet statistics for that period of time in the United States: B-707, 335,997 hours; B-727, 830,389 hours; DC-8, 325,887 hours; BAC-111, 129,199 hours. On international flights, Northwest, Transworld, and Pan American Airlines flew various versions of the B-707 for a total of 416,487 hours; and Pan Am, United Airlines, and Trans Canada, various versions of the DC-8 for a total of 113,850 hours.

These are all passenger jet totals. Cargo jets totaled 131,-887 hours domestic flying time, and a grand total of 271,100. The overall total of these American and Canadian jets' flying time is a whopping 2,771,357 hours.

Add the whine of turboprop hours and the figure is even higher, an additional 349,936, for a jet and jet-prop total of 3,121,293 hours. That's a lot of flying time—and a lot of jet noise.

Noise increases with engine power. The first scheduled American commercial jet flight took off on October 26, 1958; it was Pan American World Airways' Flight 114. The plane was a Boeing 707, the first jet airliner to fly successfully after the Comet tragedies. Each of the 707's four engines developed 13,500 pounds of thrust. Successive models had engines which developed 17,500 pounds and then 19,000 pounds of thrust each. The Convair 880, first flown in 1959, had four engines which each developed 11,650 pounds of thrust; the bigger Convair 990 had four 16,100-pound thrust engines. The French Caravelle airplane began with two 11,-600-pound thrust Rolls Royce engines; the Super Caravelle was given two American 14,000-pound thrust engines. DC-8's have the same engines as the B-707's. The shorter range 727, 737, and DC-9 airplanes each have 14,000-pound thrust engines.

In 1957, United States commercial airlines operated 1,803 propeller aircraft and no jets. In 1968 they operated that many jets plus 400 additional planes—some of them props, but most of them prop-jets.

The successors to the planes mentioned above are the Boeing 747, the Douglas DC-10, and the Boeing and Concorde supersonic transports (S.S.T.). The 747, rolled out of the hanger in September, 1968, first flown in 1969, and placed in service in January, 1970, is powered by four JT9D engines which each develop 43,500 pounds of thrust.

Lockheed's L-1011 "airbus" has three 40,600-pound thrust engines. The British-French S.S.T. Concorde, first flown March 2, 1969, has four 35,000-pound thrust engines. The three kinds of DC-10s planned as of this writing will have 40,000-pound or 40,600-pound engines, or an even bigger engine, the CF6-10 turbofan which develops 45,600 pounds of thrust. Each of these engines mentioned for the superjets develops more than three times the energy of the jet engine first used on the Boeing 707! And the engines to power the lagging American S.S.T. is even bigger—GE4 with 67,000 pounds of thrust—or five times that first 707 engine's power.

Along with the tremendous increases in the volume and comfort of air travel around the world have come tremendous increases in noise. You don't ever have to ride a jet to be exposed to its terribly anguishing noises, of course. There was my experience with the Trident taking off above me at Milan (see Appendix B). Standing on the observation deck at Orly Airport, outside of Paris, my ears got quite a jolt from the 91 and 93 dB screams of jets taxiing up and taxiing away from the parking apron just below. As for the various exposures to noise inside the airplanes, there are decided differences between the makes. For one thing, those airplanes that don't use thrust reversing to slow down after touching the runway on landing (the Caravelle as flown both by Air France and by SAS is in the category) are considerably quieter at that stage of the trip (76 to 80 dB) than were those planes that did use the thunder of thrust reversing on landing (such as Lufthansa's Boeing 737 and SAS's DC-9, 90 to 103 dB).

We are all placed in the same position as *Chicago's American* columnist Jack Mabley, who told of coming home from a trip to Washington, D.C., to shout hello to his unresponsive wife amid the din of a blaring TV set. Said his wife, "We can't hear on account of the jets." Commented Mabley, "It was a moment of mixed emotions. I hate the jets when I'm on the ground and they're roaring overhead. But what a lovely way to travel."

The price we pay for jet progress is a diminution in the quality of our lives. This was well portrayed during hearings before the Subcommittee on Transportation and Aeronautics of the U.S. House of Representatives on Tuesday, November 14, 1967, in the testimony of Rep. Herbert Tenzer of New York:

> We have personally experienced, since the flight of the first jets at Kennedy International Airport, the interference with our daily lives caused by jet noise.
> We have not since that time been able to enjoy the quiet and peaceful environment of our homes. Our

lawns, terraces, and front porches no longer serve the purposes for restful recreation on evenings and week-ends, when indoors our telephone conversations are disturbed and our television programs are interfered with.

Our children's education is disturbed at school. Our church and synagogue worship services and outdoor community activities are marred by the frequency of low-flying aircraft with their accompanying shrieks of jet noise. Who is not aware of the problems of the teacher—the minister—the priest—the rabbi—waiting with bated breath for the jet—with noise in its wake to pass overhead?

The effect of jet noise on property values; the hazard to the nation's health; the increasing volume of litigation by property owners and the disturbance of the peaceful enjoyment of our homes are some of the aspects of this problem. . . .

On Wednesday, November 15, 1967, Rep. Hale Boggs of Louisiana told of the plight of New Orleans International Airport:

When the site for this airport was chosen in 1943, it was in an area which was really almost rural—it was some 15 to 20 miles from the center of New Orleans and the city of Kenner and the surrounding area at that time was not developed by residential or business construction to any extent.

Needless to say, the noise of aircraft of that day had little adverse effect on the sparsely populated surrounding community. But then coincidentally with the introduction of jet aircraft in 1960, a tremendous expansion of population growth took place in Kenner and the surrounding area of East Jefferson Parish. Today New Orleans International Airport is surrounded on three sides by a thickly populated, well-developed residential and business community. . . .

With the larger jet aircraft being built and employed to handle the ever-growing passenger traffic, there are no hours in the day when the citizens of nearby com-

munities such as Kenner in my district may find relief
from the noise.

And now that these jet planes are being constructed
in larger sizes, with more powerful engines, there is no
doubt that the noise will increase to intolerable
levels. . . .

U.S. Congressman Roman C. Pucinski of Chicago has
deplored the noise caused by flights arriving at and leaving
from O'Hare International Airport, one of the busiest in the
world, where a jet lands or takes off every 40 seconds. He
called this "the unrelenting, unremitting, intolerable boom
and whine of tidal waves of sound."

Despite these lessons, the communities which noisy jet
airports serve continue to creep up to them. At Cranford, a
London suburb, for instance, plans were announced in April,
1968, to build 108 apartments, many for old people, directly
under the flight path of No. 1 runway at Heathrow Airport,
and only three-quarters of a mile from the end of the runway.

This, despite the experience of tortured millions who live
near airports and despite the many sound surveys taken at
airports which bear out these outraged citizens' feelings.
People in England, America, and elsewhere are apparently
pretty much the same. To quote a 1967 report of the U.S.
Federal Aviation Administration, "The airport noise problem
has continued to grow during the last decade or so not only
because jet aircraft have been and still are inherently noisy,
but also because large numbers of people choose to live and
work near airports where they are subject to the noise. The
reasons for this tendency toward high density residential
development around major urban airports are not entirely
clear. . . ."

A study by the U.S. Department of Housing and Urban
Development found that the high-noise 23-square-mile area
around Kennedy International Airport at New York included
35,000 dwelling units and 108,000 residents, at least 22

public schools, and several dozen churches and clubs. The high-noise 12-square-mile area around Los Angeles International Airport included 47,000 dwelling units and 129,000 people, 33 public schools, and a score or more of churches, as well as at least three hospitals and a college. The high-noise area around O'Hare includes 106,000 people.

In the pre-commercial jet year of 1954, K. N. Stevens, Ph.D., of Bolt Beranek and Newman, Inc., conducted a survey of noise in the communities around eight airports for the National Advisory Committee for Aeronautics (a precursor of N.A.S.A.). He found that the background noise was about 50 dB and that the propeller airliners of those days would produce up to 90 dB on take-off as measured at a distance of a mile and a half from the end of the runways, and up to 80 dB just over four miles from the end of the runways. The noise of these DC-3 and DC-6 planes was always softer on landings.

In 1959 when jets were just landing on the scene, Beranek, Kryter, and Laymon N. Miller surveyed the airport noise situation. Based on their findings, they said, "If jet aircraft were to replace propeller aircraft and if they were permitted to follow the same flight routines as the propeller aircraft, the perceived noise levels indoors in communities near the airports would increase by 10 to 12 PNdB!" PNdB is Perceived Noise Decibels, a measurement of noise as it is perceived. It is even more high-frequency weighted than dB-A. A jet-noise PNdB is about 13 units higher than a dB-A. Thus the noise of a four-engine propeller plane taking off, which they measured at 98 PNdB from 1,600 feet away, would be roughly comparable to 85 dB-A. And the 707-120 jet taking off, measured from the same distance, was 107 PNdB or about 94 dB-A.

In 1963, when jets were firmly established, Alexander Cohen and Howard E. Ayer of the U.S. Public Health Service measured the noise levels at one airport and in the surrounding community of another airport. The take-off noise as measured on the parking ramps of No. 1 airport reached 103 dB for prop and prop-jet airplanes and 110 dB for pure jets. The ramps were about a quarter of a mile from the runway. In the community near No. 2 airport, they found "flyovers of jet aircraft to be more intense, more disruptive of speech, and more annoying than that of piston engine aircraft." While the jets were higher, they still made slightly more overall noise (peaks of 99 dB versus 97 dB) and, also important, whined more strongly in the irritable upper frequencies.

A noise survey made when National Airport in Washington opened to jet aircraft on April 24, 1966, showed that both propeller and jet aircraft produced noise in the 80's and 90's of decibels. Caravelles and executive jets were the worst offenders. The U.S. Department of Housing and Urban Development in a study conducted in 1966 plotted aircraft take-off and landing noises very carefully and charted them so that the noise levels of civil and military jet aircraft take-offs could be readily seen. The noise contour patterns looked like the waves and wake of a ship and, similarly, were most intense near the planes (as high as 130 PNdB) and weakest farthest away (90 PNdB at a 7,500-foot distance).

Unlike propeller planes of old, the jets of today produce noise on landing as well as on take-off. Why planes are noisy on take-off might be obvious: their engines are at maximum power, which is required to overcome the standing inertia of the winged behemoths, to get them rolling to take-off speed (usually in excess of 100 mph), and to pull them into the air. Propeller planes have wings of high lift compared to jet planes' wings, and so to land they glide in with engines almost idling, producing noise only when they reverse the pitch of the propellers to slow the aircraft's roll on the runway. Jets, however, don't glide but are flown down with engines running, with nose tilted upward for maximum lift.

They are closer to the ground than propeller planes at the same distance from the end of the runways, and the noise they make as they reverse the thrust of their engines on landing can be louder than the noise they make when they take off.

According to William J. Galloway of Bolt, Beranek and Newman, Inc., "A typical sound pressure time history for jets near airports consists of a signal which emerges from the background noise, rises more or less smoothly to a maximum level which may be as high as 130 dB, then recedes, again more or less smoothly, back to the background noise level. . . . The signal, therefore, has a change in sound pressure level of the order of 50 or more decibels in a matter of seconds, while its frequency distribution spans the entire audible spectrum. In the early days of jet noise, the spectrum was a relatively smooth random function. . . . The aircraft engine designs of today and the near future have greatly more complex sound spectra."

A subsonic jet airplane's noise comes mainly from its engines. One of the best explanations of jet engine noise was that given in testimony before subcommittees of the Committee On Interstate and Foreign Commerce of the U.S. House of Representatives on Wednesday, July 18, 1962, by Frank W. Kolk of American Airlines:

> The jet is—well, it is quite a large squirt of air going back out, and the faster it goes out, the more noise it makes.
>   . . . "machinery noise" . . . can be any one of a number of factors. It can be screaming or whining from the compressor. It can be air rushing past the individual vanes of the compressor—any one of a number of things.

The original engines for B-707 jetliners were turbojets in which all of the air sucked in by the engines was burned and "squirted" out the back. These engines were modified five or so years later to make them fan jets, or turbofans. The converted engines take part of the air they suck in and, like a fan, blow it back without burning it. Turbofans are a little quieter than turbojets. As Kolk testified, giving the example of a jet taking off from New York to go to Los Angeles, "Now, at 2.6 miles from start and take-off the unconverted airplane made 127 PNdB. The converted made 113 PNdB, a saving of 14 PNdB. At 3.8 miles from the start of take-off, the unconverted airplane made 110 PNdB; and the converted airplane made 104 PNdB, which is a gain of 6. Now, the farther out you go, the lesser the difference. . . . So the advantage is to the airport very close in. . . ."

The noises of a jet engine can be directly attributed to its specific parts. The whine you hear when the plane faces you is caused by the compressor rotor blades which act like a siren as they slice through the air at very high speeds. It is also the most predominant noise when a jet is descending to land because the power of the engine is reduced and the noise of the escaping exhaust gases is greatly diminished—until thrust reversing. During take-off, climb, and cruise, the thunder of exhaust predominates. The roar is produced as the kerosenelike fuel, which has been mixed with compressed air, burns and rushes out the pipelike open rear end in blowtorchlike fashion.

A very useful publication, the Federal Aviation Agency's *A Citizen's Guide to Aircraft Noise,* points out, too, that "the sound from propeller airplanes and helicopters radiates nearly uniformly in all directions. The sound from jets is somewhat focused in certain directions, however, as the light from spotlights is focused. As a consequence, the angle, as well as the distance, between a jet airplane and an observer is important in determining the amount of noise heard. . . . the noise is greatest for a ground observer slightly after the jet aircraft passes overhead or to the side."

The sonic boom is an added and special kind of noise produced by the most advanced jets. As shown, it can wreak supersonic havoc in its effect on nerves and in its destruction of physical structures. Today, pointed out N. E. Golovin of the U.S. President's Office of Science and Technology, "There are two quite different kinds of jet aircraft noise. First, during take-off and landing approaches both jet and piston aircraft produce annoying noise while overflying communities near airports, and in the vicinity of some airports this has become a major problem. Secondly, during supersonic operations beginning perhaps 50 miles from the airport and continuing through cruise flight, supersonic jets produce thunderlike bang called 'sonic boom' which affects a corridor extending 20 to 30 miles on each side of the ground flight track. Thus, subsonic jet noise disturbs the relatively small numbers of citizens living or working near jet airports. On the other hand, sonic booms will tend to disturb the entire population located inside the 40- to 60-mile wide corridor. . . . For example, several tens of thousands of people may be subject to annoying levels of subsonic jet noise near a major metropolitan airport. In a transcontinental S.S.T. flight, however, all people located within perhaps 100,000 square miles, embracing perhaps ten million people in a typical ground corridor would be likely to hear and react to its sonic boom."

Bo K. O. Lundberg, Sweden's top aeronautical engineer, pointed out that "the areas of airport noise carpets are exceedingly small, almost negligible, compared to the enormous S.S.T. boom carpets which would cover major portions—in some cases almost the whole—of the countries all over the world. . . . To permit the imposition of an airportlike environment over vast recreational and residential areas—with hospitals, convalescent homes, resorts, churches, concert halls, national parks, etc., would be unthinkable."

Karl D. Kryter, Ph.D., one of America's top sonic-boom

researchers, commented, "When the British-French Concorde and the Boeing supersonic transports (S.S.T.) are fully operational . . . it is expected that about 65 million people in the United States could be exposed to an average of about ten sonic booms per day (26 million receiving ten to fifty booms, and 39 million receiving one to nine booms)." A special report to the U.S. Secretary of the Interior, however, said that approximately 125 million Americans would be subjected to S.S.T. sonic-boom annoyance daily late in the 1970's.

The sonic boom has taken the world by surprise since its beginning. Henning E. von Gierke, Dr. Eng., of Wright-Patterson Air Force Base in Ohio, explained, "When supersonic flying became a reality, the phenomenon of the sonic boom had not been predicted. It was discovered because people heard it, reacted to it with surprise, and wondered about its source. Although the shock wave associated with supersonic motion of a body through air was well known, it had apparently *not* been expected that this shock wave would reach the ground from high altitude with such intensity."

The first sonic booms, created by advanced fighter planes after World War II, were considered a novelty. They were featured at air shows. The novelty wore off when jets were built which were capable of level supersonic flight for short periods of time. Then the emotionally and physically destructive sides of sonic booms were realized.

To the unwary, being struck by a sonic boom can be an unnerving startle. It has been likened to hearing a loud, close clap of thunder from a cloudless sky. It is sudden, unexpected, and lasts but a fraction of a second. But it is not a local startle: as indicated above, it is a giant startle with a 50-mile or more radius.

Simply stated, a sonic boom is a shock wave formed by a body moving through air faster than sound. What happens is that sound waves cannot get out of the way fast enough and

so build up in front of the bullet, or bullwhip tip, or S.S.T.
But the shock wave that makes a sonic boom does not travel
through the air like a sound wave. H. W. Carlson and F. E.
McLean of N.A.S.A.'s Langley Research Center in Virginia,
explained:

> The shock wave that forms at the nose of the airplane
> must obviously begin moving forward at the same
> speed as the airplane since it must stay in front of it.
> But as it moves forward, it also moves away from the
> airplane at an angle, like the water waves that move
> away from the bow of a ship. . . . The waves assume
> a cone-shaped shock front that streams back from the
> front of the airplane. . . .
> The disturbance from a supersonic airplane involves
> more than just a single shock wave from the nose of
> the airplane. Instead, there are many separate waves,
> and, in general, each discontinuity in the shape of the
> airplane produces its own shock wave. So in addition
> to the wave that originates at the nose, there will be
> a wave that originates at the wing-fuselage juncture,
> another at the engines, another at the tail surfaces,
> etc. . . .
> At greater distances from the airplane the separate
> shock waves interact with each other and eventually
> coalesce into just two waves, a bow shock and a tail
> shock.

In technical terms, explained Galloway, the sonic boom "is
a pressure wave which suddenly, but in finite time, rises to
what is called peak overpressure, then decays to a negative
pressure of approximately the same absolute magnitude,
then abruptly, but again in finite time, returns to ambient
pressure. The whole event takes place during a time interval
of from less than 100 to as much as 400 milliseconds,
depending upon aircraft type and performance. The change
in pressure, however, varies from the background level in a
neighborhood to an equivalent of 130 or more decibels."

The power of sonic booms is measured not in decibels but
in pounds per square foot (psf). "Nominal" boom strength is

1.5 psf. During the aircraft's climb, its shock wave on the ground is more likely to be 2 psf. But at the horseshoe-shaped leading edge of the shock wave on the ground, 300 feet thick and 15 miles long, the boom is bigger—4 or 5 psf, according to Lundberg. And if atmospheric conditions are right and if there are walls to reflect the shock waves, the boom can reach and even exceed 10 psf. While he agreed that this combination of circumstances is "very improbable," nevertheless, "one cannot exclude the possibility of people on boat decks being hit by 'horseshoe booms' of the order of 15–20 psf. Such booms are extremely frightening and potentially dangerous."

More common are "superbangs" of 3 psf caused by magnification of the overpressures. These, said Lundberg in 1966, will be "extremely frequent," about 100 million a year in the United States. He added, "When, according to plans, some 500 to 1,000 S.S.T.'s are in operation, the boom carpets will cover the major part of many countries."

Each nominal sonic boom, said Dr. Kryter, "will initially be equivalent in acceptability to the noise from a present-day four-engined turbofan jet at an altitude of about 200 feet (60 meters) during approach to landing, or at 500 feet with take-off power, or the noise from a truck at maximum highway speed at a distance of about 30 feet."

All of this discussion about supersonic aircraft thus far has been solely on the boom. During take-off and landing, these planes, though of lower PNdB, are noisier. This dilemma exists because the PNdB is so weighted as to be very sensitive to high frequencies while almost ignoring the low frequencies. The very powerful engines of the S.S.T. and its kin produce tremendous roars that register deceptively low on PNdB meters, but, because of the power of the sound, spread far wider than the roars of conventional jets. As a result, in the opinion of Harvey H. Hubbard and Domenic J. Maglieri of Langley Field, Virginia, "perceived noise level concepts may need some further refinement."

The advent of the S.S.T. made many experts in noise, aviation, and law look to new ways to refine existing rules and technology. As a startling new source of noise, the S.S.T. precipitated a vast re-examination of the entire field of aviation noise and safety problems. So much so, that many people agreed with U.S. Congressman Roman Pucinski, when he told a House subcommittee in 1967:

> It is extremely regrettable, Mr. Chairman, that before we have even begun to solve the problem of jet noise, our Government has committed billions and billions of dollars on a supersonic aircraft which will make sonic booms a daily personal experience for millions and millions of Americans. I am not opposed to progress. Yet, must we blindly engage in our own mass destruction under the guise of progress?
>
> When this generation of jets was designed, no consideration was given to noise control. The only factors were payload, thrust, and speed. And now the same mistake is being made in the development of the supersonic aircraft. But at what cost in the erosion and disruption of life.
>
> . . . the problem is acute and the time for action was yesterday.

Unfortunately, President Nixon did not agree, when in mid-1969 he gave the go-ahead for funds to build America's S.S.T.

Thanks to man's ingenuity in designing, building, and operating ways to travel through the air, there are ever newer and stranger sources of noise. Among these are hovercraft, ground-effect vehicles which use downward-pointing ducted fans to keep themselves just above the earth's surface. There is regular hovercraft shuttle service between Southampton and the Isle of Man, where they are built. But the noisy craft are forbidden from operating in town and allowed only over the water. Helicopters, with their long lift-producing blades cutting or chopping wide swaths through the air, are also very noisy hovering air vehicles. As cities become more congested, the helicopter may be even more relied on for transportation to and from airports and between points in town. But such cities face the prospect of regular "chopper" chatter bouncing off buildings and disrupting thousands in their office work, as happened in Manhattan with the helicopters arriving at and departing from the Pan Am building.

Another solution to the crowded airport problem is the V.T.O.L. or vertical take-off and landing craft. These planes need little or no runway, but rise vertically, or almost so, to altitude, then speed away at velocities far faster than those of any helicopter. According to one U.S. Air Force study report, "Close to such [V.T.O.L.] ports the community noise problem will probably be worse than that experienced at our busiest airports today." As with conventional aircraft, much of the noise of V.T.O.L. planes comes from powerful engines. But the main source of their noise is the fast vortex of air discharged from their ducted propellers—a sort of man-made tornado which is blasted backwards from the vertical vehicles.

Beyond the S.S.T. in global travel may be the boost-glide hypersonic vehicle. This is a rocket-powered ship which is blasted off to the altitude of near space, then glides down the rest of the way around to the other side of the earth. This kind of vehicle, being studied even now, will produce noise when the rockets blast off, and more noise as the craft zooms along at its supersonic speeds. One estimate is that the craft will produce 140 dB during ascent to altitude, then from 105 to 130 dB during the hour and a half it is on its supersonic way.

If the noises outside of the aircraft are mighty indeed, what about those inside of the cockpit? Dick Stone, a North-east Airlines pilot, thought the new planes he was flying were noisier than the previous ones, so he took a General Radio portable sound-level meter into the cockpit and measured the noise objectively. The noise measured as low as 70 dB-A during low-power glides and up to 103 dB-A during high-power climbs. The noise was not only potentially hazardous to hearing, but also to direct voice communication in the cockpits. Stone brought his study to the attention of the Airline Pilots Association and the Aerospace Medical Association, both of which became interested enough to continue the study and to seek to determine how cockpit noises might be reduced.

Private pilots are also exposed to noise, sometimes dangerously. Noise measurements in the cockpits of 25 different kinds of small planes conducted by Ohio State University researchers showed that pilots live in noise of levels above 100 dB for 500 to 1,000 hours a year. This is far above what is considered to be an acceptable noise exposure. Another study of cockpit noise, this on crop-dusting planes in Oklahoma, showed that these low-flying pilots were exposed to excessive noise for as long as 14 hours a day. So those hedge-hopping aerial jockeys are hurting their own ears, as well as yours.

Also particularly noisy are intercoms and public address systems. It seems ludicrous indeed for a pilot to try to lull the fears of his passengers with sweet background music before take-off, then, having taken off and reached altitude, to tell them to relax via a better than 100-dB blast over the jetliner's P. A. system. They seem to be saying by this action, "Relax, blast you!" The pilot on the one BEA flight I took, London to Amsterdam, was quite quiet, by contrast, at 76 dB. If it was typical, I recommend BEA to you.

3

WHAT YOU CAN DO
ABOUT IT

(((((((((((·)))))))))))

13

KEEPING IT OUT OF
YOUR EARS

$$(((((((((\cdot)))))))))$$

Few of us can turn noise into such a positive force as did Julia Ward Howe. It is said that she was awakened one night at the beginning of the Civil War by the clatter of Federal troops marching into Washington. Rather than put a pillow over her ear, or even pen a complaint to the District administration, she sat down and wrote *The Battle Hymn of the Republic.*

As Arthur Schopenhauer wrote, ". . . noise is a torture to intellectual people. In the biographies of almost all great writers, or wherever else their personal utterances are recorded, I find complaints about it. . . . Noise is the most impertinent of all forms of interruption. . . . How many great and splendid thoughts, I should like to know, have been lost to the world by the crack of a whip?"

The biographies of some of the world's intellectuals prove

Schopenhauer's thesis: noise so disturbed them that they took extreme measures to assure their concentrating in silence. French novelist Marcel Proust (1871–1922) hermetically sealed his studio windows against noise (and germs). American poetress Amy Lowell (1874–1925) so disliked noise that she slept by day and worked by night. When she went to the theater she bought tickets to the seats on each side of her and left them empty; when staying in a hotel she took the room above hers to assure its being empty to prevent the noise of conversation and of footsteps above her head. Railroad Tycoon Edward Henry Harriman (1848–1909), father of Ambassador William Averell Harriman, so hated noise that he had a double door built to keep out noise from his bedroom in New York. (This device, incidentally, inspired a melodrama called *The Double Door*, in which the murdered victim's cries could not be heard from outside the room.)

In 1897, after Giuseppe Verdi (1813–1901), at the age of 84, moved from his estate to spend his final years in a second-floor apartment of the Grand Hotel in Milan, Italy, not far from his beloved La Scala, he worked a little every morning on sacred music. Each afternoon he walked and spoke to the people he met on the street. When he was ill and didn't appear for his walks, the city placed straw mats on the street below his room to muffle the sound of horses' hooves on the pavement. This is somewhat reminiscent of Jerusalem's erecting a road sign near the home of the late Israeli Nobel Prize writer S. Y. Agnon stating: QUIET, AGNON IS WRITING.

Irish Nobel dramatist George Bernard Shaw (1856–1950) hated noise so that he instructed his housekeeper never to use the vacuum cleaner when he was in the house, never to laugh or talk in a raised voice, and always to use the set of the two staircases in the house that was farthest away from him. Neither could he stand the sound of dripping faucets. According to his housekeeper, Mrs. Alice Laden, "If there

was any noise in the street outside, all the windows of his
room had to be shut at once. As a rule his wife and he, when
they were alone, never talked during meals. He wanted
silence and she observed it."

Noah Webster (1758–1843) compiled his first dictionary
at home with nine children running about. He did it by
working in his second-floor study which he had specially
designed with foot-thick walls lined with cork.

Joseph Pulitzer (1847–1911), the famous American newspaper owner, was phobic, or perhaps maniacal, about noise.
Like Amy Lowell, he kept vacant the rooms alongside him,
above and below him in hotels. On his European voyages,
made mainly on White Star Line steamers, a huge floor
covering made of manila rope was spread on the promenade
deck so that he would not hear any footsteps in his state-
room below. In 1895 he had added to his great house,
Chatwold, at Bar Harbor, Maine, a $100,000, four-storied,
40-foot square granite building that was so painstakingly
soundproofed that it was nicknamed the Tower of Silence by
his secretaries. The basement was occupied by a steam-
heated swimming pool. The main floor was almost entirely a
magnificent living room. The upper two stories held bedrooms for himself and his staff. Behind the tower was a little
balcony overhanging a rocky canyon through which a brook
roamed down to the sea. It was Pulitzer's favorite resting
place. The only irritating noise that penetrated his quiet
solitude was the foghorn at a nearby lighthouse. Caring even
more for silence than for the safety of ships at sea, he tried
to have the government turn off the horn, but his efforts
were in vain.

In 1902 he had built in New York City a new mansion, at
Nos. 7 and 15 East 73rd Street, which the architects assured
him would be soundproof. But despite their assurances, the
building was not soundproof enough for his sensitive ears
and temperament. The main problem was a sump pump, the

noise of which ironically focused on Pulitzer's bedroom. So
he had built a single-story annex in the yard. Its double
walls were packed with mineral wool; its windows were
triple-glazed; silk threads were stretched across the fireplace
chimney to break the sound of early morning factory whistles; the passage to the main part of the mansion was
sonically defended by three doors, and its floor rested on
vibration-dampening ball bearings. As a result of all these
measures, his New York study was so quiet as to be uncanny.

Perhaps the ultimate in contemporary quieting measures
occur aboard the Royal Yacht *Britannia*. To guard the ears
of Great Britain's queen, her family, and her guests, all
orders aboard ship are given by officers to the crew by hand
signs; all work to be done in the royal quarters must be
completed early in the day, after the family is up; and, when
the royal family is aboard, no sailor may go aft of the
mainmast after 9:00 P.M. Undoubtedly, it is the quietest ship
afloat—far quieter, in fact, than the new liner *Queen Elizabeth 2*, with its noisy propeller shafts.

These examples of how some famous people have met
their noise problems point up the two most practical ways to
deal with noise: you can withdraw from the noise, or have it
withdraw from you. In short, isolate yourself from the noise
in one way or another.

The easiest and cheapest way to withdraw from noise is to
block it from your ears. This was well shown by an April 27,
1968, item in the *Times* of London, which advised the
24,000 residents of Hatfield, Hertfordshire, to wear earplugs
(or take sleeping pills) because that night "pile drivers are
being used to drive a hole through a railway embankment
for a new bridge." (It would be nice if American municipalities were as civilized as to warn their citizens of impending
sonic disasters, rather than to make the noise, and then
merely receive complaints.) The problem with Hatfield's
temporary noise problem was that it was unlikely that there

were 24,000 pairs of adequate ear protectors or ear defenders (as the English call them) in town, or even in the entire county. Reading that news item, those Hatfielders who cared probably stuffed cotton wool into their ears at bedtime and were soon disappointed when the plugs didn't do their job for the night of noise. All of this points up the ironic fact that even though we knowingly live in a noise-polluted world, we really don't know what to do about it.

Josef Zwislocki of the Laboratory of Sensory Communication at Syracuse University, New York, has likened ear protectors to eyeglasses and said that, probably, no more people want to wear one than the other. Still, he pointed out, "personal ear protectors are probably the most versatile, effective, and the most economical means of noise control."

All ear protectors work on the same principle: they attenuate sound and thus reduce its loudness before it reaches the eardrum. The simplest is the earplug, whether it be stuffing your fingers or cotton wool into your ear canals. Earplugs can be temporary and quite simple, or reuseable and quite complicated. The best temporary and disposable kinds of earplugs are made of wax-inpregnated cotton wool or of the very fine glass wool known as "glass down."

Ordinary cotton wool plugs give very little protection to the ear, as statistics show. At the pure-tone frequency of 4,000 Hz, glass down earplugs attenuate sound by 35 dB. Waxed cotton plugs attenuate it by 32 dB. Dry cotton wool plugs, however, attenuate the sound only 12 dB. Glass down is made in Sweden by Gullhögens Mineralull AB, at Billesholm, and is marketed in the United States by Rockford I. C. Webb Inc., P.O. Box 1552, Rockford, Illinois. It comes packaged in a pocket-sized carton which contains a sheet from which you can tear two pieces, roll them, and insert them into your ears. The glass down does not irritate even the sensitive skin of the ear canal and the plugs can be thrown away after they are used. Studies at Allis-Chalmers in Milwaukee indicate that $4 worth of glass down can protect a worker for a year.

Reuseable earplugs are made of soft plastic or of rubber. Their core may be solid or hollow, and of intricate shape or filled with a viscous fluid. A common and simple kind, the V.51R *Sonex* made by Amplivox Ltd., Wembley, England, attenuates about 30 dB at 3,000 Hz pure tone. Willson Products Division of Reading, Pennsylvania, makes a vinyl earplug (*Sound Silencer*) which it claims can attenuate 54 dB at 4,000 Hz. The *Com-Fit* earplug of Sigma Engineering Co., North Hollywood, California, is supposed to attenuate 38 dB at 4,000 Hz. The *SafEar* of Human Acoustics, Inc., Carson City, Nevada, is designed to selectively reduce only loud noises. There are other brands and designs; this is merely a sampling. There are even earplugs that have valve-like internal operations designed to give added protection against gunshot and other impulse noises.

The trouble with all earplugs—points out Surgeon Commander R. Ross A. Coles of Southampton, whom we quoted in an earlier chapter—is that they are uncomfortable. They must be kept very clean and, even then, shouldn't be used when the ear is infected; they seldom seal in perfectly the ear canal and hence can let noise in through air leaks; they can also transmit sound by vibrating like a piston. "The design of earplugs is really a compromise," Dr. Coles stated. "They more easily deform under the action of sound waves and so allow the transmission of sound through them."

He and other noise-deafness experts prefer the earmuff, a rigid cup usually filled with some foam plastic or other absorbent substance. A fluid-filled cushion around the rim insures a tight fit around the external ears so as to allow no air (and, consequently, no noise) to enter the ear canal. The muffs are kept pressed against the ears by a flexible headband or are mounted inside a helmet. Well-made earmuffs, said Dr. Coles, "are the most efficient ear protectors that can be made." Muffs can attenuate 4,000 Hz pure-tone sounds by 47 dB. Their inherent disadvantages are their discomfort. Big, bulky, and tight-fitting, they cut off air, make the ears hot, and induce perspiration.

Comparing the two kinds of ear protectors, Dr. Coles recommends using the plugs at lower, and the muffs at higher noise levels. His opinion is based not so much on the degree of noise protection, but on the interference with voice communication which the ear protectors impose. "The tendency to use earmuffs exclusively irrespective of the ambient sound pressure level is wrong, as too much attenuation can reduce the signal level reaching the ear to such a level that a further reduction in intelligibility results," said Dr. Coles. The reason is that (by the Lombard Effect explained earlier) you adjust your own voice to rise above the level of the noise of your environment. If you wear muffs in, say, a 90 dB noise environment, the level of voices reaching your ears may be but 50 dB and you would tend to respond with your voice at that low level, which your muffed co-workers would not be able to hear at all because your vocal utterances would be lost in the noise around you.

A great technical advance designed to eliminate such communication problems is the earmuff with built-in head set. One, the *Ampligard* (by Amplivox of Wembley, England), comes with either a throat microphone or a noise-canceling boom microphone.

Headsets built into muffs can be cleverly used to protect the ears against impulse noises, by employing the acoustic reflex. The patent for this system* is held by John L. Fletcher, Ph.D., of the U.S. Army's Medical Research Laboratory at Fort Knox, Kentucky, and Arthur J. Riopelle, of Yerker Laboratories, Orange Park, Florida. As explained earlier, the middle ear has two muscles (the *tensor tympani* and the *stapedius*) which can stiffen the eardrum and the movement

* U.S. Patent No. 3,068,319, dated December 11, 1962.

of the tiny bones which transmit sound from the drum to the inner ear. These muscles will tighten on command from the brain. But the command and its execution come a few hundredths of a second *after* any sound of 80 dB and up reaches the ear. If this sound is an impulse sound, as from a gun, often the damage has already been done by the time the muscles poise to protect. With Dr. Fletcher's system, when a gunner presses the trigger he activates an electronic circuit which produces a protective sound in his headset. Then, milliseconds later, the weapon fires. "The Acoustic Reflex Ear Defender System (A.R.E.D.S.) is currently under test by the Army for use in Army Weapons systems," Dr. Fletcher explained. "It could be used by industry for proof firers, drop forge operations, explosive riveting, and various other impulse noise situations."

Designing a good ear protector and getting anyone to wear it are two different things. As Dr. Coles pointed out, "Dislike of wearing ear protectors is universal though varying in degree. Objections are in many cases very reasonable but have to be weighed against the hazard to hearing. In other cases the objections are less well founded and depend on such factors as self-consciousness, carelessness, bravado, tradition, and unawareness of the dangers." The objection in many situations, he points out, is that "indicator sounds"— certain engine sounds, for example—are lost when ear protectors are worn. Workers have to be shown that they can hear, say, a hot bearing; it's just that they will hear it differently, and they have to learn this. Thus, getting people to use ear protectors is largely a matter of education. In factories, aboard naval vessels, or in army tanks, this should be rather simple, since the people who are exposed to dangerous noise levels can be *required* to wear protectors as a condition of their employment or service.

Ear protectors are but one part of what should be a total

hearing conservation program. Such programs not only are for the good of the workers, but are becoming necessary because the courts are tending to award more and more damages to workers in industries where no protection against noise was afforded. At the Sixth Congress on Environmental Health held in Chicago in 1969 by the American Medical Association, Meyer S. Fox, M.D., of Marquette School of Medicine, Milwaukee (a member of the Committee on Conservation of Hearing, American Academy of Ophthalmology and Otolaryngology), stated, "On the basis of what has happened during the past twenty years, the increase in hearing loss claims and proposed legislation on the part of state and federal agencies, it is safe to say that the noise problem would be very much alive in the years ahead. Regulations and standards will most likely be established as well as safety rules for the use of ear protection where noise is hazardous."

A 1967 editorial in the *Journal of the A.M.A.* noted that "enlightened management is rapidly taking measures to control occupational hearing loss by reducing industrial noise levels. Some companies have made great strides in protecting the hearing of their workers. Others have taken the view that the problem is best left unnoticed and will somehow disappear magically. Fortunately the latter view cannot prevail long because more and more knowledge is accumulating and being published in the professional journals. In light of new evidence, industrial hearing loss will have to be faced by all as a real and serious health problem."

W. Dixon Ward, Ph.D., of the University of Minnesota's Hearing Research Laboratory, pointed out that "industrial hearing loss is now treated as an occupational disease analagous, for example, to silicosis. It is considered the duty of the employer to prevent noise-induced hearing loss, either by keeping the noise level down or by providing ear protection for his workers. If he fails—that is, if a hearing loss develops—then he is required to pay an amount of money that depends on the degree of loss and the particular compensation schedule of his state, often even in cases where it is quite evident that the worker was not using the proffered earplugs or muffs. As one might predict when tens, if not hundreds, of millions of dollars in potential claims are involved, this assignment of responsibility to the employer has engendered a feverish activity that now spawns several hundred articles yearly."

Dr. Fletcher, after organizing a hearing conservation program in a plant of 2,200 workers, concluded that "with proper indoctrination and supervision, workers will use ear protective devices and thereby prevent noise-induced hearing loss. In addition, the longer a man works in an environment of hearing conservation, the more he understands and properly uses such devices. All this is not achieved without effort, but maximum effort is necessary."

A good hearing conservation program includes not only protection of the ears in noisy environments, but also an adequate hearing measurement program. This is spelled out in the United States by the Public Health Service and the American Academy of Ophthalmology and Otolaryngology and in Great Britain by the Ministry of Labour. They are unanimous in their call not only for measurement of the extent of noise pollution in specific industrial environments, but also for tests of workers' hearing at the time they are hired and periodically thereafter. The audiometry tests should especially test hearing at the 4,000 Hz frequency and no less often than once a year.

Noise, as we detailed in earlier chapters, is perhaps the most pervasive and insidious pollution in our industrial world. Alexander Cohen, Ph.D., of the U.S. Public Health Service noted that "the number of workers subjected to potentially harmful noise levels probably exceeds the number exposed to any other significant hazard in the occupational environment." An article in *The Reader's Digest* quoted one industrialist as saying that "Noise is on every payroll," estimating that it costs American industry $4 billion annually. Industry, however, is very slow to change methods voluntarily if the changes do not appear to promise increased profits. Industries seldom change procedures for humanitarian reasons—unless forced to do so by union or legal pressures.

The shortcomings in trying to block noise at the ear become readily apparent with some thought and a few facts. For one thing, even the best of earplugs or earmuffs cannot block all of the noise that falls on the temporal bones and is then conducted to the middle and inner ear. Another point is that we are surrounded by sound we cannot hear—ultrasonic sound especially—which is finding increased use in medicine, industry, and homes. It is less costly and presumably safer than X-ray in looking for flaws in metal and for disease or foreign bodies in the human body, in surgery, for controlling manufacturing processes, and in cleaning tools and jewels. Sound of the frequencies and energies used to pierce metal, the body, and other living and nonliving materials easily pass through ear protectors—and silently as well as dangerously. Also, ear protectors at best block noise from the ear but leave the rest of the body bare to the effects of noise.

There is also the serious consideration of who should wear ear protectors—and where and when. As the noise of our lives intensifies, steadily not only in factories and other working places but in our homes and in recreational situations as well, we are fast approaching that time and place when every one of us should have his own pocket earplugs or his own initialed set of ear protectors hanging on his belt or waiting in purse or attaché case. If our noise does not lessen, ear protectors should be everyday personal equipment for everyone and as available and as ready to use as the sunglasses which are designed to protect our eyes from too much light—another sense organ and another excessive stimulus.

Inanimate objects can be spared the effects of destructive noise if they, like ears, are protected by some sort of blockade against din, or are walled in, safe from the bombardment of wave after incessant wave of sound. We do this when we place fine crystal and china in cabinets.

The same technique of protective walling is involved in the construction of buildings so as to keep noise from shooting from one living space to another. Not merely the walls, but how they are made and what they are made of are involved. This larger-than-ear blockading of noise is the concern of the next chapter.

14

BUILDING FOR QUIET

((((((((((•))))))))))

The quieting of noisy conditions has been variously called
sound conditioning, acoustical treatment, noise quieting,
and noise reduction. (It is not acoustical correction, which is
the elimination of the undesirable effects of sound so as to
provide optimum hearing conditions, as in a concert hall.)
The object in noise quieting is to reduce total sound to an
acoustically comfortable level, working substantially with
the existing structure of a room or building. There are relatively simple things that can be done to keep noise from
being transmitted into working or living spaces. Many of
these are detailed in the U.S. Department of Housing and
Urban Development's booklet on insulating houses from
aircraft noise. They include adding storm windows and
doors and weather stripping, calking and sealing cracks and
gaps in exterior siding and walls, adding brick veneer or

even concrete block to outside walls, installing insulation between, or gypsum board over, open joists in ventilated attic spaces, installing drop ceilings, and placing dampers in fireplaces.

As we explained earlier, noise (even if unwanted) is sound and as such is a form of physical energy carried by some medium. Air is a common medium for carrying noise. Sound carriers exact their price: the larger the distance, the more sound is spent along the way. The more air space between the source of noise and your ear, the weaker is the noise you hear. So, one way to lower the din is to put distances of feet, miles, or counties between you and the noise. Some people intend to do this when they move from the city to the suburbs. (The trouble with such moves is that the suburbs have become so urbanized, the noises there are little different from those of the inner city.)

A clever Chicago residential developer used this distance principle when he built a condominium complex of 24 units in the suburb of Park Ridge, Illinois (a suburb which has its aircraft noise problems, about which more later). To achieve some measure of quiet in the three-story luxury apartments, the developer, William C. McLennan and Co., placed the furnace–air-conditioning units outside the apartments. Instead of being installed in the basement, they were suspended from overhangs of the roof. The idea was to keep all of the noises of the heating, humidifying, cooling, and filtering equipment outside of the apartments. As a result, said a spokesman for the firm, the apartments are the quietest it had ever built.

Acousticonsultant Beranek pointed out that economics is a new force for quiet buildings. "In apartment buildings the errors of design are compounded by economic pressures that have resulted in a too flimsy separation between apartments. Many new high-rise apartment buildings in New York are so noisy that their occupancy rates have fallen below the profitable level. . . ."

Buildings, no matter their purpose, are made of walls (including doors and windows), floors, and ceilings. What follows are some ways they can be designed (or restructured) to keep things quiet. As you will see, many of these techniques are really a matter of correcting original construction errors. Improvements like this should be made not only in homes that are sonically assaulted by aircraft, auto, and other transportation noises from without, but also around kitchens, utility and play rooms, and at work around machinery rooms from the boiler room up to the computer room.

WALLS

The *staggered-stud* is an interior wall construction technique which eliminates the tendency of walls to transmit noise directly from one room to another. In a staggered-stud wall, the plaster or wallboard on each side of the wall is attached only to its own stud. Thus there is dead space inside the wall, and thus each wall surface can vibrate freely without directly affecting the other. The noise, in effect, spends itself in causing the closest wall to vibrate sympathetically. The National Bureau of Standards has noise-tested staggered-stud walls. One kind is made of 2 x 4 studs set on 16-inch centers and spaced 8 inches on centers with ½-inch offset from the other set; each side has ⅜-inch plain gypsum lath nailed to studs, ½-inch gypsum vermiculite plaster, machine applied, and a hand-applied white-coat finish. This wall rates a Sound Transmission Class (S.T.C.) of 43. (S.T.C. is, roughly, the average decibels of nine test frequencies that are lost in transmission, i.e., the average decibel drop.) If the space between the plaster walls is filled with sound-absorbing vermiculite, the S.T.C. is better: 48.

Electrical conduits set rigidly inside walls help transmit noise from one side to the other; if flexible plastic or BX armored cable is used instead, there is no such direct transmission.

There are other ways to let one side of a wall vibrate without the vibrations being transmitted to the other side. Usually there are flexible or resilient mountings that allow the walls to vibrate and dissipate sound energy in their springlike structure. Quiet walls can, for instance, use only a single set of studs—but instead of the lath being nailed to the boards directly, they are attached to resilient channels or clips and these, in turn, are nailed to the studs. Tests by the bureau of standards give such walls S.T.C.'s of 44 to 52.

The S.T.C. numbers get even higher when hollow gypsum blocks are used in combination with resilient clips holding the lath and plaster. When 4 x 12 x 30-inch blocks were used, the S.T.C. was a more silent 53.

Another technique is to attach sound-deadening board to the studs, then install wallboard over this. "The minimum S.T.C. of these walls is 46, which is significantly higher than the S.T.C. 38 of a conventional wall," according to R. A. LaCosse, technical director of the Insulation Board Institute (I.B.I.). This technique coupled with staggered-stud construction can yield an S.T.C. of 50, LaCosse claimed. (The sound-deadening board is related to acoustic tile in that it is made of wood or cane fibers. The S.T.C.'s of the various sound-deadening board walls were determined by a respected independent testing laboratory, Geiger & Hamme Laboratories, Ann Arbor, Michigan.)

You can also modify walls and partitions by constructing a new or false wall in front of an existing one. The new wall should be attached to the existing wall with spring clips or other flexible mountings and have sound-deadening board or insulation in back of it.

Sound-deadening board, like softer sound insulation, acts to reduce the transmission of noise by trapping it in tiny dead-air spaces which occur on the order of millions per square foot. In addition, the finely interlaced fibers of wood or bagasse vibrate sympathetically with the noise, absorb its

energy, and convert it to heat, produced by the friction of
the fibers rubbing against each other. The heat is dissipated
to the dead-air spaces. According to I.B.I., "70 percent of the
excess noise that strikes an acoustical insulation board" is
absorbed.

Lead is another material that can be used in walls to cut
down the transmission of noise; its mass and limpness are its
chief assets. According to two Canadian engineers, D. H.
Lauriente and W. L. M. Phillips, "Pound for pound, lead is a
more effective sound barrier than any other conventional
building material." Sheet lead, they point out, "was never
used extensively due to the high cost of rolling the sheet to
the thin gauges generally required. The recent development
of a continuous lead sheet casting machine has significantly
reduced its cost and made its application economically at-
tractive." Lead is more expensive than other sound-deadening materials such as gypsum board or plywood (10 cents
per square foot for boards versus 25 cents per square foot for
lead), but lead sheet is easier to install and so labor costs are
saved (80 cents per square foot for lead sheet versus $1.20
per square foot for boards).

Lead can be used as hanging sheets or as a wall covering
in leaded vinyls. Lead can also be used on doors to lower
sound transmission. Furthermore it can be hung in drop
ceilings as a sort of limp and heavy barrier which prevents
these plenums (as they are called) from tunneling noise
overhead for the length of a building.

WINDOWS

Windows can let noise in as easily as they do light, and
they usually do.

Here's a good example of the kind of a goof that can boost
noise: casement windows in adjoining apartments, if they
open facing each other, serve as excellent sound reflectors to
send noise from one apartment directly into the other. If

they both open in the same direction, however, then sound from one apartment's window is reflected away by the glass surface of the other.

Common glass window pane is transparent to sound because it is so thin and flexible. However, if the pane is made of laminated glass-and-plastic, or of two panes with dead-air space between them, they can be effective noise barriers.

Amerada Glass Company's *Acousta-Pane* is a laminated pane made of two sheets of glass with interlayers of soft, transparent plastic. The highest rated kind, which is ¾ inch thick, has an S.T.C. of 43, according to tests performed for the company by Riverbank Laboratories. Thinner versions have S.T.C.'s of 36 and 40. Libbey Owens Ford Glass Co. makes laminates which have S.T.C.'s of 33 and a triple-glass double air space *Thermopane* with a 40 S.T.C. (according to tests performed by Gieger & Hamme). Such windows have been used with some success in airport hotels and in schools located near elevated trains.

Multipane's sealed acoustical separated-pane window units, framed in aluminum, claim S.T.C.'s of 32 to 41. Similarly, in homes, double-hung windows and storm windows help reduce noise transmission because of the dead-air space between them. To be maximally effective, the windows, of course, have to be closed. Even better, they should be well-calked and sealed all around the edges so that sound doesn't enter through any air leaks.

DOORS

Doors, for several reasons, can let in more noise than the walls to which they are attached. For one thing, they are lighter in weight and more likely to vibrate sympathetically on their hinges. For another, they have openings around them through which air and noise can leak.

Hollow doors, used in most construction these days, are the poorest performers in impeding sound transmission. Na-

tional Bureau of Standards tests showed that such doors*
have the shocking (if not annoying) S.T.C. of 18!

Even such lightweight doors can be made to hold back
some noise if only soft gaskets or felt are placed on their
bottom edges to prevent noise leaks. If gaskets or weather
stripping is placed on all edges, all the better.

Folding doors, even with gaskets, are terrible, with
S.T.C.'s of 21 and 25. Obviously the best doors for keeping
noise away are those which are heaviest and best sealed.
S.T.C.'s of 50 can be achieved with doors 5¾ inches thick,
with skins of 16-gauge steel over ¾-inch plywood, filled with
cork and sealed along the edges with neoprene foam and
tubular gaskets. A more reasonable design, perhaps, is a
2⅝ inch door made of double construction—solid wood
sheets pressed against a core of ⅛-inch-thick felt—and sealed
around the edges by gaskets. Such doors can achieve S.T.C.'s
of 35–45.

FLOORS AND CEILINGS

The sound of footsteps and of dropped objects can be
disturbing indeed. The expression about waiting for the
other shoe to drop tells well the anguish that can be caused
by noises overhead.

Ceilings transmit below not only the noises from the floors
above but the sounds from walls as well. Unseen air channels where walls and ceilings meet are natural pathways for
airborne noise. Similarly, where floor and wall intersect is a
solid pathway for structural noise transmission. And when
floor above and ceiling below are rigidly connected, noise
can only be transmitted up and/or down. The Construction
Lending Guide of the U.S. Savings and Loan League expresses the problem well: "Impact noise caused by a floor or

* A 1¾ x 36 x 84 inch, veneer face, flush type, wooden door, with
hollow core installed in conventional manner, i.e., ¼-inch air space at
bottom, no drop closure, and no gaskets on ⁷⁄₁₆-inch wooden doorstop.

wall being set into vibration by direct mechanical contact is then radiated from both sides. This vibration may also be transmitted throughout the structure to walls and reradiated as sound to adjoining spaces . . . footsteps, children romping and playing, and moving furniture on floors constitute the major impact problem."

The usual floor-ceiling construction is pretty much a lay-down version of the too-usual straight-stud construction of walls. Instead of vertical 2 x 4-inch studs, the main structural floor units are horizontal 2 x 10-inch joists spaced 16 inches on centers. Sometimes they are cross-braced. The surface underneath is the ceiling, built exactly like a wall with lath and plaster. Above is the floor, constructed layer-by-layer upward of: lumber subflooring, rosin or building paper, and tongue-in-groove finished flooring or plywood. Such basic floors have S.T.C.'s in the mid-30 range, as measured by the National Bureau of Standards.

Techniques to reduce the transmission of noise through floors and ceilings borrow somewhat from wall-quieting techniques, then add a few of their own. For instance, there is a staggered-joist construction in which floor and ceiling are each supported by their own set of joists and are free to vibrate independently of each other. The basic design gives an S.T.C. of 45. When the floor is further isolated by sound-deadening board and furring strips and when sound-deadening material such as mineral wool is placed between the joists, the S.T.C. can be in excess of 50.

Another way of rating floors is the *Impact Noise Rating* or I.N.R., expressed as + or − from a standard set by the F.H.A.; + means better, − worse than the standard, and no more than −8 is allowed. The staggered-joist construction rates an I.N.R. of +3. Compare this to the rating of −16 for the standard straight-joist floor described above.

If 1 x 8-inch joists are used instead of 1 x 10 and the ceiling is suspended from spring clips instead of being nailed,

the S.T.C. is 51 (no I.N.R. available). If 8-inch steel joists
are used and the floor is made of paper pulp building board
onto which is glued hardboard, to which, in turn, is glued
felt building paper which is then covered with foam rubber
padding and, finally, with nylon carpet, the I.N.R. zooms to
+15. If the floor is made of poured concrete, the joists made
of steel, and the ceiling hung from spring metal clips, the
I.N.R. is +26. If the floor is a slab of poured concrete supported by poured concrete walls but sonically isolated by
fiberglass and covered with foam rubber pad and carpeting,
the I.N.R. is +33.

The point should be clear: the more mass a floor has, the
less easily it can be set into sympathetic vibration. The more
it is padded and carpeted, the more "cushion" a floor has to
prevent impact sounds; the more free-floating and independent a ceiling is, the less likely it is to sympathetically pick
up the noises from the floor above.

The most popular kind of noise quieting is the use of soft,
absorbent materials strategically placed to prevent noise
from being further transmitted or to cut down its reverberation time in a room or hallway. The most widespread of all is
acoustical ceiling tile. According to the Insulation Board
Institute, "Every year, retail building materials dealers sell
enough acoustical insulation board and ceiling tile to sound
condition more than one million average rooms in American
homes."

Homeowners, office proprietors, and others who install
such ceiling tile are often disappointed when they discover
that the installation did not hush the space as much as they
thought it would. Actually, ceiling tile doesn't cut down the
decibels as much as it does the reverberation time. It can
make a room a bit more comfortable and conversations less
of a chore, simply by reducing the reflection of most of the
sound waves which are imposed on it. This means that most

of the noise produced at one end of a den or office or restaurant or plant won't be reflected off the ceiling to the other end. But, needless to say, it does nothing about those sound waves which travel directly through the air.

Similar results are obtained when sound-deadening materials are placed on walls. This can be absorbent boards, or tiles, or even heavy drapes. It works with floors, too, since hard-surfaced floors can reflect footsteps and other noises upward. Resilient plastic floors help and carpets help even more—the thicker the better, and the thicker the pad underneath the better.

Be careful that you are not misled about the nature of acoustic tile and other sound-absorbent materials. The fact that they pretty much fail to reflect sound doesn't mean they also fail to *transmit* it. Remember the wall and floor construction techniques. You need mass and isolation to prevent the transmission of noise. An Englishman, Mr. H. J. Purkis of the British Building Research Station, at Garston, Herts., pointed out that "it is important to note that absorbent materials cannot by themselves be used as an effective sound insulating barrier; they have the wrong characteristics, being porous instead of airtight and generally light instead of heavy." He also added this cautionary note:

> Materials which are introduced intentionally into a room as sound absorbers are generally of the soft porous type, e.g., glass wool, mineral wool or the proprietary acoustic tiles, and these are most effective at low frequencies unless mounted over an air-space. The absorption also varies with thickness. Some foam rubbers and expanded plastics also come in this category as long as the cell structure is such that the pores are interconnected; materials with sealed cells are not good general absorbers. . . . It cannot be emphasized too strongly that most common types of absorbing materials are very ineffective insulators against sound.

There are techniques to apply in cutting down the noise within a room. These are, merely, the use of upholstered and other soft furniture (for instance, inflatable chairs) and other furnishings. This principle has been known for centuries, yet is often not applied because too many owners of homes, offices, halls, hospitals, and schools believe they save money in maintenance by purchasing hard-surfaced chairs and sofas. Actually, what they may save in upholstery they spend in inefficiency and in lost business, due to the physiological and psychological effects of noise.

Actually, anything that will impede this reflection of sound waves from ceiling to walls and other surfaces will cut down a room's reverberation time. This could be a carpet on the floor, acoustical material on the ceiling, drapes or curtains on the walls, or stuffed furniture. Anything, in other words, that is soft and absorbent of sound will lower a room's reverberation time. That is why music sounds different when an auditorium is empty from when it is filled with an audience. (One music expert complains that the miniskirt has changed the echo absorption characteristics of auditoriums; longer skirts absorbed stronger sounds.)

Drapes are very expensive to buy and clean. Yet most men who own homes can put up their own tile and can wash it down or paint it when it gets dirty. Handy homeowners can also do other projects to quiet their homes. They can, for instance, place rubber or plastic treads on uncarpeted stairs.

PLENUMS AND DUCTS

Suspended or drop ceilings can be made to transmit very little noise indeed. However, the plenum thus created, as we said earlier, is a tunnel which can transmit noise horizontally. It needs something, perhaps lead sheet curtains placed at intervals, to baffle sounds.

The ductwork of forced-air heating/cooling systems in newer homes is another form of built-in sound tunnel. Ducts

can carry not only sounds of the heating-humidifying-
cooling system, but also (particularly in apartment buildings) the conversations of people and their television sets
and radios in nearby rooms. Furthermore, if the forced-air
system has a fresh-air vent to the outside, it can also pick up
noises from the street or from neighboring buildings—
depending on where it is pointing. If the furnace is oil-fired,
rather than gas-fired, there will be even more noise sent
through the ducts, because of the high-pitched oil vaporizer.
Mounting the motors on cork or some other vibration-absor-
bent material can help greatly.

Noise can be reduced in ductwork by linings of sound-
absorbent materials. Such ducts are often made larger to
allow enough air to pass. Where the ducts are very long and
big, several walls of absorbent material can be lined up in
the direction of the airstream. These are called duct splitters. Prefabricated duct splitters and attenuators are made
and should be considered in new installations.

There are other ways to prevent duct and grille noises.
One is to have flexible sections properly placed, as at the
furnace and at intersections with walls and ceilings. Another
is to make the bends round and not square, in order to keep
air turbulence to a minimum. Still another is to keep the
velocity of the forced air at the lowest possible speed. This is
more of a problem in summer, when you want air moving
fairly rapidly so as to enjoy its cooling effects.

PLUMBING

Noisy plumbing can be quieted considerably without too
much trouble and expense. Water makes noise flowing
through pipes whenever it is set into turbulence. So, to keep
such noises down in the design of a plumbing system, it must
have as few bends, as few changes in diameter, and as few
valves as possible. Pipes—especially hot-water pipes—
expand and contract and can create noises in doing so; also,

this movement can cause creaking and other noises if the pipes rub against their supports or against walls or other structures. Swing arms should be used at both ends to prevent movement; expansion joints should be used; and washers, when replaced for worn ones, eliminate chattering or whistling sounds. Too-hot water can cause noise; try reducing the thermostat on the water heater and see if that helps. If it doesn't, it may indicate a faulty heater. Sucking noises often indicate drains that are either clogged or inadequately vented. An antisiphon trap can alleviate this.

Neoprene, cork, or other resilient material can be used wherever pipe comes in contact with something else, be it supports, walls, or fixtures. Where any pipe passes through a header (horizontal 2 x 4 which runs at ceiling height in walls and to which studs are nailed) or other structural member or through masonry, the pipe should be wrapped with insulation. Each opening should be calked or closed with a gasket to prevent airborne noises from leaking through. You can replace the last foot or so of piping with flexible tubing to isolate appliances and fixture noises from the gas or water supply system. Water hammers—that banging of pipes that can come when faucets are shut suddenly—are relieved by installing air chambers or by draining the water out of existing air chambers. Loose or worn faucet supports should be flexible or frictionless. The same is true, incidentally, for gas pipes.

While our emphasis on building quieting has been on dwellings, the very same techniques are applicable to shops, offices, restaurants, schools, hospitals, and even factories. The noise of the cocktail lounge, for instance, can be kept from spilling over to the leisurely diners in the next room if heavy enough dooring—even of the glass type—is used between the two rooms. Offices in plants and even in office buildings need not be so hard to work in because of the noise levels, if they are properly walled and windowed and doored and floored.

These same techniques can also be applied to various transportation vehicles. If engines were properly sound-insulated and barriered and if walls surrounding the passenger compartments were acoustically constructed, travelers could be moved in far more peace than they are now. Some car makers—notably Rolls Royce and Ford—say they have achieved this. There is no reason that any passenger should have to hear the noise of the powerful engines used to propel you as you sit in a jet, in a high-speed train, or even in your own automobile.

Taking all the foregoing possible measures into consideration, look at kitchens, bathrooms, and utility rooms. They usually contain the loudest noise sources in the home, and yet they have the hardest, most sound-reflective surfaces. In each, the average housewife spends most of her waking hours. What can be done about cutting the reverberation time? Not too much. Sound-absorbent tiles or boards can be placed on the ceiling, but in kitchens there is the problem of grease accumulation. Floors can be laid of vinyl backed by foam rubber or other soft material, which will not only retard some reverberation but hold down impact noises. Similar treatment can be given to the walls. The trouble is that there is little wall space in a kitchen. Most of the vertical area is made of cabinet doors. There is little reason that softer material can't be used on cabinet doors, but the trend now is away from somewhat resilient wooden doors to stiff plastic laminates because they "wipe easier."

As for bathroom and kitchen design, there are a few essentials. Bathrooms, kitchens, and laundry rooms should not be placed next to quiet rooms, such as bedrooms. They should be stacked, rather than put back-to-back, even though the latter is done to save dollars (if not decibels). If this is not possible, medicine cabinets should be staggered; so should plumbing fixtures. Walls around these rooms and their doors should be of high S.T.C. construction.

Heating and cooling equipment, together with washing machines and driers, should be placed in isolated or walled-off utility rooms, usually in the basement or at one end of the house. (But not always. Sometimes all this noisy machinery is placed right in the middle of the house, where it can annoy everyone all the time. And why those terribly noisy dishwashers are not located with clothes washers, I don't understand. It would both free cabinet space in the kitchen and remove a major noisemaker from that sonically unbearable room.)

That still leaves the oven, range, refrigerator, blenders, and miscellaneous other appliances which not only contribute their own considerable noises, but also reflect each other's. One of the major contributions to American home life which appliance designers and manufacturers could make would be not to redo their packages so that they merely *look* more appealing, but redo them so that they *sound* more appealing. Why not resilient (if wipeable) surfaces for kitchen, utility, and even bathroom appliances?

To quote Jack Mowry, publisher of the journal *Sound and Vibration,* "Economic and technical means are available to produce quiet equipment and to control noise sources inside and outside of the home. The equipment manufacturers have the staff and programs to respond to market requirements. . . . Vibration isolation and vibration damping materials and components are in common use in industry and can be adapted to home construction and equipment." So, why aren't they? Why, he asks, can't you "get as excited about noise and vibration control as you were about hi-fidelity and TV some years ago?"

If you are a purist about silence, you may not like this last suggestion. A "white noise" of mixed frequencies, which (unlike conversation) carries no information, can be used to mask the noise you can't keep out. The first thing required is that all windows be closed; this alone will cut down on noise from without. Then, turn on a window air conditioner, an electronic circuit and loudspeakers, or a circulating fan. Sometimes the registers of central heating/air-conditioning systems create enough "white noise" to mask any offending sounds. "White noise" is not preferable to silence, or no noise, but it is preferable to noise which carries bothersome information, such as conversation in an adjoining room.

Moving away from your ears and from the buildings in which you spend your time, there are other kinds of barriers which can help keep noise away, grander in scale than the walls of a room.

Some people think that a hedge in front of their home will keep out the noise of traffic. Unfortunately, the same physical laws apply to greenery as to acoustical tile, masonry walls, and every other material. To keep from transmitting sound waves, the material of which the barrier is made has to have either a great mass, or else be free-floating. The leaves and branches of bushes and trees don't fill either requirement very well. The trunks of trees, further, can even act as sound wave reflectors. Perhaps 50 to 100 feet of dense growth might achieve a 5 to 10 dB reduction in noise transmission—and then mainly at the higher frequencies!

You might be better off if you built a solid brick or concrete wall around your home. It could stand the force of noise without transmitting much of it. The question is, how high should the fence be? Mufflers and engines on the street or highway outside your home are, at most, perhaps three feet above the surface of the pavement. But the vehicles would not all likely be right up against your wall, so there is the problem of the angle upward to you from as far away as they are—perhaps across the highway. Also, what about trucks, with their exhausts high in the air? There is the additional problem of the reflection of their noises off nearby buildings, causing the noise to travel upward in a sort of curve and not in a direct line.

There is also the phenomenon known as *sound focusing*. An example of how this works is at the National Aeronautics and Space Administration's Mississippi test facility, which is surrounded by five miles of dense forest—intended to serve as a barrier to protect nearby communities from the shattering noise of rocket engine firings. However, peculiar combinations of wind and temperatures can make the atmosphere transmit the noise upward and outward to distances beyond five miles—there to break windows, offend ears, rattle china, and perhaps cause structural damage.

Also, consider the vibrations that trucks and cars and buses and even trains make as they travel near your house. These are transmitted through the ground—in effect, *under* your wall.

Embankments and neighboring buildings or similar solid structures make even better barriers to noise. If road traffic and trains are run in cuts, instead of at or above ground level, the sloping embankment serves the purpose of a noise barricade. How effective the embankment is depends on its angle and on the depth of the roadway or the tracks below the ground. These measurements will determine the angle at which the noise will rise from the traffic. The steeper the angle up from the depressed roadway or railway, the less likely is the noise to be directed at those who live alongside. (There is, of course, the sound-focusing effect to take into consideration.) One study, which measured the difference of the noise levels 100 feet away of the same train running at grade level and in a cut 12 feet below grade, showed that the latter resulted in a lowering of as much as 23 dB.

As for super-barriers, they have been suggested in the form of eight-story apartment buildings as long as, and parallel to, runways (but not too close to them). Such 100-foot-tall structures would protect the community on the side away from the airports by 25 to 30 dB. Of course, the buildings themselves would need elaborate treatment to keep sound out. There would also be the problem of air safety, which might be threatened by tall buildings so close to airport traffic.

The subject of barriers against roadway traffic has also been studied by the National Swedish Institute for Building Research in Stockholm. The researchers concluded that barriers, rather than 100 feet or so of strips of open space, were most practical in today's urban areas. But which form of barrier—a 10-foot-high mound, or wall, a continuous row of four-story buildings, or depressed roads—was not decided by the researchers.

Another form of barrier to noise is zoning. The law (which we'll discuss in a later chapter) is going to have to require that residence-free areas be left around airports and around other intense noisemakers in the city (and elsewhere), and absolutely prevent creeping residential communities from building alongside of them, as has been the case with so many airports in America, notably Kennedy in New York, Midway and O'Hare in Chicago, and International in Los Angeles. As long ago as 1926 the U.S. Supreme Court declared that zoning was a legitimate means to "decrease noise and other conditions which produce nervous disorders." It affirmed this opinion in 1954.

We have the means, we know the techniques, we have the reasons and the motivation. We need only do it. But we haven't. A 1911 book on Daniel Burham's great city plan for Chicago notes that "it must do away with unnecessary noises, smoke, dust, dirt, confusion. . . ." Almost the same wording was used in 1967—more than half a century later— by the U.S. Task Force on Environmental Health and Related Problems: "Therefore, the Task Force recommends that, by 1973, the Department develop, through research, basic data sufficient to establish human levels of tolerance for crowding, noise, odor. . . ."

15

QUIET BY DESIGN:
AT HOME AND AT WORK

((((((((((•))))))))))

A barrier against noise—whether you put it in your ear, over
your ear, in a room, in your garden, or around an airport—is
really a last-ditch stand. Like a Maginot Line, it can easily
be penetrated by new and unexpected force. Even better
than barricading is lowering noise at its source. In other
words, the prevention of noise is far more effective than is its
suppression. It is also more humane, for though you may be
lucky enough to be able to shut out noise at your ears or at
your walls, others may not be so fortunate—or so affluent.

With materials and labor as expensive as they are today,
we tend to settle for decibel reductions instead of insisting
on absence of decibels. The result is that we compromise not
only our ears but the health of our hearts and our nerves.
For instance, we settle for lowering the transmission of noise
between walls and floors to a comfortable level during the
day. But what of the night, when even sounds that seem

faint during the day can keep us awake or prevent our restful sleep?

Besides, there is no one source of noise. In our society today, noise surrounds us, engulfs us; noise from many sources imposes upon our every waking and sleeping moment. The need for designs for quiet is imperative. If the din climbs, as some say it has, at the rate of a decibel a year, modern civilization in a few years will become an unbearable environment in which to live. Not only might the rate of noise deafness, heart disease, and nervous breakdowns increase by then, but also the rate of suicides. They have already been climbing. In the United States more people kill themselves (annual suicides: 20,700, or 10.5 per 100,000 population) than kill others (annual murders: 13,100, or 6.6 per 100,000). Suicide rates have increased in recent years in America, as they have in many advanced, noisy countries, including (from most suicides to least) West Germany, Sweden, Australia, Belgium, England and Wales, Poland, and Canada. International statistics show that more than 76,000 human beings—most of whom live in noisy surroundings—take their lives every year. Who is to say that the unbearable noises of our society do not in some major way help convince many emotionally afflicted that this life *is* simply too unbearable?

There is some evidence that in quarters of our Western Civilization, the "Think Quiet" movement is having some effects. Here are some examples:

El Jardinero, the bulletin of the Men's Garden Club of Tucson, Arizona, told its members that hand-powered, rather than motor-powered lawn mowers are "a decent, civilized way to mow a lawn." It added, "Many lawnowners—and may their numbers rapidly increase—are turning away from that noxious noisemaker of so many neighborhoods, the sputtering, smelly gasoline mower. Many of these seekers after peace and quiet are discovering the Silent

Scotts mower is just what they need and want." To O. M. Scott & Sons, of Marysville, Ohio, goes the credit for developing and marketing a quiet manual lawn mower.

The Christian Science Monitor of April 12, 1968, in an article by Roderick Nordell, pointed out that those buzzing, vibrating, chugging air motors and devices are really not necessary for home aquariums if the tanks have but enough green plants in them to provide oxygen for the fish.

The Dentists' Supply Co. of New York introduced The Silencer Cartridge for its high-speed (300,000 rpm) dental handpiece. Says the company, "The new Silencer Cartridge insulates the rotating turbine from the handpiece housing with a rubber cushion. Vibrations are absorbed. And the high-pitched whine of ball bearings is eliminated."

Bethlehem Steel Corp., itself a profound noisemaker, announced early in 1969 its application for a patent on the quieter steel garbage can developed by its noise control engineer, James H. Botsford. The can, which makes a thud instead of a clang when it or its cover is dropped, was introduced in New York in April, 1968, at 51st Street near the Avenue of the Americas by Citizens for a Quieter City (about which more in a later chapter). It was demonstrated again in Washington, D.C., in June, 1968, at the National Conference on Noise as a Public Health Hazard, at which Botsford was a speaker. The bottom of the can has a mastic, like that which is used to undercoat automobiles; it has six rubber feet to cushion shocks; a one-inch-wide steel-and-asphalt felt belt encircles the midriff of the can to dampen vibrations there; a similar belt is attached to the lid. Dover Stamping Co. of Fall River, Massachusetts, makes them to sell for slightly more than noisy conventional cans.

Noise was substantially reduced at 500-bed Walsall Hospital in England with a pilot quieting program, which included covering the clattering wooden floors with foam-backed sheet rubber, replacing squeaky metal curtain

runners with ones made of plastic, and relocating the nursing office and linen rooms between kitchen (which was
quieted) and patient ward.

The Vier Jahreszeiten Hotel in Hamburg, Germany, is one
of the world's most famous, in part because it delivers break-
fasts to guests in their rooms on leather trays, so as to
prevent morning dish clatter.

With thought and design, even the terrible demolition
construction sounds which reverberate through the concrete
canyons of Manhattan and other metropolises can be substantially reduced. An excellent example of the application
of quieting techniques was one manufacturer's use of decibel-
lowering walls around air compressors. You've seen these
terribly noisy, ubiquitous machines in the streets, near men
who were working those infernal pneumatic drills. The new
Spiro-Flo DL900S portable compressor by Ingersoll-Rand
makes only a hundredth of the noise of previous models: at
full power it produces 85 dB-A of noise at 3 feet; the old one
produced 110 dB-A or more at that distance. At the machine's unveiling in New York City in mid-1969, Neil H.
Anderson, chairman of that city's Task Force for Noise
Abatement, said that for the New Yorkers who are subjected
to 80,000 street repair jobs and 10,000 demolitions and construction projects every year, the new compressor "will help
minimize the unwanted sounds that these projects produce.
Its development represents a significant step forward by the
equipment manufacturing industry and the construction
industry."

The DL900S achieves its noise reduction not by any
changes in the compressor mechanism but simply in better
muffling and enclosure. The entire unit is surrounded by
panels of glass fiber with an aluminum-sheet backing coated
with a vibration-damping mastic material. Two engine-
exhaust filter silencers are clad in glass fiber and wrapped in
asbestos. The cooling fan is made of glass fiber, and there are

two 90° sound traps to help dissipate the sound of air rushing in and out of the unit.

A truck-mounted machine, nicknamed the "cookie cutter," because of the way it works, can be used to replace jackhammers and their air-driven, eardrum menacing staccato. The Road-Bor device cuts a 5-foot diameter circle into asphalt and concrete pavements and roadways. Another kind of impact construction noise can be eliminated by the replacement of the usual drop-hammer kind of pile driver with a vibrating kind. Besides being quieter it is also quicker. The hammering kind can take an hour to knock a steel beam 50 feet into the ground; the sonic kind can drive a steel beam 30 feet into the ground in only 45 seconds. The vibrating pile driver produces an audible rumble which is far more acceptable than is hammering. Reportedly, a fifth of all construction jobs in the eastern United States employ the vibrating pile driver, and Russia has a version in use.

A construction company in New York City pleasantly surprised Manhattanites in 1966 by placing special steel mesh blankets, each weighing several tons, over sites where explosives were used to blast through bedrock. This resulted not only in muffling of the blast noise, but containment of debris to keep it from flying. In the same building, incidentally, the steel frame was welded rather than riveted together, effecting a further prevention of noise.

These are just random examples. Botsford has pointed out that "purchasers can encourage manufacturers of noisy equipment to produce quieter products by requesting that product noise data be supplied with quotations or by including noise specifications in purchase requisitions. This approach has been successful in obtaining quieter products from manufacturers of excavating and hauling equipment used in mining."

Alas, the individual consumer cannot demand such decibel specifications for each vacuum cleaner, lawnmower,

dishwasher, or garbage disposer he buys. And manufacturers' claims about their products are often more fanciful than
factual. For instance, a leading appliance manufacturer
boasted that it had developed a quiet dishwasher and quiet
garbage disposer. I inquired about details, but after six
months of correspondence, in which I was referred from the
Chicago plant to the Louisville, Kentucky, plant, and from
product planner to engineer to product redesign, no meaningful information—not even on decibel reduction, if any—
was forthcoming.

When organized, though, consumers can exert force to
add low maximum decibels to low maximum price demands,
or to rate products, as does Consumers Union, by quiet as
well as by cost.

At the same time, we consumers have to be educated to
the realization that we *should* demand quieter products and
that noise does not mean strength and power. As Ray
Donley, principal engineer with the Acoustical Engineering
Division of Hearing Conservation, Inc., told the American
Medical Association's Sixth Congress on Environmental
Health in mid-1969, "A vacuum cleaner which is nearly
silent, which is technically feasible, is not likely to sell very
well . . . today's housewife wants to hear the sound of
power." Similarly, her husband, when he buys a car, wants
its door to slam with a solid thump, not a quiet squish. Our
values are backward.

The fact is that quieter vacuum cleaners have been designed. So have quieter power lawnmowers. For example,
Dr. Tony Embleton, of the National Research Council of
Canada and of the University of Ottawa, told a science
writers' seminar in New York in 1967 that he had worked on
the problem of a quieter upright vacuum cleaner and had
solved it. The blades of this impeller for the centrifugal fan,
which creates the suction, are sloping and slightly tilted,
rather than upright. The result, he said, was not only a
quieter, but a more efficient vacuum cleaner.

Similarly, a quieter blade for an 18-inch rotary power mower was developed more than a decade before the publication of this book by two Illinois Institute of Technology researchers, William C. Sperry and Guy J. Sanders. The blade noise is the aerodynamic noise generated by the blade as it cuts through the air in the mower frame. They found that while a sharp leading edge is necessary to cut the grass most effectively, a sharp trailing edge of but 4 to 5 inches effectively reduces the noise—by as much as 20 dB at 4,800–9,600 Hz octave bands. Changing from a straight blade to an S-curved blade (20° sickle) achieved a further 20 dB reduction to the astonishing level of 42 dB. Even a slightly S-curved blade was much quieter than was the straight blade still in use. (They left to others the problems of the noise created by the engines of power mowers.)

Courses in noise control for engineers and industrial designers are given at various centers, some on a regular basis. Among them are the courses given by the U.S. Public Health Service; the Center for Professional Advancement; Massachusetts Institute of Technology; Pennsylvania State University; Bolt Beranek and Newman, Inc.; the University of Missouri; and Consultants Kodaras and Lindahl. Yet, estimated consulting acoustician Lewis S. Goodfriend of Cedar Knolls, New Jersey, "these are available to less than three hundred people a year."

Attempts at holding national and even regional noise control symposia regularly have faltered. Noise journals have a tortured and unsuccessful history, as you may have gathered if you tried to look up details of the original papers cited at the back of this book as references. The list of now-silent noise journals includes *Noise Control* (1957–1960); *Sound, Its Uses and Control* (1962–1967); and the *Proceedings of the National Noise Abatement Symposium,* of which there were at least four, sponsored by the National Noise Abatement Council, which was disbanded in 1961. "Only a tiny section of the scientific community is concerned with noise. It's just not popular," Alexander Cohen, Ph.D., of the U.S. Public Health Service, told me. Few universities offer curriculum in noise control, he pointed out. The subject is mostly taught on the job.

When industrial planners, designers, and managers start to Think Quiet, they can accomplish much in the way of noise prevention or reduction. Machines, for instance, should be mounted on vibration- and sound-absorbing pads; all pipe connections to the machines should have flexible couplings; in every case possible, the machine should be enclosed by a high-S.T.C. wall, ceiling, and floor, or by more closely fitting enclosures. Industrial buildings should be constructed so that both airborne and structure-borne noises are not transmitted from space to space on the same story or between floors.

But, as Goodfriend pointed out, "Noise control in industry is like quality control. The personnel are not usually greeted with delight by the production department. They are often viewed with suspicion as cost raisers and troublemakers. I ask you what kind of satisfaction is there in that for the new graduates, especially when they can go into computer work or value engineering and show how to save money?" Furthermore, there is no financial or industrial support for postgraduate noise education for those who missed it in college.

Two systems development experts from I.B.M., R. E. Jelinek and K. S. Nordby, told a 1967 meeting of the Acoustical Society of America about their fight for quieter computer equipment such as printers and reader/sorters. These machines, they pointed out, "operate in engineering offices, hospitals, libraries, and general business offices. The machine noise levels should be acceptable in all customer environments."

They made the very important point that the earlier in a project that engineers and designers can Think Quiet, the better. As they express it, the "dollars per decibel" in noise reduction "are lowest during the early design stage. At that time, there are drawings only and it is least costly to make changes. The cost of noise reduction rises as prototype hardware is built and changes become more difficult. After Phase I, it becomes increasingly difficult and costly to get noise reduction recommendations implemented. Initial tooling has begun and many parts of the machine design have been frozen. The cost of noise reduction increases rapidly as the machine approaches full-scale production. By Phase III, the cost of noise control is usually prohibitive. The conclusion is that for minimum cost, noise control must be implemented before Phase I." To prevent products from being noisy means giving development engineers an acoustic education and therefore making them conscious of noise and the need to prevent or reduce it. Otherwise, said the I.B.M. pair, the designers/engineers "wait until they can hear the noise of actual hardware, but then it is too late for economical noise control because hardware changes may be required."

Using construction as the example again, here is what the Wilson Committee suggested: "We feel that designers should consider, in preparing their designs, whether there are alternatives which will involve less noise in construction. They should be specially careful to avoid the use of very noisy processes such as sheet steel piling, if the circumstances of the site and the costs make this feasible."

As for machinery used in factories, the Wilson Committee affirmed that "the noise output is rarely considered seriously when machines or plant are designed and installed. It is important that it should be, as it is often at these stages that most can be done economically." An example of planning was given by Pierre Lenard, Mr. French Acoustics, as he is called, who works for O.N.E.R.A. (Office National D'Études et de Recherches Aérospatiales), the French equivalent of America's N.A.S.A. His agency located its giant, high-speed wind tunnel in part in consideration of a waterfall on the site which could provide needed hydroelectric power, and in part because there was not much of a population around the site to disturb. The site is at Modane in the Alps near Italy. This biggest wind tunnel in Europe, called S-1, is 8 meters in diameter at its test section and can "fly" even some full-sized planes at speeds of 0.98 mach. S-2 is a sister wind tunnel of smaller size (2 meters) but producing speeds up to 3.0 mach. S-3 tunnel, also on the site, is for hypersonic speeds, 12–15 mach. "All this," pointed out Professor Lenard, "makes a lot of noise. But there is, essentially, no one around for it to disturb."

The O.N.E.R.A. model is a good one for governmental and industrial noisemakers the world over to emulate. The location of a noisy factory, the Wilson Committee suggested, "is an important factor in reducing the disturbance caused, and planning authorities can play a constructive part in this by giving due weight to noise as one of the matters to be considered when dealing with applications for planning permission for industrial development."

Engineer Botsford agrees that "programs for modernization of facilities or new construction when noise can be considered in the design of operations and selection of equipment provide the best opportunities for noise control. But the possibilities for noise control are still limited since materials and equipment currently available embody little consideration of noise control."

All too often noise is not prevented in factories, but has to be controlled just the same. Botsford gave as example six gigantic blowers (1,500 hp each) located on the side of a plant for the purpose of drawing air in from outdoors. The fans were so noisy that they interfered with telephone conversations in an office across the street. The problem was relieved by placing baffles in front of the blowers to contain the aerodynamic noise created by the turbulence of the incoming air. The shield, which would allow air in, was made of steel to diminish the transmission of noise directly to the street and was lined with sound-absorbing material to prevent reflection of the noise back to the building and then to the street. In addition, vent pipes to the blowing air were covered and acoustically isolated. As a result, the noise reaching the offices across the street was 19 dB fainter.

W. Ian Acton and three colleagues from the Institute of Sound and Vibration Research at Southampton had to recommend drastic means in 1966 to reduce the almost pure-tone whine produced by giant motors at a pumphouse known as Blyth "B" power station. The 3,250-hp motors produced a ringing-bell type of magnetic reverberating noise which measured 104 dB in the station and which was clearly disturbing to residents in nearby private houses. As a result of the noise researchers' recommendations, the rotors of these large motors were modified by rewinding them, the entire motor was fitted with a silencing enclosure, and the entire pumphouse was modified to contain the remaining noise. As a result, the noise level in the building was reduced to 77 dB, and outside the building it was considerably less—38 dB outside the nearby houses—when the wind blew directly from the pumphouse.

Altering installations such as these to quiet them is far more expensive than designing them for quiet in the first place, but it should be done more often. This is eminently true of the very loud textile industry, the effects of which on workers' hearing was described in a earlier chapter.

Robert Crawford, also of Southampton, spent the years 1965–1968 with Great Britain's Imperial Chemical Industries' I.C.I. Fibres subsidiary in a somewhat successful attempt to reduce the noise of, especially, drawtwist machines used in the manufacture of nylon. In the drawtwist stage of manufacture, the fresh plastic strands are literally pulled to align the nylon molecules so as to give the yarn strength, then twisted into thread and wound on a bobbin. Each machine is 50 feet long with bobbins aligned in two rows, 4 feet apart, each row consisting of 64 bobbins spaced on 6-inch centers, each bobbin spinning at about 10,000 rpm.

The bobbins, Crawford found, make the most noise. To find out why, he had to go down to the basics and learn about the construction of the bobbins and the spindles that hold them, and the fine details of their operation. He found that the noise of the bobbins was made by very small deviations from perfect of the bearings, on which they rotated so rapidly. He measured differences of as much as 0.002 inch, which meant that on each machine 128 swiftly spinning bobbins produced 128 maddening, discrete frequencies of noise. He also found that noise was being produced by rollers and by a chain-and-gear drive mechanism.

Thanks to his recommendations, significant noise reduction was made by using flexible bearings on the spindle so as to dampen the out-of-balance rotational forces that were producing noise; by replacing the spindle shafts with those made of a dampening type of alloy (30 percent copper, 70 percent manganese); by developing a cast polyurethane gear; by replacing high-speed chain drives with tooth belts; and, by using many smaller, lower-powered motors, instead of a gigantic central motor. As a result, he reduced the noise the textile machines produced from about 100 dB to 85 dB, and altered the nature of noise to more bearable lower frequencies.

But if he or some other acoustical consultant had been called in at the time the machines were being designed, there would have been effected not only a quieter drawtwist machine at the beginning of the plant's operations, but at far less expense in terms of hearing loss and money spent in damage claims and in needed design alterations.

Professor W. Taylor of Queen's College, Dundee, whose study of weavers' hearing we related earlier, was not so fortunate in reducing the noise level of jute looms, which generate noise at the dangerous 100 dB level. After a careful analysis of the machines' noise and noisemakers, he replaced 17 kinds of key metal parts with plastic ones. He achieved, however, a noise reduction of only 3 dB. He concluded, somewhat pensively, "Even small noise reductions of the order of 2-3 dB are desirable and worthwhile. Every effort, especially on the part of loom manufacturers, must be made to reduce overall loom-noise levels, however small the increments."

Again, the lesson was plain: quiet should be built in from the beginning at the design stage, and not be an afterthought.

Important if somewhat neglected sources of noise in industry are gears and ball bearings. This was one of the ingredients of the problems in the textile industry, as we have seen. Mr. G. Berry of the National Engineering Laboratory, Glasgow, Scotland, after studying the problem in detail, concluded that "the greatest single factor contributing to bearing noise is the departure from sphericity of the balls." He recommended closer tolerance specifications when ordering balls for bearings, of the order of 0.0000025 inch to 0.000005 inch. He also pointed out that gears are a particularly vexing noise problem. Replacing metal gears with plastic ones does not solve the problem because such gears need to be operated at lowered loads even if at higher speeds, which only produces new noise problems. It seems incredible, indeed, that studies of bearing and gear noises should only have begun in the 1960's!

Underground mines are another inherently noisy working place, essentially because the miners work with pneumatic hammers and drills in a confined space with hard walls and, thus, long reverberation times. The percussion drills used by miners deliver 2,200 hammer blows per minute, and the rotary drills whine like the turbines they are. The result is noise of the level of 105 to 120 dB. Studying the problem at the Sullivan Mine in British Columbia, E. M. Cantwell of Uniroyal Ltd., Montreal, found that most of the noise was radiated by the machine's exhaust, essentially a continuous explosion of compressed air. This sudden adiabatic expansion, together with high humidity, could cause severe icing problems, particularly if an exhaust muffler of the type used in automobiles were put on the drills. Instead, he found that he could reduce the noise level at the miners' ears by piping the exhausted air through a hose and placing the opening 50 feet away. Also, he designed a rubber jacket which, when placed around the drill, lowered its radiated noise by about 10 dB. At the same time, the miners were required to wear ear protectors.

The miners at first complained about the added weight of the rubber jackets and the inconvenience of the ear protectors, but, as Cantwell reported, "When a miner returns home after four hours of drilling, without protection, he is aware that he cannot hear the television at a normal sound level. He also experiences a disagreeable ringing sound in his head for several hours after leaving the mine. It is easy to demonstrate the benefit of protection."

Air-conditioning systems also move large amounts of air, and the large rotating fans and running water of cooling towers in canyons between skyscrapers can generate much noise. In a heavily populated urban business environment, they can affect far more people than can pneumatic equipment in mines. It took several years of living and suffering with noisy rooftop cooling towers and centrifugal fans which push cool air through the miles of ductwork in office buildings before air conditioning, heating, and ventilating engineers learned to Think Quiet.

In the meantime, noise experts were consulted. Among the

innovations that had to be added were air-intake and air-discharge silencers and the various kinds of duct silencers described in a previous chapter. But all were installed after the fact. Until the new era of Quiet Engineering really arrives, industries throughout our civilization will have to learn how to make up for lost quiet, to noise-control their machines and plants. They will have to learn to put mufflers on machines, to put asphalt or other dampening material on noisy parts, to place machines on noise- and vibration-absorbing pads so as to isolate the noise and prevent it from being transmitted to walls and floors, and, thus, prevent building members from acting as sounding boards. This means, too, they will have to learn not only to quiet their machines through redesign or by building noise-containing enclosures around them, but to modify the factories and design new quiet ones for future use. They will have to learn to operate their machines at the proper speeds, or use bigger but slower machines. They will have to, instead of using one big force to cut or shape a part, use several smaller, quieter forces in stepped operations. They'll have to replace impact tools with quieter rotating ones. They will also have to maintain their equipment properly, since worn bearings or other parts, or those that are lubricated inadequately or not at all, cause excessive noise. The first thing to consider, when modifying a machine to cut down its noise, is whether it is properly lubricated and maintained.

16

... ON THE GROUND
AND IN THE AIR

(((((((((·)))))))))

The principles enumerated in the last chapter also apply to motor vehicles. General Motors's David C. Apps threw some of the blame for truck noise back at operators when he reminded them: "The responsibility for maintenance is that of the owner or operator. He must replace the muffler with original equipment units; he must select new or re-tread tire designs which do not broadcast tire noise that can be heard for miles. He must not allow loose cargo or cargo tiedowns and hardware to add to the level of the basic truck noise. We submit that these things have not been done."

He added that "industry recognizes the tire noise problem." But facts don't support this statement. Tire makers are more concerned with sales than satisfaction. In Southampton, again, considerable study was conducted into the problems of tire noise, but, because of manufacturers' erroneous notions about consumer attitudes, little was done to alleviate the problem.

Earlier we told how Christopher G. Rice, of Southampton's Institute for Sound and Vibration Research, explained that a tire is very much like a siren: it rotates rapidly and has a regular tread pattern that cuts the air at certain speeds so as to cause an annoying whine. One way to attack tire whine, in his view, is to vary the tread pattern of the tire, so that it does not repeat itself. Also, by eliminating the smallest cuts or slits, the higher frequency whines can be eliminated. Thus, if tire manufacturers wanted to, they could produce quiet, or nearly quiet tires. But they won't. One prominent tire manufacturer who was approached with the solution, Rice related, said a tire has to be noisy or have a noisy tread to be safe. Another leading manufacturer said its sales managers specified that in order to be sold, tires must look "sexy," and that meant treads with regularness and not randomness of tread pattern.

Another way to cut down the noise of cars is to modify street surfaces. How much noise a tire makes depends on the road as well as on the tire. Siren noise is only part of the problem. The other problem is the noise of the rubber on concrete, or on whatever material the road is made of. Roadway noise is also transmitted through the body of the car to the driver and passengers.

Dr. Cohen of the U.S. Public Health Service pointed out that "little interest has been directed toward developing roadway surface materials which could reduce structure-borne and airborne roadway noise emission. The application of soft plastic coatings to highway surfaces has been mentioned as a possible means of absorbing tire noise, but no evaluative work has been done as yet."

As related earlier, the modern automobile engine is a noisy affair that has been governed by considerations of power; there is little evidence that it has *ever* been designed

for any degree of quiet. Rotational balance, bearing toler-
ances, radiator fan design, valve rockers, carburetors, and so
forth have been designed for more power or less break-in
time, or for masculine identity, but never for less noise. Car
manufacturers have limited their noise control efforts to
placing sound-absorbent materials in the firewall and floor so
as to sonically isolate—not always so successfully—the
people in the car from the whines, rumbles, swishes, grunts,
slurps, clicks, and roars under the hood. Car manufacturers,
in fact, often tend to pull in the other direction, making
engines roar "powerfully" and exhaust "mufflers" rumble
meaningfully. How often does a salesman say to a prospec-
tive car buyer, "Listen to that engine's power?"

New sources of automobile propulsion power are being
investigated. But while turbines and jet engines should be
ruled out, at least at this stage of their technology, because
they are such horrendous noisemakers, the steam-powered
car, using modern steam engine techniques, holds promise of
being silent, as well as being efficient and not polluting the
air. In addition to automobiles, new steam engines might
well be adapted to power trucks and taxies—and perhaps
even boats; their relative silence would be quite a contrast to
today's noisy outboard and inboard marine motors. The electric auto would also help solve the smog problem while
giving considerable relief to the decibel problem. Its motor
would start quietly, idle almost silently, and run quietly. A
quiet electric motorcycle developed by Karl Kordesch,
Ph.D., of Union Carbide Corp., used the space-age fuel
hydrazine and air, went 25 mph, and had a range of 200
miles for each gallon of fuel.

At least one diesel engine, more inherently noisy than is
the gasoline-powered engine, was sonically tamed—or,
rather, barricaded—by British navy engineers. They effected
decibel reductions by cladding the huge engines with 2-inch
layers of polyurethane open-cell foam, sandwiched between

an outer layer of lead sheet and glass-reinforced polyster resin and an inner sheet of reinforced resin.

As it rolls along its assembly line, a raucous horn is automatically installed on every car in the world. So, too, is an automatic siren on every ambulance, fire engine, and police car. There is much evidence that these emergency sounds serve to panic drivers and pedestrians and provoke them into doing the wrong thing—which is probably why so many of these emergency vehicles get into accidents. One problem is that you can't get a clue about direction from sirens. And what purpose does a blast of the horn do, except to make you feel better because you protested to the driver ahead of you? As for warning people, you're fooling yourself. Drive defensively, and place your foot on the brake instead.

Lee E. Farr, M.D., head of the State of California's Disaster Health Services, wonders why horns are still left on autos at all, especially since more and more cars have air-conditioning units and thus are operated with the fans running (and radio or tape player blaring) and the windows closed. He suggests that visual warning signals would be not only easier to live with, but far more effective. After all, we use visual signals now to regulate traffic—in the form of lights, signs, and policemen's hand motions. Visual signals are seldom misconstrued, as are audible signals. "When you hear a traffic policeman's whistle, do you know at whom it is directed?" asked Dr. Farr. Yet, he pointed out, "When you drive through a yellow light, you know it." There is no question that Dr. Farr not only is a competent complainer against noise, but is a profound thinker for quiet.

The clickety-clack of the railroad is caused when the steel tracks run over expansion gaps. The expansion joints are necessary in temperate areas of extreme changes in climate because of the rails' expansion and contraction. In these places the temperature can have a range of 200° F. The expansion joints used to be spaced every 6 feet, which represented as much rail as a man could carry unaided. Then it was standardized to 39 feet, which was the right length to fit in a 40-foot railway flatcar. Now, even in Canada, where temperatures swing wildly, rails are being welded together into one continuous steel ribbon, so as to remove the clickety-clack and to reduce maintenance needs. The technique was developed in Canada by the National Research Council.

There are many other things that could have been done to quiet railway travel, which did not rely on new technology as does this advanced welding-and-stressing technique. Among them are cushioning the tracks, using rubber instead of steel wheels, better suspension for the cars, and better insulation of the car walls.

The worst noise offender of our generation, as far as the general public is concerned, the aviation industry, has never tried to Think Quiet. Never, that is, until public, regulative, and legislative pressure was applied. Since man's first successful powered flight at Kitty Hawk in 1903, airplanes have grown more and more powerful, and more and more noisy. Even in World War II's golden era of aviation, a quiet plane which could sneak in and attack without audible warning was not successfully developed. The nearest things to it were the glider (which had no motor at all) and the jet, which swept in fast and apparently silently (until it was close) at nearly the speed of sound. But as planes exceeded the speed of sound, their presence was announced by the sonic boom, that most devilish of all of aviation's noises.

No one, apparently, thought of a quieter engine for the great B-29 or the thunderous B-36 or the menacing B-52 or the screaming F-100. "Banshee" was an excellent name for a Navy jet. "Noise is something we'll have to live with," was the attitude of those who gave us the 707, DC-8, and other jet transports. In the very development of the jet turbine engine, conquest over the speed of sound, not its loudness, was the main thrust. Finally, with enough public indignation, engineers began late in the 1960's to see if they couldn't contain some of the noise of ever more powerful jets right inside the engines.

As Peter A. Franken, a vice president of Bolt Beranek and Newman, Inc., expressed it—and this is true not only of aviation, but also of motor vehicles and railroads—"It is now common practice to regard noise control as an add-on item that is considered *after* a transportation system has been designed or even constructed. The manufacturer, the owner, and the general public are then often surprised to discover new noise problems *that could have been predicted*. The greatest progress in transportation noise control will be made when noise is considered early in the design state of a transportation system [italics his]."

In a way, he was echoing the feelings of the Aeronautics and Space Engineering Board of the National Academy of Engineering, which in a monumental report issued in August of 1968 "noted the randomness by which new technologies found their way into the total air transportation system." The report called for "a resolution of the noise problem that depends upon the development of quieter aircraft, improved methods of operation, establishment of federal noise standards, development of consistent land-use practices near airports, and development of less expensive building and air-conditioning techniques for residences to reduce noise penetration."

In an attempt to control noise made by jets taking off and landing at Kennedy International Airport, the Port of New York Authority installed noise-measuring and recording equipment at five locations around the airport. But the airlines retaliated by what they called Operation Test Able in which spotters stationed on the ground near the noise-recording boxes communicated with pilots over the radio and told them, when they were near enough, to temporarily reduce the power (and the noise) of their engines. In one month (September, 1967) this teamwork beat the box 1,686 times.

Commenting on this operation, U.S. Congressman Richard L. Ottinger of New York told the Subcommittee on Transportation and Aeronautics of the House of Representatives in November of 1967 that "if the airlines invested half the ingenuity in solving the noise problem that they expend evading the Port of New York's monitoring system, we might have had the problem licked by now. . . . We are spending millions on new and bigger airports and new and bigger jets. We have embarked on a program to build the biggest aircraft bang in history, the $5 billion supersonic S.S.T. But we don't know how to live with the engines we have today, and jet noise remains the poor cousin of the aeronautics industry."

As we explained before, there are two kinds of noise from a jet engine: the whine from the sirenlike compressors at the front of the engine, and the roar of the burning fuel-and-air mixture as it thunders out of the rear of the engine to give forward thrust in accordance with Newton's Third Law of Motion.

In typical add-on tradition, airlines bolted noise suppressors on jets long after the jets were flying and were creating so much noise that public pressures demanded them. The suppressors worked by either attenuating in tubes the noise created by the jet exhaust or by slowing down the exhaust gases so as to reduce noise-making shearing caused when the fast, hot gases collided with still cold surrounding air. There were airborne suppressors hung on the back of the engine nacelles and large, landbound suppressors to cut down the terrible noise of engine run-ups. By 1965, America's airlines had spent nearly $150 million to install added-on jet engine suppressors. The most commonly used was of the multiple tube and lobe design, which gave 10 to 15 dB reduction (corresponding to 5 PNdB). Most of these engines were scrapped when they were replaced by the newer kind, the turbofan or fan jets. These engines, as we said in an earlier chapter, are not only more powerful but are slightly quieter than turbojets. This is because in the turbofan engine, energy is taken from the exhaust gases (thus slowing them) and given to a large fan section at the front of the engine which moves a massive, but slower, stream of air. This slowing of the gases which squirt back from the jet results in less noise.

As an example of the futility of added-on devices, the noise suppressors of turbojets never did quiet the jets much in practice. John M. Tyler of the Pratt & Whitney Aircraft Division of United Aircraft Corp. pointed out that the noise suppressors added weight and drag, necessitating more fuel: roughly 1,000 pounds for a transoceanic flight. "Now, taking into account this extra thousand pounds of fuel, the extra weight of the noise suppressor, the reduction in thrust which the engine has as a result of having the suppressor added, the airplane is at a lower altitude when it passes over the nearest [to the airport] neighbor's house which offsets the noise reduction of the suppressor. . . . on long flights it turns out that in some cases the noise is actually higher on the ground when a suppressor is used than it would be if the suppressor were not used," Tyler explained in December, 1962, to subcommittees of the U.S. House of Representatives. From an engineer, that was an amazing admission of the futility of half-measures. He then made the shocking statement that, "Looking into the future, we feel that as the state of the art improves some small noise reductions will be achieved using improved engine designs based on present engine cycles, but no marked noise reduction is anticipated."

While the fan jet design kept exhaust roar down somewhat by increasing mass flow and reducing the velocity, it increased the problem of jet whine on approaches, because of the enlarged fans and compressors at the front of the engine. As a result, considerable research dollars and effort were expended to reduce these noises. Engineers at various engine manufacturing firms experimentally altered the number of vanes in the compressors, and their angles and their configuration, to see if such design changes could reduce noise. They also worked on design changes in the engines' inlet and exhaust ducts. The results seemed promising enough that the Federal Aviation Agency set a 10 EPNdB (Effective Perceived Noise Decibels) noise reduction as a tentative goal, then set regulations to insure its achievement in the current new generation of aircraft, the Jumbo Jets and Airbuses, which began operations in 1970, should saturate the airlanes in 1980, and probably will be phased out after 1990.

Both Boeing and Douglas engineers, under quiet-engine contracts from N.A.S.A.'s Langley Research Center, Hampton, Virginia, worked on lowering jet inlet noises by lining jet engine ducts with sound-absorbing materials. The sound-absorbing ("acoustic") lining of the ducts were made of porous material sandwiched between honeycomb cells, designed to trap and dissipate sound. Experiments were conducted on the perforations and cavities to see how "tuning" their size and shape might increase their absorption of the specific sounds of the engines for which they were designed. At Boeing in Seattle, the take-offs and landings of the 747 during its test flights were actually measured and recorded by engineers on the ground so that its noise profile could be studied and examined for such purposes. Interestingly enough, in reports to the Acoustical Society of America in 1969, Boeing engineers claimed a 30 dB whine-noise reduction, while Douglas engineers predicted a 7 to 10 PNdB reduction using applications of the same technique. One unforeseen problem was the distortion on the engine nacelles produced when the planes flew; this did not occur on ground tests of the engines.

Laudable and audible as these meager but necessary achievements in noise reduction might have been, they again point up the failure to design quiet into engines from the beginning. Even after all of the experience—the complaints from the public, the investigations by Congressional committees, and the blaring publicity—the jet engine designers of America still approached noise control with techniques, not much more sophisticated than lining your basement ceiling with acoustic tile. What was and is needed is some real Think Quiet philosophy in this very noisy segment of our technology. Despite the Rolls Royce ads, European aircraft manufacturers are no better. Apparently, the engineers who design new jet engines say, as do the French who built the first Concorde, "Noise is *their* problem [here, Britain's]."

Despite the publicity about its Quiet Engine program, there was even evidence that somewhere along the way the Federal Government had lost its nerve or its idealism on jet engine quieting. In 1967 the Secretary of Transportation, Alan S. Boyd, told Congress, "I do not believe there will ever be such a thing as a quiet airplane." He pointed out, "Despite our far longer experience with the problems of truck noise and railroad noise, we have not been able to produce quiet vehicles in these modes of transportation. But I am convinced that we will be able, by technological and regulatory means, to reduce the impact of aircraft noise." He added, "The present technology we have to produce a quieter engine, and that we believe will be available within the short-range future, will not solve the complete aircraft noise problem. We believe that the eventual range of noise reduction may be between 10 to 20 perceived noise decibels [PNdB's]."

The preponderance of learned wisdom supported his hands-in-the-air opinion. Noise fighters turned their attention away from the noisy engines and concentrated instead on take-off and landing patterns and buffer zones around airports. This seemed rather amazing in the space age when technology was seen as mankind's salvation. In fact, there was supposed to be an actually quiet plane, the Wren 460-B, purchased by the U.S. Air Force for service in Vietnam. Essentially it was a modification of the Cessna 18 business executive's aircraft. The modification details were a defense secret when the news leaked out in May of 1969, and perhaps that is why the quieting techniques were never allowed to be applied to the domestic war against aviation noise.

Progress in quieting hovercraft, which are inherently very noisy, was reported about the same time. The craft was described as using centrifugal ventilation fans rather than propellers. By moving lots of air at slower speeds, it achieved substantial noise reduction at similar lift.

The prospects for finding a technological breakthrough to eliminate or reduce the sonic boom are even more dim than are those for a quiet jet engine. A small ray of brightness in the picture was a concept belatedly proposed in 1968 by Edwin L. Resler, Jr., the director of the Graduate School of Aerospace Engineering at Cornell University. His suggestion, not so radical, was that the engine nacelles be much larger in cross section than were called for in the designs of the Boeing and Concorde S.S.T.'s. This would cause air sucked in by the inlet ducts to be compressed farther back in the engines and thus be exhausted out the rear more rapidly. The idea is to draw in air which surrounds the S.S.T. and thus prevent its build-up on the leading edges of the wing; this piling up of air causes the shock waves which make the boom. Unfortunately, there was no evidence that the S.S.T. builders ever took heed of this suggestion.

In the meantime, the battle of airport flight patterns

continues and has reached no settlement in the aircraft noise war. Compounding the problems are the facts that jet transports continue to grow bigger and go faster as their airborne population increases. Over the years the irony has been that as the outer cities crept closer to the airports (which, in most cases, had been originally located in rural areas), the speed, load, configuration, and loudness of airplanes extended out from the airports. Congressman Pucinski of Illinois expressed it well before a subcommittee of the U.S. House of Representatives in 1962: "Congress cannot go back and undo the rezoning law of two or three or four decades ago, but I think that this Congress had better give some serious consideration as to the minimum and maximum standards of the size of airplanes that can be used at these airports near urban areas, because if they develop a 270-passenger carrier, you are going to see that while we have a problem now 10 and 12 miles away from the airport, you are just going to extend that problem back 20 miles from that airfield. So you are going to create more problems . . . the time has come when the legislation on the books has to start reflecting some rights of people on the ground."

Pratt & Whitney's Tyler told the same committee: "We should get away from this 'house that Jack built' procedure for accommodating modern aircraft near our large cities. The airports must be near the cities if they are to be effective in providing fast transportation. However, we should do the best job possible of keeping noise close to the airport and not spread it over the whole city."

Five years later, in 1967, President Johnson sent to heads of all Federal departments and agencies a memo which said, in part, "Air traffic in the vicinity of airports has increased enormously in recent years, and the expansion of air commerce and air travel promises to continue. One of the results is that persons and property in the vicinity of airports are being exposed to an increasing amount of aircraft noise. At the same time our growing economy and population create pressures for increasingly intensive land use near transportation facilities, including airports. . . . Various agencies of the Federal Government . . . must all be deeply concerned with seeking solutions to the problems of noise and compatible land use around airports."

Thus, at all levels, the problem is well defined and well described. But, as in the case of engine noise, the solutions have been added on and thus are of limited effectiveness. The philosophy that pervades aviation the world over—"If some want to fly, others will have to stand the noise"—prevails. The solution, then, obviously, is to alter the take-off and climb, glidepath-and-landing patterns of airports so that planes will not fly low over built-up communities, or at least, so that they fly over the least-populated areas. The suggestion has not been so easy to apply, however, since, at great expense, runways are built aligned in the direction of prevailing winds. Even the power of modern jets doesn't obviate this need. Perhaps a criteria for future land development around airports should be to build homes, etc., along roads and highways that are at right angles to the prevailing winds!

It is more than interesting to note that the city of Washington, D.C., the heart of the Federal Government, is well protected from aviation noise. In terms of jet noise, one might call it the nation's quietest city. At the end of every Washington National Airport runway, before the pilot revs up his engines for take-off he sees clearly the sign:

AVOID P-56 PROHIBITED AREAS
OBSERVE NOISE ABATEMENT PROCEDURES

Security reasons (ostensibly) keep airplanes from flying low over the city. Both take-offs and landings are along the Virginia side of the Potomac. The story has been often repeated that during a solemn service for Carl Sandburg at the Lincoln Memorial, President Johnson became disturbed as across the Potomac somehow came the sound of jets. He asked a Secret Service agent to call the airport and have the planes rerouted until the services were over. Silence prevailed for the rest of the ceremony.

What about satisfying the rest of the country's yen for quiet? In 1967 Transportation Secretary Boyd told a Congressional committee that less noisy take-off and landing procedures had been imposed on airports and airlines by the F.A.A. He explained: "This so-called segment noise abatement climb profile consists of a maximum take-off climb to a specific altitude, followed by a reduction in power and lower rate of climb to an altitude where the generation of noise is not annoying and thereafter a resumption in the normal climb procedure. In addition, research is now underway to provide a noise abatement approach [landing] profile . . . there is, as yet, a safety hazard in increasing the rate of descent with today's aircraft instrumentation and performance. It is hopeful that this hazard can be overcome. We also intend to continue our efforts to ensure that Federal funds will not be expended for airports which have not provided for adjacent land utilization compatible with future noise exposure."

An interesting aspect of this problem is that the local agencies that operate airports have not had any authority to regulate the flight of aircraft into and out of them. This authority resides in the Federal Government, particularly the F.A.A. But local agencies do have, or can try to get, authority to regulate the use of land around their airports. Dr. Cohen suggested that local governmental agencies keep undeveloped land around airports zoned for nonresidential use, or else buy up land around the airports to keep them as noise-buffer zones. Recognizing the financial problems that would be involved, he suggested that "there are some acute

airport community noise problems which can only be corrected through purchase of extensive residential land areas.
While this remedy may be extremely costly, the eventual
resale of this land for more compatible land usage might
offset any financial loss involved in such transactions." That
was not so wild a suggestion. After all, Federal and local
governments stepped in to help private and public devel-
opers raze city blocks of slums and replace them with new
apartment buildings. Why couldn't there be similar funds
for leveling areas in which reside those whose lives are
impoverished by the noise of low-flying jets?

Governmental agencies have considered locating new airports out in large bodies of water, miles off shore and away
from people. Specifically considered have been an airport in
Lake Erie to serve Cleveland, one in Lake Michigan (perhaps below the surface of the water, surrounded by a coffer
dam) to serve Chicago, and one on the island of Saltholm in
the narrow Öresund sound between Copenhagen, Denmark,
and Malmö, Sweden. Among the reasons proposed for locating these airports on the water was that the jets using them
could take off and land over water, sparing the nearby cities.

This seemed to be a valid application of Think Quiet,
except that there is a phenomenon—a variation of the noise-
focusing mentioned earlier—which may nullify the noise
protection intended. Fritz Ingerslev and Christian Svane, of
the Acoustics Laboratory of the Technical University of
Denmark at Lyngby, made careful studies of the transmission of sound from Saltholm island to the mainland 6.6 km
(4.1 miles) away. They found that the water reflects sound
for long distances, whereas land is likely to absorb the
sound. So, under certain common conditions in the lower
atmosphere, sounds from Saltholm are carried to land by
being reflected between the air and the water. A similar
effect may have carried the noise across the Potomac to
President Johnson at the Sandburg service.

Altering procedures by which aircraft are put into the air and landed may be somewhat effective in reducing noise around airports, but they contain inherent dangers. As Volrath Holmboe, manager of aircraft analyses for Scandanavian Airlines System (S.A.S.) in Stockholm, explained, "There are other considerations in flying an airplane than noise. When you reduce power at 700 feet to lessen the noise you are making, you always have to consider what would happen if you lost an engine. You need the safety factor of having the potential to maintain level flight with one engine off. If you reduce power too much and then lose an engine, you may have to lose precious altitude in order to maintain enough speed to stay in the air."

At Bromma, the airport at which S.A.S. has its headquarters, as at many airports, there are time limits on landing and take-offs so as to keep the nighttime hours peaceful. Such was proposed for Chicago's O'Hare International Airport by a delegation to Washington in 1968, which met with little success. The airport is just too busy to have all its traffic stopped between 11:00 P.M. and 7:00 A.M., they were told. However, as promised by Secretary Boyd, special instruments for assuring that airplanes stay on their appointed flight paths and not come lower—called Visual Approach Slope Indicators—were installed at O'Hare and other airports. And for each airport, pilots were instructed that certain runways were preferred over others, in the interests of lessening noise over nearby communities.

For all these reasons, it seems that the best approach to reducing noise near airports is, as Dr. Cohen suggested, the control of the land around the airport. This means, again, thinking and planning ahead. It means tight, effective zoning laws for land use around airports; it also means strict anti-aviation noise zoning laws for property within the cities. How, for instance, did New Yorkers ever allow the (happily, now still) Pan Am Heliport to be constructed and be put into operation, creating the daily havoc of noisy helicopters? And, how did New Yorkers ever allow a V.T.O.L. fighter, the British Harrier jet, to land at an East River pier, "screeching like an angry bird," as *The New York Times* of May 6, 1969, described it? Even if it was a promotional gimmick for the Great Trans-Atlantic Air Race, it could be a dangerous precedent for the future. If V.T.O.L.'s arrived in Midtown Manhattan regularly, the Pan Am Heliport would be remembered fondly, in comparison.

With the S.S.T. a reality, there are still few noise considerations being applied to its operation. Its archfoe, Bo Lundberg of Stockholm, was first to say that operation of the S.S.T. over any inhabited land was entirely unacceptable. He remained a staunch enemy of the S.S.T. since its conception. He said that back in 1943 he was first to advocate jet air transportation because it made sense; he said the S.S.T. doesn't make sense since it causes more inconvenience, more noise, and more of a safety hazard than it is worth. He suggested letting the Russians gain experience with their S.S.T. and its boom before the British, French, and Americans put theirs into operation.

One of his weapons against the S.S.T. was convincing governments such as his own to ban the flight of S.S.T.'s over land, even provisionally. The provision in the case of Sweden is if S.S.T. booms disturb the sleep of people on the ground. West Germany passed a similar law, prohibiting the overflights of S.S.T.'s if the booms were a hazard to health. Switzerland promised to follow with a similar law, and Canada was also considering one. The United States has no such law, but has the feelings expressed by Transportation Secretary John A. Volpe and confirmed by President Nixon that S.S.T.'s should not fly supersonically across populated areas.

Lundberg hoped to confine the routes of S.S.T.'s to overwater so they wouldn't be worthwhile. He pointed out that in a flight from London or Paris to New York, via the Great Circle route, a third of the distance covered is over or alongside land. Banning the take-off and landings of S.S.T.'s to far outlying airports would also help, he felt, by requiring so much ground travel time as to nullify any airborne time-saving advantages.

Finally, he suggested that S.S.T.'s be only the size of military fighters, able to carry perhaps a dozen passengers. According to his calculations, such a smaller plane would impose only nominal boom overpressures on the ground, about 0.2 psf, or about a tenth of that produced by the larger S.S.T.'s that are in existence.

But best of all, in his mind, would be the absolute banning of S.S.T.'s from the skies.

The same kind of measure—banning—would keep the streets of central cities quieter. No municipality has done this on any great scale, but Miami Beach did convert the Lincoln Road shopping area into a pedestrian mall. Jack Mabley, columnist for *Chicago's American* newspaper, reported, "It was exhilarating to stroll up and down the mall. . . . The absence of the noise and turmoil of heavy auto traffic, more than anything else, transformed what is usually a tiring chore into a pleasant episode. I kept thinking how much greater State Street would be with wide sidewalks, plants, and art works fronting the stores instead of trucks, cars, and harassed cops trying to herd pedestrians through the congestion." He and others have suggested the complete banning of autos and trucks from busy central areas such as Chicago's downtown and Manhattan's midtown. People would have to rely solely on public transportation to get to stores and offices located there. As a result, public transportation would be convenient, reliable, and reasonable. There is no question but that cities should concentrate on this instead of building more and more expressways which funnel cars in to clog them up.

Goodfriend put it well when he stated, "The various states and municipalities which have had noise problems arise from highway route alignments, have served commercial interests and nebulous 'public's' benefit while disregarding the various negative effects of highway noise on the noise-exposed public who receive little or no direct economic benefit from the highway."

In the next chapters we'll discuss the ultimate weapon against noise—the law—which becomes a weapon in the fight for quiet only when there is enough pressure from the public to make it so. And the public is *you*.

17

THE PEOPLE VERSUS NOISE

((((((((((•))))))))))

The victims of sonic assault—those violated by noisemakers who will not voluntarily take measures to down the din that they produce or broadcast—ultimately turn to the law for relief. More and more, the legal trend in the United States and throughout the world has been to come to the aid of the noise victim, but it has been only a trend. There are too many situations in which the law offers no relief. What is especially maddening is that the progress of the law is so much slower than technology's increasing capacity to make more noise.

Legal rights to quiet came essentially after World War II, not as broad, sweeping, anticipatory legislation, but as individual court decisions here and there, often counterbalanced by a court decision against any relief.

Still, the legal victories against noise have been notable.

Mathew Slawinski, a drop forge worker for J. H. Williams and Co., who had lost a good measure of his hearing from his noisy working conditions, filed a claim for compensation against his employer. In July, 1948, the Court of Appeals, the highest court in New York State, awarded Slawinski $1,661.25.* It was a precedent-setting decision, since Slawinski was still on the job and since it did not involve, as had previous hearing-damage decisions, *sudden* loss of hearing—as from an explosion. For the first time, a court of law in the United States recognized occupational loss of hearing due to chronic noise and allowed that there could be a compensable disability without loss of earnings.

Even America's first effective state compensation law (passed in Wisconsin in 1911) only covered deafness caused by accidents. But in 1951, one Albert Wojcik filed a noise hearing-loss claim in Wisconsin against the Green Bay Forge Co. Taking its cue from New York, the Wisconsin Industrial Commission awarded him $1,575.46—even though he had not lost any wages or time from work, "only" part of his ability to hear. The Wisconsin Supreme Court upheld the Commission's decision.†

The New York and Wisconsin disability awards opened the door to a flood of similar claims filed all across the country. Alarm shivered through the management of the noisiest industries. A member of the Wisconsin commission estimated then that the total claims for occupational loss of hearing due to noise in the United States would rise to billions of dollars.

More and more the law was standing on the side of noise victims. And more and more each year in the United States, effective city ordinances, state laws, and federal legislation were and are being passed, not just to compensate for the harm done by noise, but to prevent harm from noise and to make sure that effective protection against noise was offered

* 273 App. Div. 826, N.Y. 546, 81 N.E. [2nd] 93.
† 265, Wis. 38, 60, N.W. [2nd] 409.

and taken. At the same time, other countries advanced in this respect ahead of the United States. The rest of this chapter will show how the law has helped fight noise at work, at home, in the streets, on the roads, and on the ground under airplanes. It will become quite clear to you that more pressures need to be brought to bear on government by its citizens for even better and stronger laws which would be even more effective weapons in the Fight for Quiet. The weight of evidence of the harm of noise, as presented in the first part of this book, is so heavy that such legal weapons can be forthcoming, but only if aroused citizens will demand them.

A man has a right to work in an environment which will not harm him, and there is no question but that noise which is loud enough and consistent enough will harm him.

In the early years of the Industrial Revolution, a workman injured on the job might be financially compensated by his employer, but only if he sued and proved that his employer had been negligent. The employer, in turn, had some wonderful defenses which too often resulted in dismissed cases and in an injured worker's family seeking support from welfare agencies during his hospitalization and/or convalescence.

Great Britain passed a Workmen's Compensation Law in 1897. The United States lagged pitifully behind. In 1910 every state finally had an employers' liability statute, but these laws were fragmentary and perfunctory at best. Many applied only to railway accidents, and almost all merely served to mitigate the harshness of the common law decisions. Not until 1948 did every state finally have workmen's compensation laws which made employers remunerate any employees injured while on the job. With time the laws changed to also include diseases and bodily harm other than injury. Aram Glorig, M.D., explained, "As the progress of industrialization continued and more workmen were employed, it became evident that many industrial processes produced specific diseases as a direct result of occupation. Such conditions could not be defined as an injury. They did not have a specific date of injury, nor in many cases did they produce a wage loss. . . . Most of the recent problems encountered in establishing equitable compensation laws are a result of provisions declaring that occupational disease may be compensable. Noise-induced hearing loss is a good example of this. It is unquestioned that hearing loss reduces a man's capacity to live a normal life, and in some specific instances may reduce his earning capacity . . . there is no question that hearing loss can be occupationally induced."

The courts began to agree, starting with the 1948 New York case, and confirming it in the 1951 Wisconsin case. And the legislators had to follow suit. Thus, as Dr. Glorig stated, "Both labor and industry realize that as a result of this decision, Wisconsin industry faced a serious problem. . . . a new law written expressly for noise-induced hearing loss was passed and became effective in July of 1955 . . . it is the most advanced law in the country today."

Some states reacted more conservatively as a result of the Slawinski and Wojcik cases. They passed laws which made the workers retire from their jobs for six or so months before they could file a noise-deafness claim, so as to determine whether or not the hearing loss was permanent or temporary. This helped hold back the tide of compensation claims filed, since there were few workers willing or able to afford to give up half a year's wages, even if they knew they had a good case. At the same time, as an authority, Meyer Fox, M.D. of Milwaukee, stated, "Industry and the insurance carriers learned that while they did not have to protect the hearing of the workers they could be held responsible for the hearing loss." Because the states vary so, Dr. Fox and Ralph Gintz, director of Workmen's Compensation for Wisconsin, surveyed the United States and Canada in 1963 and again in

1969. They found the trend was toward greater coverage for occupational hearing loss.

In both nations, however, there were gaping holes in the picture. Dr. Fox said, "The states of Illinois, Ohio, Pennsylvania, Michigan, Rhode Island, Massachusetts, and Texas do not provide compensation for hearing loss, either from noise or trauma, unless the loss in one or both ears is total. From a medical standpoint I have had considerable difficulty in attempting to learn just what is meant by total hearing loss. Does this mean inability to hear sound at the intensity limits of the audiometer, or does it mean hearing loss, of sufficient extent and degree, to interfere with the ability to carry on one's duties?"

In 1969 the states and Canada were lined up, according to the Fox-Gintz statistics, as follows:

—39 states recognized as compensable, hearing loss due to noise exposure over a period of time.

—Only 5 states, a territory, and Canada specified the level of noise, the type of noise, or the period of exposure considered as hazardous (California, Oregon, Puerto Rico, Utah, Washington, Wisconsin). In addition, New Hampshire and Texas were preparing such rules.

—6 states and Canada had the 6-months away-from-work requirement for filing claims.

—for the two years (1967–1968) previous to the survey, the following total claims were reported by 5 states and a province: Californ. a, 790; New Jersey, 434; Oklahoma, 106; Washington, 52; Virginia, 42; and Ontario, Canada, 289. In addition, while New York State and Wisconsin processed many cases, they had no statistics. Not included in any of the data were cases settled by compromise.

In his report, Dr. Fox told the A.M.A.'s Sixth Congress on Environmental Health in Chicago that, as had been true in the previous 20 years, he foresaw an increase in hearing-loss claims and proposed legislation.

The Canadian provinces have regulations requiring ear protection be worn in noisy working conditions, but only six states and Puerto Rico had such requirements (New Hampshire, in addition, had one in preparation at the time of the survey), and only Utah and Washington specified the decibel level. Therefore, Dr. Fox felt, the future held much promise of activity in the way of state-enforced safety rules for ear protection in noisy industries.

As a postscript, no one has a law requiring the noise of a working place to be held down to a certain maximum. Thus, the most liberal rulings and laws deal with awarding money to noise-deafened workers, and in a few cases they direct the employers to provide ear protection, but nowhere in the American law is there a requirement for more quiet—the best protection against deafness, the cure of which no money can buy.

Money exerts its force only insofar as it makes deafness expensive in economic terms. Often profit-making companies are more strongly motivated toward change and improvement by financial rather than by humane considerations. The same was true in industries in which silicosis, asbestos lung diseases, lead poisoning, and blindness are industrial health hazards. Noise deafness produces no coughing and no telltale shadows on an X-ray film, yet it is just as real. If governments spent as much effort and money to prevent noise deafness as they did to prevent these other occupational diseases, the toll of noise deafness would have dropped as sharply in this "medically/socially enlightened" age as did these other industrial health afflictions.

The professions of scientific research and medicine stand ready, with their criteria for noise exposure for the prevention of deafness, if only government would ask for help in formulating the protective laws. Progress has been slow, if faintly promising. Late in 1968, for instance, the Department of Labor revised its health-hazard regulations of the Walsh-Healey Public Contracts Act applicable to corporations holding United States' government contracts of more than $10,000. The new regulation required that such employers guarantee that their employees would work at noise levels no greater than 85 dB-A. Actually that was the maximum noise level to be applied in 1972. In the meantime, employers could have noise environments of 92 dB-A for three years from the time the regulation went into effect. Supposed to start in January, 1969, the regulation's initial date was delayed by the Secretary of Labor until mid-May 1969.

Despite its emphasis on quiet, backed by laws, Great Britain has not had a compensation case come to trial of a worker whose noise deafness was job-inflicted.

In Sweden, the Workers' Protection Board has patrols of factory inspectors who roam through plants, taking measurements of noise and advising managers how to lower it. As Dr. Bengt Kylin of Karolinska Institute explained, "We are hoping that industry by itself will take on private consultants to help solve their noise problems." He cited, among those companies practicing excellent hearing conservation, the Volvo car manufacturing firm.

On paper, at least, the U.S.S.R. has very fine set of regulations for keeping the level of industrial noise down. In fact, it sets permissible noise levels as follows: low frequencies (below 300 Hz), 90–100 dB; middle frequencies (300–800 Hz), 85–90 dB; and high frequencies (above 800 Hz), 75–85 dB. The regulations also specify that noisy worker stations be made less noisy, set strict noise-exposure criteria for workers, and specify that "in designing new machines and plant units, means must be sought to reduce their noise as much as possible and, in any event, to reduce noise at operator posts near the units to levels not exceeding those permissible."

In the densely populated and highly industrialized Federal Republic of Germany (West Germany), the Industrial Code (Section 120a) requires all plants to be operated in such a way that workers are protected against dangers to life and health—including noise-induced hearing loss. Directive No. 2058 issued by the Ministry of Labor under the code set maximum at-ear noise levels for industry: 50 dB for persons engaged in constant mental activity, 70 dB for those in office or similar work, and 90 dB for all other workers.

Alan Bell, the Australian occupational health specialist mentioned earlier in this book, who surveyed industrial noise around the globe for the World Health Organization, found:

> In Austria very noisy machines or manufacturing processes must be physically separated from other places of work, and in certain circumstances the authorities may require specialized control measures. In Czechoslovakia, it is recommended that, wherever possible, risks should be reduced by the introduction of automation and remote control. Low noise levels are considered an index of quality in factory operation, and acoustics and vibration experts must advise on factory construction. Machines, etc., may not be imported if they exceed allowable noise limits. In Finland, if a harmful noise cannot be adequately dealt with otherwise, the process must be intermittently reduced or interrupted. . . . Turkey prohibits the entry of those not directly involved into noisy machine rooms. . . . Brazilian legislation classifies any noise above 80 dB as hazardous enough to justify a higher salary—an incentive to employers to reduce the hazard.

A man's home is his castle. It should be a quiet castle, free from the noises of his neighbors and the noises of the community and the world outside. Yet at this writing there is no national building code in the United States with specifie noise control requirements. But there has been some progress since 1957, when this statement by Richard V. Waterhouse, then of the Sound Section, National Bureau of Standards, Washington, D.C., was published: "It is perhaps surprising that although the building codes of Canada and several European countries contain noise control requirements, in the United States, where mechanization and noise levels are so great, the building codes possess none. . . . an apartment block in Manhattan needs as much sound insulation as an apartment block in London. At present the chances are that it does not get it. . . . none of the four principal national codes of the United States, nor any of the city codes, contain noise control requirements at the time of publication." The only bright light at that time was the State of New York's advisory building construction code of 1953. Since Waterhouse's words were published, the Federal Housing Administration's construction detail recommendations, called F.H.A. No. 2600, revised August 1964, have been published. They have the status of a quasi-law. Any builder who wants to apply for an F.H.A. mortgage has to comply. Also, many banks have automatically adopted the recommendations as requirements. What happened in New York in 1967–1968 was as, or more, important.

On Thursday, June 22, 1967, Robert A. Low, chairman of the New York City Council's Buildings Committee, presented Proposed Local Law Int. No. 436, a comprehensive new revision of the city's building code, which for the first time in any American city included strong noise control measures guaranteeing some degree of quiet for every resident of a dwelling erected in the future. The pertinent section was "Sub-Article 1208.0, Noise Control in Multiple Dwellings," which set specific S.T.C. requirements for walls and I.N.R. requirements for floors and ceilings; called for such noise control measures as air duct linings, noise isolation of building equipment, proper separation of machine rooms and apartments; set maximum noise output levels for equipment placed outside the building; and called for isolation of all pipes from solid contacts.

On November 23, 1967, while Low was conducting hearings on the proposed code's changes, Senator Robert F. Kennedy wrote him (and the newspapers) that the noise control sections should be even stricter. The late senator asked for noise-suppression standards closer to those of Europe. On October 23, 1968, the New York City Council did adopt, and on November 7, Mayor Lindsay signed the code, requiring an S.T.C. of 45 after January 1, 1970, and of 50 after January 1, 1972. Of this passage, Martin Hirschorn, of Citizens for a Quieter City, Inc., also president of Industrial Acoustics Co., said, "The present compromise constitutes a major step forward in eliminating acoustical slums in New York City . . . the New York City Council are to be congratulated on adopting this code. . . . We trust, however, that the code will be further refined to include outside walls, windows, and dwelling entrance doors."

New York may have set a trend. Oak Park, Illinois, a suburb of Chicago, proudly passed its new building code in March of 1969. It represented two and a half years of work by a committee which was headed by a man highly appreciative of the need for noise control, Frank Niles, who at the time was medical records librarian for Michael Reese Hospital and Medical Center in Chicago. The Oak Park code sets specific S.T.C. standards for party wall construction (a wall between apartments, or between an apartment and a space common to other apartments).

Across the country, acoustic mistakes are occurring less and less frequently, mainly because of regulation of construction details by the Federal Housing Agency and other bodies. F.H.A. No. 2600, Section M40504, for instance, contains this paragraph among its noise control construction requirements:

> Electrical receptacles, heating grilles and medicine
> cabinets shall not occur in the same stud space unless
> sufficient sound absorbent material is installed or the
> wall thickened to restore the partition to the minimum
> loss impedance required.

Great Britain and Canada have more stringent noise control construction requirements for homes, offices, factories, hospitals, and all sorts of buildings.

Canada in particular has a very specific national building code. This is, explained T. D. Northwood, head of the Building Physics Section of the National Research Council of Canada, "a model document prepared by a committee of experts from across the country. Formal jurisdiction over building standards is a provincial matter and the provinces generally delegate authority to the municipalities. Practically all the major municipalities have by now adopted the code." The code, first issued in 1965 and revised in 1967, was scheduled to be revised again in 1970. Section 5 of the code deals with sound control. It consists merely of three specific paragraphs and of a very detailed appendix of charts which designate S.T.C.'s for specific kinds of wall construction. Besides stating that E90-66T of the American Society for Testing and Materials is the method of sound rating, it states that party walls of dwelling units have an S.T.C. of at least 45. Further, that "every service room or space such as storage rooms, laundry, workshop or building maintenance room and garages" be separated from the dwellings by walls with an S.T.C. of 45 or better. The appendix to the section lists different kinds of exterior and interior wall construction and floor-ceiling construction, gives its sound or impact rating class, and tells whether or not this is acceptable.

In 1965 Britain passed a set of building regulations which went into effect in 1966. However, Part G, Sound Insulation, is nonspecific and says only that a party wall "shall be so constructed as to provide adequate resistance to the transmission of airborne sound." Ditto for floors. That country does have a Standard Code of Practice for building construction, the third chapter of which is devoted to "sound insulation and noise reduction." The code gives very detailed data on the noise control effectiveness of various kinds of construction. But the British code is a set of recommendations and not a law—although some Building Bylaws require compliance with some of the details of the Code. Still, home construction is largely a locally regulated activity in Britain, and local authorities can grant approval to build, conditional on noise control—or they can ignore it. In an international survey published in 1967 by the National Swedish Institute for Building Research (in agreement with the United Nations), the United Kingdom was quoted as stating that a standard of 50 dB insulation would be desirable, although difficult to enforce.

The same publication noted that Belgium had a standard (NBN 576.40) which enabled architects to demand satisfactory sound insulation; Poland had a special standard to determine the sound insulation of dwellings in blocks of flats; Romania had a government standard for sound insulation; and in Sweden, which has a specific code of 48 dB loss through walls, local housing committees approved blueprints and inspected workmanship and could measure sound transmission after construction was completed.

As long ago as 1938, Germany had a building code with the requirements for specific decibel losses through walls at various sound frequencies. A series of standards, starting in 1953 with DIN 52 210 (*Deutsche Industrie-Norm*, or German Industrial Standard), have been in effect. The newest as of this writing is DIN 4109 of 1964.

Norway has had sound transmission loss requirements of 50 dB in its building code since 1948. The Netherlands has had a code requiring sound transmission losses, and specifying how much, since 1952.

There are two weaknesses in all of these codes. First, the

required S.T.C.'s are rather nominal. Second, they are enforceable only as municipalities do or do not see fit.

For Americans, the conclusion is inescapable: we can send men to the moon, passing, as they do, through the quiet of Outer Space. But we are powerless to launch laws which would guarantee throughout America the quiet of the private Inner Space that is our dwelling place.

18

CITIES VERSUS NOISE

$$((((((((((\cdot))))))))))$$

When noise leaves your neighbor's home and imposes itself on you, it becomes a community problem. One of the world's authorities on the laws of noise, Hans H. Wiethaup, a Dortmund, West Germany, lawyer and author, wrote, "In various countries there are articles in the penal code providing for fines or imprisonment for disturbing the peace with noise. However, these are not very effective, and attempts to sue for grievous bodily harm are even less effective." He pointed out that the penalties for disturbing the peace were so light as to be no deterrent. In France, for example, the fine may be 40 to 60 NF, about $8 to $10, and perhaps an imprisonment of five days. Of Austria, Belgium, Denmark, England, Finland, France, Italy, Luxembourg, the Netherlands, Norway, Sweden, and Switzerland: "none of these countries has so far enacted a special comprehensive anti-noise law."

Wiethaup pointed out in a special international publication on noise produced by the Geigy pharmaceutical company of Switzerland, that "public law with its sanitary regulations constitutes the only really effective protection of the individual."

While Great Britain, as I found with my portable noise meter, is not so quiet, that nation does have more and better legal weapons to fight noise than does the United States or many other nations. Its biggest stick is the Noise Abatement Act of 1960, which makes irksome noise a statutory nuisance in England, Scotland, and Wales. Under common law for a long time before, noise could be the subject of a civil action for nuisance, defined as the wrong done to a man by unlawfully disturbing him in the enjoyment of his property. In a 1930 decision Mr. Justice Luxmoore* wrote, ". . . every person is entitled as against his neighbour to the comfortable and healthful enjoyment of the premises occupied by him." The 1936 Public Health Act provided a procedure for the abatement of statutory nuisances, and, since the 1960 act makes noise a nuisance, the same procedures apply to it. A noise-bothered person can go to his local authority and file a complaint. If the authority is satisfied of the existence of a noise nuisance, he serves an abatement notice on the noise-maker or on the owner or occupier of the noise-making premises. If the abatement notice is not complied with, the authority must bring proceedings in Magistrate's Court for its enforcement. If the court upholds the complaint, it issues a noise abatement order and may impose fines, both total and daily, for noncompliance. If the local authority refuses to act in the first place, three or more noise-bothered citizens can complain directly to the Magistrate's Court.

In France, the Minister of Social Affairs, J. M. Jeanneney, in a public health circular dated November 17, 1966, directed the governors of all provinces to assess fines against

* Vanderpant *vs.* the Mayfair Hotel Co. Ltd. (1930).

noisemakers, especially Frenchmen who disturbed their neighbors with loud radios, record players, television sets, and unruly pets. It also forbade noisy construction work at night. Violators could be brought before a tribunal and, if guilty, fined from 300 to 2,000 francs.

Furthermore, Paris and its region have a special regulation which enables Parisiennes to complain about noise to the *gendarmerie* or the Paris police. Statistics from one month which was surveyed (July, 1964) show that police courts received 789 such complaints from the city and 300 from the suburbs.

Ideally, one of the best ways for cities to fight noise is to enact and enforce anti-noise ordinances, and in the United States more and more cities that didn't have them before are enacting such ordinances. James J. Kaufman, a Rochester, New York, lawyer who became an expert on noise as special legislative assistant to U.S. Congressman Theodore R. Kupferman of New York City during the 89th and 90th sessions of Congress, pointed out in a speech in Washington in mid-1968: "It is at the city code level that noise sources of garbage collection, construction noise, motor vehicles, loudspeakers, and many other noise sources can be effectively controlled. It is important, however, to exercise extreme caution when attempting to solve a problem by simply passing a law. We should inquire whether all is being done which can be to otherwise deal with the problem."

The City of Chicago has various anti-noise sections in its Municipal Code. So does Memphis, Tennessee, and yet the latter and not the former is known as The Quiet City. Most of the provisions of the ordinances of both cities do not deal directly with decibel levels, but are rather general. In Chicago, for instance, "No person shall make, or cause, permit or allow to be made, upon a public way, or in such close proximity to a public way, any noise of any kind . . ." except alley peddlers between 11:00 A.M. and 6:00 P.M.

Memphis's ordinance says, "Yelling, shouting, hooting, whistling or singing on the public streets, particularly between the hours of 11:00 P.M. and 7:00 A.M. or at any other time or place so as to annoy or disturb the quiet, comfort or repose of persons in any hospital, dwelling, hotel or any other type of residence or of any persons in the vicinity is hereby prohibited."

The point is: it is the *intent* of the city which counts most. Memphis was intent on maintaining its reputation for quiet. It awarded prizes for anti-noise essays and ideas, honored "Silent Citizens" who did such things as muffle their power-mowers, and arrested horn-honkers (most likely to have been out-of-towners). It started not with the passing of the anti-noise ordinance in 1938, but with enforcement of it in 1940, when the late City Commissioner Joseph P. Boyle got fed up with young men blaring their auto horns to summon their dates. In every year since, about 1,000 motorists have been ticketed for noisy horns and/or mufflers. But mostly, its success in the Fight for Quiet was due to the education of its citizenry and the pervasion of Think Quiet throughout the city.

Similarly, when any city opens war on noise, the result is usually successful. Three South American towns are good examples of this. A one-man campaign was launched in São Paulo, Brazil, which has a population of four million. The director of its Acoustics and Phonetics Laboratory, Dr. João Lillis Cardoso, put up signs on the busiest streets to admonish motorists not to lean on their horns, and introduced a new kind of bus with a pleasant "harmonic" horn, non-screeching brakes, and silent doors. He also sponsored on-the-spot hearing tests on the streets to give people an idea of what the city's noises were doing to them. Dr. Cardoso said that in a big city "people get used to the noise and justify it as the price of progress. What we have to develop here is an 'acoustic conscience.'"

In Cordoba, Argentina, where noise is *ruido,* 10 percent of the population of better than half a million have motorcycles and motorscooters. Professor G. L. Fuchs, director of acoustic research at the University of Cordoba, pointed out that the city's "municipal regulations on noise were introduced many years ago and had long been ineffective." This, combined with increased population and industrialization, made Cordoba among the noisiest cities in Argentina. "Noise is a social problem, and its solution calls for intensive campaigns to alert the public to the need for action," Professor Fuchs said. In 1960 he began his campaign for public action with a symposium on the subject. An official Silent Week followed. In 1964 Professor Fuchs helped establish Argentina's Noise Abatement Council, which was promptly admitted to the International Association Against Noise. With the educational campaign came a new anti-noise city ordinance which classified fifteen unnecessary noises for which the perpetrator could be penalized without the city's needing noise measurement or analysis. It also classified as excessive noises those that exceed the limits that affect the well-being and tranquility of citizens, a criterion largely based on time of the day or night. Another provision of the law was that not only the noisemaker but those associated with him at the time are liable. Penalties for noise-making included fines, closing of the shop, club, or other loud business, and revocation of driving license.

In Rio de Janeiro in January, 1970, quiet was helped when all horns on buses were disconnected and leaky mufflers were replaced.

Ithaca, New York, (population, 29,000) has an ordinance which states that "no person shall play an instrument, device, or thing so as to disturb peace or quiet in any neighborhood." In 1964 a bank there installed an outdoor electronic carillon. In January, 1968, the bank was brought to trial in City Court for violating the ordinance by having the chimes

peal every day at 9:00 A.M., noon, and 5:00 P.M. for three
and a half minutes each time, after heralding the hour. To
make a point during the trial, the defense attorney called the
president of the bank to the stand at noon, then asked, as the
carillon played in the background, "Does the sound of those
bells interfere with your hearing the testimony that's being
presented in this room?"

"What?" the banker replied. Both sides were then given a
week to file their briefs. The banker later said he had heard
many more favorable than unfavorable remarks about the
chimes.

Tokyo, called by one reporter "a deafening bedlam of
familiar and exotic sounds," for some years had a giant
electric sign at the Nishi-Ginza underground station to publicly report the noise level, just as electric signs elsewhere
tell the temperature. A 1968 dispatch from there quoted
Minora Matsumoto, chief of the city's Noise Control Section,
as saying that "Tokyo is not only the biggest city in the
world [11 million], it is also the noise capital of the world."
For the previous decade Tokyo had an anti-noise ordinance,
but it was largely unenforceable. In 1968, however, the Diet
passed a new noise control law that set jail sentences and
other penalties for noisemakers. But the people's attitude
was still pro-noise, Matsumoto explained, so the new law
could only mitigate the noise problem.

Another way cities can help keep the peace is to set up
zones of quiet around special facilities, such as hospitals and
schools. The Chicago ordinance, for instance, states that
"there is hereby created and established a zone of quiet in
all territory embraced within the block upon which abuts
the premises of any hospital . . ." and "during school hours
in all public ways surrounding every block within which is
located a building used, controlled, leased or operated for
free common school education in the city."

Zoning, in fact, can be one of the most potent tools a

municipality has to confine noisemakers. Chicago, again, in the mid-1950's instituted a zoning ordinance which established a set of decibel and frequency-band limits for manufacturing zones: ". . . at no point on the boundary of a Residence or Business District shall a sound pressure level of any individual operation or plant . . . exceed the decibel levels in the designated octave bands shown below for the districts indicated." The maximum allowed is 79 dB at the low 0 to 75 Hz octave band; above 4,800 Hz, it is 39 dB when businesses are nearby, and 32 dB when residences are nearby. However, the weakness of the zoning ordinance is the phrase: "other than background noises produced by sources not under the control of this ordinance, such as the operation of motor vehicles or other transportation facilities." Thus, the ordinance is concerned with factory noises more than with noises of motor vehicles, which pervade the city rather than being confined, as are factories, to specific areas.

"Zoning towns for noise levels has much to commend it," R. S. Forster, the town clerk of Willesden, Middlesex, England, told the Symposium on the Control of Noise held at the National Physical Laboratory in 1961. "In the first place its educational value is very considerable. The uninitiated gradually hear of something they have hitherto heard very little about. They become aware of a new standard. . . . Zoning areas by noise levels would also enable responsibility to be considered more objectively. If ten factories together exceeded the zone level by 20 percent, which one should be guilty of exceeding the zone level? . . . If nine of our ten factories reduced their noise, the tenth one might be visited by the local council and asked why they should not do the same."

To be most effective in the Fight for Quiet, zoning ordinances should be in force before cities are built, or rebuilt, and land should be used to buffer the noise of airports, factories, and other noisemakers from people in homes, schools, hospitals, libraries, and other peaceful quarters. According to architect Constantin Stramentov, "Town planning in the Soviet Union complies strictly with the principle of separating industrial and residential areas, and in this way city dwellers are spared the harassment of excessive noise. . . . Reconstruction and renovation of cities offer opportunities for eliminating or reducing many sources of noise. Green spaces and protective screens are incorporated in street designs so as to surround buildings with a 'wall of silence.'" In his studies, he has found that "squares are usually thought to be the noisiest places in town, yet tests show surprisingly that they are less noisy than streets. City streets may be likened to canals, with houses acting as walls, between which all sounds continue to reverberate until they finally die out. In squares the extra space helps to disperse the sound waves."

The problem with motor vehicles is that they are so mobile that they broadcast their noise wherever they go. Hirschorn, commenting on the benefits of New York's building code revisions, said after its passage that the City Council needed next to limit "traffic noise, often exceeding 100 dB, which is essential if acceptable noise levels are to be assured for city apartment dwellers."

Most cities and states have some legislation requiring every motor vehicle to have an adequate muffler in good working order to prevent excessive noise, and forbidding any device on the exhaust system which amplifies the motor sounds. The trouble is that the laws are useless for any effective prevention of noise because they are so vague. The first specific laws—all for 95 dB—were enacted by Milwaukee in 1956, Cincinnati in 1958, and Beverly Hills, California, in 1959.

European countries have been way ahead of America in

having specific, comprehensive national laws. Thus, in 1956 West Germany put into force the very specific requirements for maximum noise levels of new vehicles, then, in 1959, revised the figures downward. The unit of measurement is the DIN-phon, roughly equivalent to dB-B (which discriminates somewhat against higher frequencies, but not as much as does the dB-A). Each vehicle's full-throttle noise is measured with a portable sound-level meter from a distance of 7 meters (23 feet), at full throttle, both as the vehicle is standing still and moving by.

Since October 25, 1962, France has had a "road code" (Code de la Route), which also specifies the maximum decibels motor vehicles can make. (The use of a horn except for emergencies has been forbidden since 1959). In July, 1968, Great Britain enacted similar noise maximums.

The French, German, and British noise limits are surprisingly alike:

	FRANCE dB-A	W. GERMANY dB-B (at 23 ft.)	G. BRITAIN dB-A (at 17ft.)
Motor bicycles	80	75	
Motorcycles	86	80/82	80/90
Trucks			
over 2.5 tons		87	
under 3.5 tons	83		92
over 3.5 tons	90		
All other vehicles		82	92
Private autos	83		88

In 1965, New York State passed a law intended to start in 1966 which limited truck noise to 88 dB at a distance of 50 feet. In 1967 the state of California passed regulations limiting motor vehicle noise, which went into effect January 1, 1968: motorcycles and trucks 92 dB-A; all other vehicles, 86 dB-A—as measured at 50 feet.

Don't be impressed with the wonderful way traffic noise is

controlled in Germany, France, Great Britain, New York, and California. A visit to any of these with a noise meter before and after the laws were put into effect would show few decibels of difference. Look at my decibel diary (Appendix B) and you'll see how noisy the streets of Paris and London were, for instance. In each case, unfortunately, while the law was willing, the enforcement was weak. Take France: if a Parisian car is too noisy (and too many of them are), a gendarme could issue a ticket which required the owner to bring it to Bois de Vincennes, a park outside of Paris where its noise level would be measured. If the car's decibels, indeed, exceeded the maximum allowed, the owner would be required to fix his muffler, or whatever, and return in a fortnight for a follow-up test. If he failed to return, or if he did and the car was still noisy, he was liable for a fine which was set, cleverly, just over the price of a good muffler—approximately $20.

Professor Lenard explained, "The problem is that our police don't carry noise meters. And besides, they are too busy directing traffic." He told the story of a lawyer he knew who found a particular motorcycle operated in his neighborhood very noisy. So, he summoned a policeman and took him to the motorcycle and its owner. Because he knew nothing of the traffic noise regulation, the policeman refused to issue a ticket. The lawyer wound up taking the policeman to his own prefecture and pointing out the regulation to him.

The same thing happened with anti-noise laws in America. The police don't have sound-level meters with them and anyway are busy trying to direct traffic and prevent accidents, or saving lives. The *Wall Street Journal* in 1968 pointed out that New York State "is still waiting for a court test of the law before it sinks huge sums into noise-measuring devices. In the two years since the law took effect, only 48 citations have been written for noisemaking. In every instance, the violators—mostly truckers—have

pleaded guilty or jumped bail. A state police official suspects
the truckers would rather pay the $5 or $10 fine rather than
challenge the law and have it upheld." In California, the
state patrol decided to investigate noise *meters* first, before
they measured noise*makers;* by the end of 1969 the noise of
but half a million vehicles on the road were measured, with
1,500 violations discovered. California's neighbor to the
north, Oregon, "does not have any statutes concerning noise,
except for the prohibition of 'unnecessary' noise in the
operation of a motor vehicle. I am not aware of any legislative proposals in this field at the present time," Governor
Tom McCall informed me in 1968.

To a noise-fighter, it is a sad thing to see specific anti-noise
laws, one of the potentially most useful weapons for silence,
rust with disuse. The lesson is clear enough: not only are
effective and specific laws needed, but people in government
and in law enforcement agencies eager enough to use them
are needed. Otherwise, it is as though the laws and ordinances did not exist.

19

LEGAL ANTI-AIRCRAFT WEAPONS

$$(((((((((((\cdot)))))))))))$$

The U.S. Constitution protects every landowner against the government's taking his property without paying for it. Article 5 of the Bill of Rights states "nor shall private property be taken for public use without just compensation." The press of the growth of aviation made Congress declare, in the 1938 Civil Aeronautics Act that the Federal Government had the right of "free transit" in the navigable air space. In effect, this made the air over the ground—even private ground—a public highway, or airway. But early common law had held that an owner's claim to his land extended not only to the boundaries of the land and below its surface, but also above it, to infinity. Lawyers call this the *ad coelum* (to-the-sky) theory. Common law and aviation legislation had their inevitable confrontation in 1946 in *United States vs. Causby* [328 U.S. 256 (1946)].

Mr. Causby owned a chicken farm located off the end of

279

the main runway of a World War II air base from which
operated four-engine propeller-powered bombers. The
thundering of the bombers low over his farm day and night
made him and his family nervous wrecks and provoked the
deaths of so many chickens that his farm became a useless
venture. In its decision in favor of the chicken farmer, the
U.S. Supreme Court said that by operating its airplanes so
low and so frequently, the government had indeed taken
property, or trespassed, without just compensation, and so
awarded Causby losses. At the same time the court declared
that in the modern world, private ownership of the sky is
unrealistic.

The courts got involved again when jets appeared, with
their even longer landing approaches and take-off climbs.
The 1958 Federal Aviation Act superseded the 1938 act and
extended the definition of "navigable air space" belonging to
the public to include the take-off and landing paths. But in
1962 the U.S. Supreme Court again ruled for the owner of
private property. The case, *Griggs vs. County of Allegheny*
[363 U.S. 84 (1962)], involved a landowner's complaint
against the operator of the Pittsburgh, Pennsylvania, airport.
Airplanes from the airport came as close as 11 feet above the
top of Mr. Griggs's chimney. Justice Douglas, writing for the
majority of the court, said, "Without the 'approach areas' an
airport is indeed not operable. Respondent in designing it
has to acquire some private property. Our conclusion is that
by constitutional standards it did not acquire enough."

The first person in the world to receive compensation
($58.44) for injuries caused by a sonic boom was 3-year-old
Richard David, in 1968. The English lad was thrown from
his pony when the animal bolted from the boom of a Royal
Air Force supersonic jet. Explained New York lawyer
Morris L. Ernst (with writer David Loth), "Law has just
begun to prepare itself for contests over damages caused by
the greatest threat of supersonic air travel: the sonic boom.

. . . is the sonic boom a noise or an explosion? The semantics are important. Insurance often covers damage from one but not the other. . . . By the time a ceiling falls down in Indiana, the plane that caused it may be on the far side of the Mississippi River, or preparing to land in New York. And where traffic is heavy, how will the courts decide *which* plane caused the damage? . . . The law, often charged with an inability to move as fast as some people desire, will be matched against planes flying 2,000 miles per hour!"

The courts will see thousands of cases against operators of S.S.T.'s, as well as those of supersonic bombers, as these craft increase their airborne populations and routes. French writer Bouille's stories are a forecast of what is to come. One concerns a village where the roof of the *mairie* (mayor's office) was damaged and its clock destroyed by a sonic boom. When village officials approached military authorities for compensation for the damages, they were told that in order to file a claim they must submit the guilty plane's number. They proposed, in turn, to mount a telescope on the roof and keep it constantly manned so as to identify the planes in future claims—and to deduct the cost of this operation from that part of the village's annual tax assessment which went to the defense budget. The stories tell of other cases in which the sonic booms supposedly caused death by fright, the rupturing of abdominal wounds after surgery, sudden development of diabetes, a broken leg after being thrown by a mule, and a series of traffic accidents started by the bolting of a horse.

It will, of course, be up to the courts of the world to decide how to settle these claims and whether the boom is an explosion and what is the best way to assess damages. But looking at the preliminary data, you would think that the legal entanglement which is just over the horizon would have been enough to deter those who so compulsively instead of thoughtfully developed the S.S.T.

Great Britain's Noise Abatement Act of 1960 may have sounded quite appealing when I mentioned it earlier, but it will lose much of its appeal when you understand two important facts about it: It exempts "statutory undertakers," which are railroads; and, Subsection 7 of Section 1 of the law states that "nothing in this section or the said section sixty-six shall apply to noise or vibration caused by aircraft." As the Wilson Committee found, "The major difference from the law relating to other noise is that, in general, there is no right of legal action for nuisance from aircraft noise." This was merely a continuation of the feeling in Britain's 1949 Civil Aviation Act, and the Air Navigation Acts of 1920 and 1947, which broadly prohibited actions for nuisance from civil aircraft in flight or at air fields because of noise. France, Germany, and Great Britain all have similar regulations which prescribe that airplanes should take off and turn away, if possible, from the most populated areas on their power climbs. England sets a 110 PNdB (about 96 dB-A) limit on aircraft operating out of Heathrow Airport near London. This is almost identical to Kennedy Airport's 112 PNdB (about 98 dB-A) limit at three miles from start of take-off roll established by the Port of New York Authority in the mid-1950's. These are only minimal legal safeguards for protection against noise for those living near these busy airports. West Germany in 1968 passed a law which promised to be more helpful. It stipulated that around each airport there would be two zones. In one, housing would be entirely prohibited. In the other, homes could be built if adequately insulated from the aircraft noise, but the construction of hospitals, schools, kindergartens, and homes for the aged was prohibited.

Zoning-in airport noise is an excellent idea for cities that have not thought of it. One of the problems here is that usually more jurisdiction than a city's is involved. O'Hare Airport, for instance, belongs to the city of Chicago, but the land outside its fence belongs to suburbs. LaGuardia and Kennedy Airports are under the jurisdiction of the Port of New York Authority. As suggested in the last chapter, what is needed in America, and elsewhere, is an anti-noise super-authority which can create zones around airports in which residential buildings would be prohibited. In fact, why not allow around each airport the construction of the community's loudest industries? This would, in effect, relegate the worst offenders of our ears to their own little islands located away from the cities.

The legal weapons against airport noise in the United States are meager. Lyman M. Tondel, Jr., a lawyer who represented many airlines in airport noise matters, explained that "there are necessarily some property owners who feel that noise created by arriving and departing aircraft has interfered with the enjoyment of their homes to such a degree that they should be compensated. . . . Most complainants seek only noise reduction and an understanding attitude rather than relief in the courts. When suits for damages are actually brought they present only another example of the age-old question of how far the individual must tolerate public improvements that interfere with the use or enjoyment of his property before he is entitled to compensation."

Except for a few landmark cases (two of which were related earlier), the courts have regrettably sided more with noise-making airports and airlines than with the citizens they disturb. And citizens who live under flight paths sue successfully more often than do their neighbors just to the sides of the flight paths! The reasoning is that private comfort must often give way to public good. Thus aviation is a legalized noise nuisance. Few injunctions against airports or operators have ever been issued, especially in recent times, because of the great national desire for air transportation.

However, any citizen can complain to the F.A.A. about

violations of its own rules, among which are the turning-away patterns. As of this writing, this has only happened once with success, in New Orleans in 1962. That same year, there were more than a thousand lawsuits involving noise at nineteen airports. In the 11 years preceding 1966, when Tondel's report was published in the *Journal of Air Law and Commerce,* damages were actually recovered in only nine cases. Eight were against civil airport operators on the legal ground of unconstitutional taking, for a total of $470,334; the ninth was $12,500 against Lockheed Aircraft Corp. on a nuisance theory. In addition, three quarters of a million dollars were recovered in 22 cases against the U.S. Government involving military airfields. At least 100 cases are always pending. It's also interesting that in 1968 aircraft noise was the dominant subject among 29 noise abatement bills introduced to the U.S. Congress.

(The plight of people who live in communities near airports and suffer from the noise, is so widespread as to have been a subject of concern in a popular 1968 novel, also made into a movie—*Airport* by Arthur Hailey. In the story a lawyer, Elliott Freemantle, arouses a dinned community, Meadowood, to demonstrate at the airport, while collecting enormous fees to represent each homeowner. The book's portrayal of an unscrupulous lawyer is questionable, but the explanations given by airport authorities to the citizens' delegation on the subject of aircraft noise is well done.)

Two new suggestions for legal weapons against airborne noisemakers came from a famous British economist and from a U.S. Government high official, the first in 1967, the second in 1968. In his book, *The Costs of Economic Growth,* Chicago-educated Ezra J. Mishan of the London School of Economics and Political Science, suggested that the law recognize what he called inviolable "amenity rights"—the rights to peace and quiet, to privacy, and to clean air. He wrote, "No effective legislation putting the onus on airlines has been contemplated. The noise created is limited only by what the authorities believe people can be made to put up with. And the public may be conditioned over time to bear with increasing disturbance simply (i) because of the difficulties and cost of organizing protests; (ii) because of the apparent hopelessness of prevailing upon the authorities to put the claims of the residents before claims of 'progress,' that is, the airlines; and (iii) because of the timidity felt in pressing one's claims against so effective a retort as 'the national interest.' If there is a national interest, however, our discussion reveals the case for the Government's bearing the cost of its safeguard."

Professor Mishan suggested that airport authorities and airlines compensate in advance all the victims of aircraft noise, since the noise is an invasion of their amenity rights. Further, he said, "Privacy and quiet and clean air are scarce goods—far scarcer than they were before the war—and sure to become scarcer still in the foreseeable future. . . . Clearly if the world were so fashioned that clean air and quiet took on a physically identifiable form, and one that allowed it to be transferred as between people, we should be able to observe whether a man's quantum of the stuff had been appropriated, or damaged, and institute legal proceedings accordingly."

Charles H. Haar, assistant secretary for metropolitan development in the Department of Housing and Urban Development, suggested, "Instead of a permanent right to make noise at a level prevailing at the time of the condemnation proceeding, the airport would lease the right to make noise for a stated period of time, perhaps two or three years. At the expiration of the period, the property owner would be required to prove loss in value suffered due to noise. By settling claims at the expiration of the period, it would be easier to determine accurately the amount of damage, taking into account changes in noise level, up or down, that might have occurred." There was legal precedent, he said, through cases of lands flooded for reservoir areas, in which the government, or whoever does the flooding, makes permanent settlement for damages in advance. In the case of airports, the damages would be reviewed periodically, since routes, traffic, and types of aircraft keep changing so.

As Haar so well said, "Jet noise is an anxiety-inducing problem—and one which our legal system has handled with woeful inadequacy."

20

CONCLUSION: MAKE
YOURSELF HEARD!

((((((((((•))))))))))

It's probably legally impractical, but there ought to be a simple law against the making of noise that disturbs anyone. It should be an enforceable law which would be perfectly constitutional, would hold up in court, and which would be effective on a person-to-person level. It should be a law that allows you to take to court the person at the next desk who always shouts over the phone so loudly that you can't conduct your own phone conversation, or the next door neighbor who constantly makes annoying noise, or the operator of a jet which whines over your home every night at 1:30 A.M. (as one does over mine when the wind is right), or the hot-rod driver who screeches his tires as his exhaust resonators roar down the street, obviously faster than safety allows—ad infinitum. How sweet it would be if we could instantly arrest noisemakers on the spot and take them to a magistrate who would ask them to defend themselves.

A campaign theme during the 1968 national elections in the United States was Law and Order. Perhaps it's time for someone to run on a campaign pledge of Peace and Quiet.

Perhaps what we need even more desperately is an education of the people, starting when they are children, of the common courtesies that quiet brings. We teach our children how to say "thank you" and "please" and "yes, sir" and "yes, ma'am," but we don't teach them when not to talk at all. We have to teach everyone that noisiness is the rudest behavior and that loudness, especially in music, is detrimental, not enhancing.

My thesis really can be reduced to your RIGHT for quiet, and the fact that noise invades your privacy and trespasses on that right. Even the International Music Council, at an October, 1969, UNESCO Symposium in Paris, proclaimed that every man has a right to quiet, and that music has been misused.

Fortunately, there are around the world organizations of interested citizens who have strived to make the world a quieter place in which to live. There are too few such organizations but they are there, exerting their influence. With your support they will proliferate and increase their influence on lawmaking and law-enforcement agencies.

What can be accomplished when citizens rise up to fight for quiet was well illustrated by writer Sam Blum in his article on noise in *McCall's* magazine in 1967. As he described it:

> About eight in the evening, not long ago, in New York's Chelsea area, a housewife marched out of her apartment house and in cold fury informed a gang ripping up the street that they were keeping her child awake. Said the foreman: "Thanks, lady, I was afraid we were going to be here all night. Our orders were to keep working until someone complained."
> In the quiet that instantly followed, our heroine was

stricken with a sense of cause. "Is it possible," she asked herself, "that we are all needlessly suffering noise in silence. If a 93-pound woman can single-handedly silence six men built like pile drivers, what might a whole neighborhood of aroused femininity accomplish?" In just such a fashion do all revolutions snowball. . . .

Blum overstated the situation a bit. The Fight for Quiet is certainly a movement, but it has not yet achieved the status of a revolution. If the decibel-a-year din rise keeps up, though, it will.

There are other examples of effective individual actions against noisemakers. Take Helmut Winter, who in 1967 opened war against the U.S. Air Force, N.A.T.O., and the Luftwaffe because jet fighters were flying low (400 feet) over his Bavarian home as they landed. He had built a Roman ballista, a crossbow weapon, and began silently firing potato dumplings at the aircraft and announcements to the press. Before long the military surrendered and retreated back to their prescribed altitudes (1,000 feet).

The Manhattan lady and the German gentleman were practicing the singular activity that can best effect changes in democratic societies. Such societies are governed by what are essentially bureaucracies, and bureaucracies respond best and fastest when pressures are applied from the people, individually and in groups. Those noise-fighters who have thus organized and applied pressures on governments at local, state, and national levels, and even at international levels, have achieved some success.

John Connell of London first realized this in 1959. As he explained it, "One afternoon in the hot summer of 1959, for some unaccountable reason, they [the six telephones on his desk] all stopped and, thankful for the break, I picked up *The Daily Telegraph*, one of our national newspapers, and following my usual custom looked first at the Readers'

Letters column, which to my mind gives news of the future as opposed to the history printed on other pages. This particular day there were two letters from folk complaining against noise and the phrases were 'Why do THEY allow it?' 'Why don't THEY do something about it?' "

Connell did some research, found that a Noise Abatement League formed in 1933, which had been the only fighter against noise in Great Britain, had been dead for many years. He wrote his own open letter to the newspaper and asked the readers if noise bothered them. In the first four days he received 4,000 replies. That convinced him of the need, so he founded the Noise Abatement Society, which soon enjoyed the support of women's organizations, labor unions, county governments, taxpayers, the British Medical Association, and many other Englishmen. Six months after the Society was formed and fighting, the national government convened the Committee to Enquire into the Problem of Noise, under the jurisdiction of the Minister of Science, presided over by Sir Alan Wilson, chairman-elect of Courtaulds, and run by staff seconded from the Ministry of Health. (The Wilson Committee's fine document, *Final Report on Noise*, has been quoted throughout this book.) Fourteen months after the Society was formed, said Connell, "in face of great opposition from certain exceedingly powerful commercial interests we instigated and got passed through Parliament, the Noise Abatement Act."

As Connell told me, the main accomplishment of the Society was to make people aware of the fact that if they spoke up, they could do something about noise. "We've given the public the courage to complain," he said.

The International Association Against Noise was formed in 1959. Its secretary-general, O. Schenker-Sprüngli of Zurich, is also director of the Swiss Anti-Noise League. He said, "Noise can be tackled with some hope of success only with the backing of public opinion and proper laws and regulations. Lawmaking is therefore a vital factor in the anti-noise campaign. But laws are effective only when they are rigorously enforced." Since its founding, the international association has established close working relationships with existing national anti-noise groups and with the major international bodies, including the United Nations, World Health Organization, and the Council of Europe.

As always in this Fight for Quiet, the United States limps behind Europe. In 1968 the National Council on Noise Abatement was formed, as some sort of a successor to the line of national noise abatement organizations which have lived for a short time and then died, as related in a previous chapter.

Locally in the United States some organizations have had some success. The Property Owners Noise Abatement Committee of Park Ridge (Illinois) was founded in 1961 to fight the jet noise over that suburb, which lies next to O'Hare International Airport outside of Chicago. Through testimony at Congressional hearings and by legal pressures, this organization was able to get an agreement from the airlines using O'Hare to fly around Park Ridge or to fly high enough above it to reduce the noise.

Tall, broad Robert Alex Baron couldn't take anymore the terrible noises of the construction of a new subway at his door at 55th Street and Avenue of the Americas (Sixth Avenue) in Manhattan, so he mobilized his equally suffering neighbors and formed the Upper Sixth Avenue Noise Abatement Association. That was in 1965. A year later he and Dr. Samuel Rosen (who, remember, studied the noise-free Mabaans) and a few others formed the Citizens for a Quieter City, Inc. During its first year, C.Q.C. (mainly with Baron as its leader) spoke with manufacturers about quieter versions of such ear-offenders as outboard motors, sports cars, and pneumatic drills; elicited much local and national publicity on the noise problem; testified at hearings at vari-

ous governmental levels, including those on the New York
City building code revisions; and published articles and
booklets. Because of this organization's pressures, the mayor
established the Task Force on Noise Control, the state legis-
lature included quiet in its Conservation Bill of Rights, New
York City purchased quieter garbage trucks, held the
first Conference on Urban Noise Control, and in January 1970
issued its recommendations report, *Toward A Quieter City*.

The reaction to aircraft noise is so strong that several
organizations were formed just to fight it. In 1967 an Emergency Committee Opposing the Pan Am Heliport was
formed. It had some good success, since that heliport was
closed two years later. In 1967, too, a Cambridge, Massachusetts, physicist founded the Citizens League Against the
Sonic Boom. Armed with statistics and his ability to use
them, William A. Shurcliff, Ph.D., provided a strong voice
against the S.S.T. Most of its efforts in its first years went
into a comprehensive study of aircraft noise problems in the
United States; into the publication of hard-hitting but reliable fact sheets; and into the giving of speeches before
groups and investigating bodies. Among its major successes
was its pressing of the F.A.A. and other governmental
agencies against the wall and forcing them to publicly discuss the painful facts about sonic booms and other of aviation's acoustic atrocities. The British Association for the
Control of Aircraft Noise has local branches which have
been somewhat effective in bringing pressures to bear to
prevent the noise of aircraft at airports which were being
built or being enlarged.

Many people have been fooled by names. An organization
which never represented the public, but sounded like it did,
was the National Aircraft Noise Abatement Council, headquartered in Washington, D.C. Formed in 1959, it actually
was sponsored by the Air Line Pilots Association and the
Airport Operators Council International. Many in the aviation industry and many noisefighters knew it to be a propa-

ganda and paper agency with the sole purpose of minimizing aircraft noise problems. It reflects the contempt for the public epitomized by the remark of Col. Robert L. Stephens of Boeing and the USAF: "People will get used to sonic booms. It will be just like a train passing their homes."

Citizens who are serious about joining the Fight for Quiet should be wary of such organizations. Before you join or contribute be sure you know what the organization stands for. (A list of legitimate American anti-noise agencies follows this chapter.)

This is not to say that some industry groups are not truly anti-noise. There are some that are. Chief among them in the United States is the Acoustical and Insulating Materials Association, which in 1969 assumed the work, anti-noise and otherwise, of two separate industry organizations, the Insulation Board Institute and the Acoustical Materials Association. The Acoustical Society of America remains the leading American scientific organization for revealing, through its meetings and its journal, the problems of noise and effective ways to control it. In addition, international congresses against noise are sponsored every two years by the International Association Against Noise.

Government has also entered the anti-noise fight officially, if reluctantly. We've already mentioned the English experience. In the United States the Public Health Service, which should be vitally concerned, is only mildly so, and in 1968 it heaped on Dr. Cohen at his Cincinnati headquarters the responsibility of a National Noise Study. The mother agency of the health service, the Department of Health, Education, and Welfare, threw noise in as a lesser concern of its Consumer Protection and Environmental Health Service when it was formed in 1968. Similarly, the U.S. Department of Transportation and the F.A.A., which reigns over the nation's worst noisemakers, each set up their own feeble Office of Noise Abatement.

The only way to convert any government reluctance into

action is to convince it of the need for action and of the strong desire of the people for it. It happened before in pure foods and in auto safety. If you want to join the Fight for Quiet, write to your governmental representatives at every level, join an appropriate anti-noise organization, and contribute your energy and money. Only through massive public participation and education can the people win the Armageddon with din. Only by fighting can we win the struggle for quiet. And we will win, or we will all drown in the rising sea of noise which our mainstreams of technology are feeding.

APPENDIX A

LIST OF ANTI-NOISE AGENCIES IN THE U.S.A.

((((((((((•))))))))))

Citizens Against Noise (C.A.N.)
2729 Wilunt Avenue
Chicago, Illinois 60645

Citizens for a Quieter City, Inc.
345 Park Avenue
New York, N.Y. 10022
Robert Alex Baron, Executive Vice President

Citizens League Against the Sonic Boom
19 Appleton Street
Cambridge, Mass. 02138
William A. Shurcliff, Ph.D., Director

Charles C. Johnson, Jr., Administrator
Consumer Protection and Environmental Health Service
U.S. Department of Health, Education, and Welfare
Washington, D.C. 20204

National Council on Noise Abatement
1625 K Street N.W.
Washington, D.C. 20006
William D. Hurley, President

Alexander Cohen, Ph.D.
National Noise Study
U.S. Public Health Service
Cincinnati, Ohio 45202

Office of Noise Abatement
U.S. Dept. of Transportation
Washington, D.C. 20553

APPENDIX B
ONE MAN'S NOISE EXPOSURE DIARY
NOISE-LEVEL MEASUREMENTS

*Made with a General Radio Type 1565-A Sound-Level
Meter during 1968 (All readings in decibels on
A-weighted Scale)*

$$((((((((((\cdot))))))))))$$

Explanation of Symbols: * Flying Exposure; ** Train Exposure;
*** Music Exposure.

30 March 1968

House party:
4-piece rock band in tiled solarium	115 dB-A***
Conversation in parlor	80–90

8–9 April 1968 (Chicago-London-Amsterdam)

O'Hare Airport, Chicago
Ambassador Lounge TWA	58

Aboard Flight 770 (TWA)
to London (707)
Standing, engines off	63
Purser speaking on intercom	96*
Plane ahead of us taking off	80*
Our plane taking off	94*
Climbing to altitude	85*

Pilot on intercom	106*
Gliding in at London	68*
London airport	95
Departure lounge	84
BEA Vanguard	
At airport, engines off	53
Engine start-up	76*
Voice on intercom	76*
Take-off	86*
Pilot on intercom	96*
Prop reversal, landing at Amsterdam	84*

10 April 1968 (Amsterdam-Utrecht-Soesterberg)

| Taxicab | 72 |

Amstel RR station	
Birds	62
Train arriving	90**
Screeching stop	100**
Utrecht	
Street	76
Small car	82
Volkswagen	81
Soesterberg, restaurant	52
Naarden (restored ancient city)	78
Amsterdam, tram (trolley car)	
Inside	82–88**
Outside	90**
de Wenteltrap Restaurant	58
Bar, piano background	82***
Bar, band background	90***
Bird's Place	
Live band	102***
Electric guitar	106***

11 April 1968 (Amsterdam-Dusseldorf)

KLM bus to airport	76
Airport terminal	60
Lufthansa Boeing 737	
Inside	70
Take-off	86*

In flight	86*
Landing at Dusseldorf, thrust reverse	90*
Essen, Dr. Jansen's office	52
Dusseldorf	
Traffic horn	86
Koenigsallee	62
Graf Adolf Str.	72
Schlüssel Restaurant	72

12 April 1968 (Dusseldorf-Copenhagen)

Otto Bittner coffee house 11:00 A.M.,	
Good Friday	56
Restaurant at Flughafen	68
Aboard SAS Caravelle to Copenhagen	70*
Landing	76*
Taxi	72*
Inside Morris Minor	76
Dr. Køster's home	50

13 April 1968 (Copenhagen)

Outside Royal Hotel	72
Main Street	to 88

14 April 1968 (Copenhagen)

Bispibjerg Hospital grounds	45
Dr. Køster's office	40
Brønnum Restaurant	45
In bed in Royal Hotel, 3:00 A.M. as	
car passes in street below	52

15 April 1968 (Copenhagen to Stockholm)

Bus to airport	
Still	54
Moving	76
Departure lounge	52
SAS Caravelle	
Still	52
Engine start-up	74*
Intercom	86*

Take-off   91*
Power reduction   78*
Climb   82*
Landing   80*
Stockholm
   Baggage claim area   65
   Bus from airport   65
   Traffic, on street outside Carlton Hotel   76
   Bus   92
   My room in hotel   40
   Inside cafeteria   66
   Shopping mall   56
   Old Town   45
   Seagulls at Strom Bron Bridge
      at dinnertime   74

16 April 1968 (Stockholm)

Bus outside hotel   92
In taxi   70
Dinner, music background   55***
Baldakinen Restaurant   70
Edge of dance floor, band playing   92***

17 April 1968 (Stockholm)

Dr. Kylin's office   40
Staff cafeteria, Karolinska   54
Dr. Kajland's office   40
   In his car   72–82
Dr. Johansson's office   40
Cab to Bromma   74
Holmoe's office
   Normal   45
   T-28 taxiing outside   60
Bo Lundberg's office   45
   Inside his Volvo, with radio playing
      Home on the Range   74
Völlingehus Restaurant, lunch   58
Commuter train (tube)
     coming into station
     Blackeberg Street   84

Inside train	74–76
Doors opening	80
Centralen Station (train 12 ft. away	
pulling out)	92
Afternoon rush hour	
Kungsgatan & Vasagatan	90

18 April 1968 (Stockholm to Milan)

Bus to Stockholm airport	74–78
Transit lounge	64–76
Boarding via tail SAS DC-9	92
Seat 14E	
Engines still	66
Engine start-up	74*
Taxiing	75–79*
Take-off	85*
Climb	82*
Cruise, at window ear	84*
Cruise, at aisle ear	77*
Landing at Copenhagen	
Air brakes	88*
Thrust reversal	90–103*
Take-off from Copenhagen	86*
Climb	83*
Cruise	77*
Descent to Milan	78*
Thrust reversal	90–100*
Baggage area	65–75
Bus stop	85
BEA Trident taking off	
obliquely overhead	102
My second floor room, Continental Hotel	45
Occasional traffic sounds	68
Sidewalk in front of hotel, trolley car	88
In Dr. Straneo's Fiat sports car	78–82
Dr. Maugeri's office in Pavia	45
da Giulio Restaurant, Pavia	58

19 April 1968 (Milan-Stresa-Borromeo-Como)

Inside Europa tour bus	72–78
Open market, Stresa	72

Motorboat to Isola Bella   82 stern
                                                      79 bow
Palazzo Borromeo   62
Ferry across Lake Maggiore   68
Lake Como shore   48
Main street, Como   78–84
Milan, galleria shopping mall   64–72
Pam-Pam Restaurant   66–76
Duomo Square, 10:00 P.M.   76–82

20 April 1968 (Milan)

Standa Department Store   74
Duoma Plaza, Communist Party rally   86–90

21 April 1968 (Milan to Paris)

Bus to airport   74–84
Air France Caravelle, Seat A-19
   Engine start-up   81*
   Taxiing   85*
   Take-off   94*
   Cruise   84*
   Air brakes open   88*
   Landing at Orly, Paris   84*
Sound of jet taking off, heard inside still bus   74
Bus to Paris   80
Cab to Hotel Astor   76

22 April 1968 (Paris)

10:00 A.M. Sounds coming into hotel room
   through open window from street below 50–64
Lunch at open-air restaurant, Petite
   Alsacienne on Rue d'Artois   88
In business office on Champs Élysées   62–68
Ambulance passing   70
Compressor in street, 50 ft. away   86
5:00 P.M. traffic at Avenue Marigny and
   Champs Élysées, Place Clemenceau   75–86
                                                      (Peak 94)
5:45 P.M. traffic at Eiffel Tower   75–85
   Lower tower elevator   65

Platform, second stage	64
Elevator to ground level	75
Birds in Park Champ du Mars	56
7:00 P.M. Avenue de la Motte Picquet and	
Avenue Duquesne by École Militaire	75–85
Sidewalk cafe, Blvd. Raspail and Babylone	75–85
8:00 P.M. Bridge to Notre Dame Cathedral	70–76
In Metro subway car, equipped with	
rubber wheels	
Running	73**
Stopping	79**
Strasbourg-St. Denis platform, train	
arriving at other side of platform	86**
Balard Line (steel wheels) arriving	
at station	80–90**
In car	96–99**
Doors closing	94**

23 April 1968 (Paris, Paris to London, London)

Cab (Mercedes 200D)	60
Prof. Lenard's ONERA office	48
ONERA cafeteria	67
Breadcutter	76
Dishwashing room	75–85
Mlle. Moreau's office	55
Wimpy's hamburger restaurant on	
St. Michel	66
Orly airport lounges	60
P.A. system	76
Observation deck, El Al 707 pulling	
away to taxi	93
Arriving Air France Caravelle	91
Air France Caravelle, Seat 12A	
Still, on ground	61
Engine start-up	74*
Intercom	76–79*
Taxiing	77*
Take-off	88*
Power reduction	73*
Air brakes	75*

Landing	75*
London, BEA omnibus	68–72
In tunnel	76
Cab to hotel	65–75

24 April 1968 (London-Southampton)

Train to Southampton	
In open	72–78**
In tunnel	88**
Dr. Acton's office	35
Birds outside	40
Senior Commons Room	78–84
London Underground, Bakerloo	78–88**
8:30 P.M. Oxford Street at Hotel Stratford	
General traffic	78
Omnibus passing	86

25 April 1968 (London and Southampton)

Underground train arriving Bond St. station	92**
In Bakerloo line car	65–90**
Train to Southampton, stopped in rural area	40**
Train passing	72**
Running again	70–80**
Southampton, traffic at Old Main Gate	55
London, 8:00 P.M. Berkeley Square	
Sports car zooming by	86
Shepherd's Restaurant	50–60
Shepherd's Bar	70
Midnight, Selfridge's on Oxford	
Traffic noise measured at curb	75

26 April 1968 (London)

Lunch at Ye Olde Cheshire Cheese, Fleet Street	75

27 April 1968 (London & Manchester)

Euston RR Station	
Walking past pavement-sweeping machine	92

Train to Manchester
   In open   86**
   Through underpass   92**
Inside Dr. Rodda's Cortina auto   70–72
Train arriving at Tottenham station   90**
London: 8:00 P.M., Golden Egg Restaurant,
   Leicester Sq.   72–78
Wyndham's Theatre, Seat N-13,
     pre-curtain   65–70
Applause, final curtain   86
Movie, *Charge of the Light Brigade,*
     measured in balcony   75–80
2:30 A.M. Sunday, Oxford Street traffic   80

28 April 1968 (London)

Jack Straw's Castle, noon   75
British Museum   50–60
Group walking through the King's Library   68

29 April 1968 (Chicago)

TWA Boeing 707, Seat 7A, landing at
     O'Hare Airport, thrust reversal   90*
My home, son screaming   92
Traffic at California & Touhy Avenues
     at 5:00 P.M. rush hour   82
Ear level, me pushing my power mower   96

12 May 1968 (Chicago-San Francisco)

TWA Convair 880, Seat 1A
   Parked   64
   Music on P.A. system   72*
   Take-off   94*
Helicopter, San Francisco to Berkeley
   Standing   86*
   Taxiing   88*
   Cruise   92*
   Walking away from heliport   104
Radio in Berkeley cab   97
Dr. Farr's office   40
   Typewriter from office across from his   60

Bus arriving at curb   80
In bus to San Francisco   80

13 May 1968 (San Francisco)

Market Street   72–82

16 May 1968 (San Francisco to Chicago)

American Airlines Flight 222, Seat 7A
   First Class, Boeing 707
      Take-off   82*
      Cruise   76*
      Captain on intercom   75–85*
      Thrust reversal   86*
      Taxiing   68*

12 June 1968 (Chicago, New York, & Washington)

United Air Lines, Flight 900,
   Boeing 727, Seat 14A
      On ground   75*
      Take-off   82*
      Descent   80*
      Landing at New York   90*
New York taxi   70
Eastern Air Lines Shuttle,
   DC-9-31, Seat 14E
      Taxiing   71*
      Take-off   80*
      Thrust reversal   94*

13 June 1968 (Washington)

10:00 A.M., 18th & L Streets, NW   74–84
National Conference on Noise as a Public
   Health Hazard, Mayflower Hotel
   Before meeting, hallway conversation   70–74
   Before opening, meeting room   65
   Speaker   60–70
Crane at 18th & L St., walking behind   106
Sidewalk repair across street   84–90

30 July 1968 Chicago subway train: (windows open)

Above ground	85–95
In tunnel underground	92–109
Chicago Transit Authority bus	80–90
Garbage truck, 200 ft. away	85

November 1968 (Chicago)

Walking 6 ft. from pneumatic hammer breaking up street pavement at Peterson & Central Park Aves.	108

APPENDIX C
PRINCIPAL SOURCES

(((((((((((•)))))))))))

PART ONE   What Noise Is and Does
Chapter 1   Introductions and Definitions

Encyclopaedia Britannica (1964), XIII, 586.

Heinrich G. Kobrak, *The Middle Ear* (Chicago: University of Chicago Press, 1959), pp. 25–26.

Harvey Brace Lemon, *From Galileo to the Nuclear Age: An Introduction to Physics* (Chicago: University of Chicago Press, 1946), p. 379.

Cyril M. Harris, ed., *Handbook of Noise Control* (New York: McGraw-Hill Book Company, 1957), pp. 2–5.

Encyclopaedia Britannica (1964), XXIII, 236.

Robert Bruce Lindsay, "Sound," *Encyclopaedia Britannica* (1964), XXI, 5–35.

Glossary of Terms Frequently Used in Acoustics (New York: American Institute of Physics, 335 E. 45th St., 1960), pp. A–26.

Hallowell Davis, ed., S. Richard Silverman, co-ed., *Hearing and Deafness*, rev. ed. (New York: Holt, Rinehart & Winston, Inc., 1965), p. 34.

Alexander Wood, *Acoustics* (New York: Dover Publications, Inc., 1966), p. 313.

Davis, *Hearing and Deafness*, p. 34.

Kobrak, *The Middle Ear*, p. 27.

Davis, *Hearing and Deafness*, pp. 34–35.

A Primer of Noise Measurement (West Concord, Mass.: General Radio Company, 1966). Free.

Wayne Rudmose, "Primer on Methods and Scales of Noise Measurement," National Conference on Noise as a Public Health Hazard, Washington, D.C., June 13–14, 1968.

Arnold P. G. Peterson and Ervin E. Gross, Jr., *Handbook of Noise Measurement* (West Concord, Mass.: General Radio Company, 1967). $1.00.

John D. Dougherty and Oliver L. Welsh, "Community Noise and Hearing Loss," *N. E. J. Med.*, CCLXXV (October 6, 1966), 759–65.

Chapter 2   Hearing and Deafness

Aram Glorig, Jr., *Noise and Your Ear* (New York: Grune & Stratton, Inc., 1958).

Edward R. Hermann, "An Audiometric Approach to Noise Control," *Indust. Hyg. J.*, July–August, 1963, pp. 344–56.

Hallowell Davis, ed., S. Richard Silverman, co-ed., *Hearing and Deafness*, rev. ed. (New York: Holt, Rinehart & Winston, Inc., 1965), Chapter 3.

Heinrich G. Kobrak, *The Middle Ear* (Chicago: University of Chicago Press, 1959), pp. 21–22.

Encyclopaedia Britannica (1964), XI, 214.

Samuel Rosen, and others, "Presbycusis Study of a Relatively Noise-Free Population in the Sudan," *Ann. Oto.*, LXXI (1962), 727–43.

Samuel Rosen and Pekka Olin, "Hearing Loss and Coronary Heart Disease," *Arch. Otolaryng.*, LXXXII (September, 1965), 236–43.

"Dr. Rosen's Medical Safari," *Roche Medical Image*, V (December, 1963), 25–28.

"Guinea Pigs Measure Rocket Noise Effects," *Science Newsletter*, July 20, 1968.

A. J. Philipszoon, "On the Cause of Presbycusis: A Case of Unequal Presbycusis of Both Ears," *J. Laryng. and Otol.*, LXXVI, 8 (1962), 593–95.

John L. Fletcher and Arthur J. Riopelle, "Protective Effect of the Acoustic Reflex for Impulsive Noises," *J. Acoust. Soc. Am.*, XXXII (March, 1960), 401–4.

Interview with R. Ross A. Coles in his laboratory at the University of Southampton, April 24–25, 1968.

Alan Bell, *Noise—An Occupational Hazard and Public Nuisance* (Geneva: World Health Organization, 1966), p. 20.

Interview with Bengt Kylin in his office at Karolinska Institutet, Stockholm, Sweden, April 16, 1968.

John L. Fletcher, "Reflex Response of Middle-Ear Muscles: Protection of the Ear from Noise," *Sound,* I (March–April, 1962), 17–23.

John L. Fletcher, "Protection from High Intensities of Impulse Noise by Way of Preceding Noise and Click Stimuli," *J. of Aud. Res.,* V (1965), 145–50.

B. Johannson, B. Kylin, and M. Langfy, "Acoustic Reflex as a Test of Individual Susceptibility to Noise," *Acta. Otolaryng.,* LXIV (1967), 256–62.

Harlow W. Ades, and others, "Threshold of Aural Pain to High Intensity Sound," *Aerospace Med.,* XXX (September, 1959), 678–84.

Davis, *Hearing and Deafness,* p. 104.

Hallowell Davis, and others, "Temporary Deafness Following Exposure to Loud Tones and Noise," *Acta. Otolaryng.,* Suppl. XXCVIII (1950), 1–56.

Michael Rodda, "Role of Test Tone in Producing Temporary Threshold Shift," *Arch. of Otolaryng.,* XXC (August, 1964), 160–66.

Michael Rodda, *Noise and Society* (Edinburgh: Oliver and Boyd, Ltd., 1967), p. 27.

John D. Dougherty and Oliver L. West, "Community Noise and Hearing Loss," *N. E. J. Med.,* CCLXXV (October 6, 1966), 759–65.

Aram Glorig, "The Effects of Noise on Hearing," *J. Laryng. and Otol.,* LXXV (May, 1961), 447–78.

Dougherty and West, "Community Noise," p. 764.

Davis, *Hearing and Deafness,* p. 104.

George E. Shambaugh, Jr., "Effects of Noise on the Ear and Hearing," *Proc. Third Annual Nat. Noise Abatement Symp.,* Chicago, October 10, 1952.

H. Engstrom and H. W. Ades, "Effect of High-Intensity Noise on Inner Ear Sensory Epithelia," *Acta. Otolaryng.,* Suppl. CLVIII, 219–29.

Dougherty and West, "Community Noise," p. 764.

Shambaugh, "Effects of Noise."

Interview with Dr. W. Ian Acton in his office at the University of Southampton, April 24, 1968.

Dougherty and West, "Community Noise," p. 764.

Davis, *Hearing and Deafness,* p. 89.

Interview with Dr. Bertil Johannson in his office at the Royal Institute of Technology, Stockholm, April 16, 1968.

Dougherty and West, "Community Noise," p. 764.

Mark Ross and Jay Lerman, "Hearing-Aid Usage and Its Effect upon Residual Hearing," *Arch. Otolaryng.,* XXCVI (1967), 639–44.

Davis, *Hearing and Deafness,* p. 91.

Harlow W. Ades, and others, "Non-Auditory Effects of High Intensity Sound Stimulation on Deaf Human Subjects," *J. Av. Med.,* XXIX (June, 1958), 454–67.

Davis, *Hearing and Deafness,* p. 91.

Chapter 3   Who Goes Deaf—And Why

Noise—Sound Without Value, Report of the Committee on Environmental Quality of the Federal Council for Science and Technology, Washington, D.C., September, 1968, p. 32.

Aram Glorig, *Noise and Your Ear* (New York: Grune & Stratton, Inc., 1958), p. 4.

Jean Roberts and John Cohrssen, *Hearing Levels of Adults: By Education, Income and Occupation, United States, 1960–1962* (Washington, D.C.: National Center for Health Statistics, U.S. Public Health Service, Series 11, No. 31, May, 1968).

"The Noise of Farm Equipment Could Prove Deafening," *Medical World News,* May 24, 1968, p. 13.

Charles D. Yaffe and Herbert H. Jones, *Noise and Hearing: Relationship of Industrial Noise to Hearing Acuity in a Controlled Population,* Public Health Service Publication No. 850 (Washington, D.C.: U.S. Government Printing Office, 1961).

M. Rodda, L. J. Smith, and G. D. Wilson, "Occupational Deafness in Weavers," *N. Z. Med. J.,* LXII (April, 1963), 183–86.

W. Taylor, J. Pearson, and A. Mair, "Study of Noise and Hearing in Jute Weaving," *J. Acoust. Soc. Am.,* XXXVIII (July, 1965), 113–20.

W. Taylor, J. C. G. Pearson, R. Kell, and A. Mair, "A Pilot Study of Hearing Loss and Social Handicap in Female Jute Weavers," *Proc. Roy. Soc. Med.,* LX (November, 1967), 1117–21.

Fred Ottoboni and Thomas H. Milby, "Occupational Disease Potentials in the Heavy Equipment Operator," *Arch. Environ. Health*, XV (September, 1967), 317–21.

Paul LaBenz, Alexander Cohen, and Benjamin Pearson, "A Noise and Hearing Survey of Earth-Moving Equipment Operators," *Am. Ind. Hyg. Assoc. J.*, XXVIII (March–April, 1967), 117–28.

The Lancet (1960) ii, 417.

Denis L. Chadwick, "Acoustic Trauma—Clinical Presentation," *Proc. Roy. Soc. Med.*, LIX (October, 1966), 957–63.

Edward R. Hermann, "Acoustical Aspects of the Environmental Spectrum," in *Interactions of Man and His Environment*, Plenum Press, 1966 (proceedings of the Northwestern University conference: Interactions of Man and His Environment, January 28–29, 1965), p. 95.

"Noise and Its Health Effects," news release, American Medical Association, October, 1964.

William M. Shearer and George H. Stevens, "Acoustic Threshold Shift from Power Lawnmower Noise," *Sound and Vibration*, II (October, 1968), 29.

R. Plomp, "Het lawaai van pneumatische boormachines voor tandheel jundige behandeling," Institute for Perception RVO-TNO, Report No. 1ZF 1959–10, Soesterberg, The Netherlands.

J. S. Lumio, and others (Helsinki), "High-Speed Dental Drill—Small High-Range Hearing Loss Noted in Some Constant Users," *Monatsschrift für Ohrenheilkunde und Laryngo-Rhinologue*, 99/4 (1965), 192–99.

James H. Flugrath, "Modern Day Rock-and-Roll Music and Damage-Risk Criteria," 76th Meeting of the Acoustical Society of America, Cleveland, Ohio, November 19–22, 1968.

Charles P. Lebo and Kenward S. Oliphant, "Music as a Source of Acoustic Trauma," *Laryngoscope*, LXXVIII (July, 1968), 1211–18.

Charles P. Lebo, Kenward S. Oliphant, and John Garrett, "Acoustic Trauma from Rock-and-Roll Music," *Calif. Med.*, CVII (November, 1967), 378–80.

Ben Zinser, "Ears Suffer from This Rock 'n' Roll Clatter," *Independent Press-Telegram*, Long Beach, Calif., April 17, 1967.

Flugrath, "Modern Day Rock-and-Roll."

Charles Speaks and David A. Nelson, "T.T.S. Following Exposure to Rock-and-Roll Music," 76th Meeting of the Acoustical Society of America, Cleveland, Ohio, November 19–22, 1968.

"Going Deaf from Rock 'n' Roll," *Time*, August 9, 1968, p. 47.

"Teeners 'Deaf' at 25?" Gainesville *Sun* (Fla.), January 12, 1968, p. 18.

James F. Jerger, Susan Jerger, and Kenneth C. Pollack, "Hearing Loss and Rock-'n'-Roll Music." Unpublished.

Don Dedera, "Teen Ears Tuned Out," Arizona *Republic*, Phoenix, December 29, 1966, p. 19.

James Stacey, "The Big Sound is Bad for You," Chicago *Tribune* Magazine, August 4, 1968, p. 21.

"U-T Research Links Ear Damage to Go-Go Music," University of Tennessee news release for morning newspapers, Friday, August 9, 1968.

Private communication from David M. Lipscomb dated November 8, 1968.

Chapter 4   Why Noise Annoys You

Michael Rodda, *Noise and Society* (Edinburgh: Oliver and Boyd, Ltd., 1967), p. 3.

Sanford J. Freedman, "Perceptual Changes in Sensory Deprivation: Suggestions for a Conative Theory," *J. Nerv. Ment. Dis.*, CXXXII (January, 1961), 17–21.

Alexander Cohen, "Physiological and Psychological Effects of Noise on Man," *J. Boston Soc. Civ. Eng.*, LII (January, 1965), 70–95.

Donald E. Broadbent, "Effects of Noise on Behavior," in Cyril M. Harris, *Handbook of Noise Control* (New York: McGraw-Hill Book Company, 1957).

Alan Bell, *Noise—An Occupational Hazard and Public Nuisance* (Geneva: World Health Organization, 1966), p. 33.

Rodda, *Noise and Society*, pp. 3–4.

Francis I. Catlin, "Noise and Emotional Stress," *J. Chron. Dis.*, XVIII (1965), 509–18.

Sir Alan Wilson, and others, *Noise—Final Report* (London: Her Majesty's Stationery Office, 1963).

Catlin, "Noise and Emotional Stress."

"Noise and Its Effects," *Brit. Med. J.*, September 11, 1965, p. 605.

"Scared Sheepdog Always Runs Home," London *Observer*, March 5, 1967.

James Bond, "Effects of Noise on the Physiology and Behavior of Farm-Raised Animals." Symposium on the Extra-Auditory Physiological Effects of Audible Sound, held at the 134th Annual Meeting of the American Association for the Advancement of Science, Boston, December 30, 1969.

R. B. Casady and R. P. Lehman, "Response of Farm Animals to Sonic Booms," Appendix H in *Sonic Boom Experiments at Edwards Air Force Base, Interim Report* (Arlington, Va.: National Sonic Boom Evaluation Office, 1400 Wilson Blvd., 1967).

Irving Kupfermann, "Eating Behaviour Induced by Sounds," *Nature*, CCI (January 18, 1964), 324.

E. Grandjean, "Biological Effects of Noise," *Proceedings of the Fourth International Congress on Acoustics* (Copenhagen: J. H. Schultz, 1962), pp. 109–14.

Robert M. Cunningham, Jr., *The Third World of Medicine* (New York: McGraw-Hill Book Company, 1968).

Michael Short, "Noise Expert Demands Less of It," Chicago *Tribune* (via Associated Press), April 23, 1967.

"Noise in the Hospital," *J.A.M.A.*, CLXXII, March 5, 1960.

P. Hugh-Jones, A. R. Tanser, and C. Whitey, "Patient's View of Admission to a London Teaching Hospital," *Brit. Med. J.*, September 12, 1964, pp. 660–64.

Duane R. Carlson, "Noise Control Program Is Quiet Success," *The Modern Hospital*, CV (December, 1965), 82–85.

Noise in Hospitals, Publication No. 930-D-11, U.S. Public Health Service (Washington, D.C.: Government Printing Office, 1963).

H. A. Denzel, "Noise and Health," *Science*, CXLIII (March 6, 1964), 992.

D. Chapman, *British National Building Studies, No. 2* (London: Her Majesty's Stationery Office, 1948).

Interview with Dr. Kajland in his office at Karolinska Institute, Stockholm, Sweden, April 16, 1968.

Erland Jonsson and Stefan Sörensen, "On the Influence of Attitudes to the Source on Annoyance Reactions to Noise," *Nordisk Hygienisk Tidskrift*, XLVIII (1967), 33–45.

Rune Cederlöf, Erland Jonsson, and Stefan Sörensen, "On the Influence of Attitudes to the Source on Annoyance Reactions to Noise," *Nordisk Hygienisk Tidskrift*, XLVIII (1967), 46–59.

Erland Jonsson, Anders Kajland, Bruno Paccagnella, and Stefan Sörensen, "Annoyance Reactions to Traffic Noise in Italy and Sweden—A Comparative Study" (in press).

D. E. Broadbent and D. W. Robinson, "Subjective Measurements of the Relative Annoyance of Simulated Sonic Bangs and Aircraft Noise," *J. Sound Vib.*, I (1964), 162–74.

Cohen, "Physiological and Psychological Effects of Noise on Man."

Broadbent, in Harris, *Handbook of Noise Control.*

CHABA Report No. 4, Proceedings of the Second Meeting of the Armed Forces–National Research Council Committee on Hearing and Bio-Acoustics, "Noise and the Community," held at the Armour Research Foundation, Chicago, October 25–26, 1954.

Paul N. Borsky, "The Effects of Noise on Community Behavior," National Conference on Noise as a Public Health Hazard, Washington, June 13–14, 1968.

J. W. Little and J. E. Mabry, "Human Reaction to Aircraft Engine Noise." *Sound and Vibration*, II (November, 1968), 14–22.

Chapter 5   What Noise Does To Your Mind

N. R. French and J. C. Steinberg, "Factors Governing the Intelligibility of Speech Sounds," *J. Acoust. Soc. Am.*, XIX (1947), 90–119.

G. A. Miller, "The Masking of Speech," *Psych. Bull.*, XLIV (1947), 105–29.

Irwin Pollack and J. M. Pickett, *J. Acoust. Soc. Am.*, XXIX (1957), 1262.

William R. MacLean, *J. Acoust. Soc. Am.*, XXXI (1959), 79–80.

Sheila Drummond, "The Effects of Environmental Noise on Pseudo Voice After Laryngectomy," *J. Laryng. Oto.*, March, 1965, pp. 193–202.

J. C. Webster, "Effects of Noise on Speech Intelligibility," National Conference on Noise as a Public Health Hazard, Washington, D.C., June 13–14, 1968.

J. C. Webster, "Speech Communications as Limited by Ambient Noise," *J. Acoust. Soc. Am.*, XXXVII (April, 1965), 692–99.

Thomas H. Fay, Jr., "Preliminary Analysis of Talker-Listener Aspects of the Fire Alarm Radio," Report to the Bureau of Fire Communications, New York City Fire Department (unpublished), March, 1963.

Interview with A. R. D. Thornton in his laboratory at Southampton, April 25, 1968.

Sir Alan Wilson, and others, *Noise—Final Report* (London: Her Majesty's Stationery Office, 1963), pp. 64–65.

Alexander Cohen, "Noise and Psychological State," National Conference on Noise as a Public Health Hazard, Washington, D.C., June 13–14, 1968.

Nathaniel Kleitman, "Sleep," *Encyclopaedia Britannica* (1964), XX, 791–94.

H. R. Richter, "The E.E.G. and the Impairment of Sleep by Traffic Noise During the Night: A Problem of Preventive Medicine," *Electroenceph. Clin. Neurophysiol.*, XXIII (1967), 283–91.

G. Jansen, "Measuring the Physiological Effects of Noise," *Documenta Geigy* (special issue on noise), 1967

Anonymous, "Sleep-Sound Study," *Research News*, National Research Council of Canada, XXI (May–June, 1968), 6–7.

George J. Thiessen, "Effects of Noise During Sleep," Symposium on Extra-Auditory Physiological Effects of Audible Sound, at the 134th Meeting of The American Association for the Advancement of Science, Boston, December 28, 1969.

Kleitman, "Sleep."

Anonymous, "Learning to Live with the Boom," *Stanford Research Institute Journal*, June, 1968, pp. 1–6.

Reported by syndicated Cleveland medical columnist David Dietz in July, 1965, and commented on by syndicated Washington satirist-columnist Art Buchwald in August, 1965.

Seminaire Interregional Sur L'Habitat Dans Ses Rapports Avec La Santé Publique, World Health Organization, PA/185.65. Summarized in *WHO Chronicle*, October, 1966.

Kleitman, "Sleep," p. 793.

Wilson, *Noise—Final Report*, p. 7.

Congressional Record, 112:8362, April 21, 1966; 112:17431, 17440, August 4, 1966, Washington, D.C.

Silvan S. Tomkins, *Affect, Imagery, Consciousness*, Vol. II (New York: Springer Publishing Co., 1963), pp. 21–22.

Sam Blum, "Noise—How Much More Can We Take?" *McCall's*, January, 1967, p. 113 .

Anonymous, "Some Airlines Find Why Most People Don't Fly," *Air Transport World*, November, 1968, p. 68.

CHABA Report No. 4, Proceedings of the Second Meeting of the Armed Forces–National Research Council Committee on Hearing and Bio-Acoustics, "Noise and the Community," held at the Armour Research Foundation, Chicago, October 25–26, 1954, p. 12.

Henning E. von Gierke, "Effects of Sonic Boom on People: Review and Outlook," *J. Acoust. Soc. Am.*, XXXIX: S43–S50 (May, 1966).

Karl D. Kryter, "Psychological Reactions to Aircraft Noise," *Science*, CLI (March 18, 1966), 1346–55.

Jerome S. Lukas and Karl D. Kryter, "Awakening Effects of Simulated Sonic Booms and Subsonic Aircraft Noise." Symposium on Physiological Effects of Audible Sound (Extra-Auditory), American Association for the Advancement of Science, Boston, December 29, 1969.

Report on Human Response to the Sonic Boom (Washington, D.C.: National Academy of Sciences, 1968).

William A. Shurcliff, "Sonic Booms," *New Eng. J. Med.*, September 28, 1967, p. 714.

"Booms," *The Lancet*, August 5, 1967, pp. 295–96.

Leo L. Beranek, "Street and Air Traffic Noise—And What We Can Do About It," *UNESCO Courier*, July, 1967, pp. 13–16.

Kenneth R. Henry and Robert E. Bowman, "Early Exposure to Intense Acoustic Stimuli and Susceptibility to Audiogenic Seizures." Symposium on the Physiological Effects of Audible Sound (Extra-Auditory), 136th meeting of the American Association for the Advancement of Science, Boston, December 29, 1969.

Francis M. Forster, "Human Studies of Epileptic Seizures Induced by Sound and Their Conditioned Extinction." Symposium on the Physiological Effects of Audible Sound (Extra-Auditory), 136th meeting of the American Association for the Advancement of Science, Boston, December 29, 1969.

Interview with Dr. Maugeri in his office at the University of Pavia, April 18, 1968.

Alexander Cohen, William F. Hummel, Joan W. Turner, and Francis N. Dukes-Dobos, "Effects of Noise on Task Performance" (Cincinnati: Occupational Health Research and Training Facility, U.S.P.H.S., 1014 Broadway, January, 1966).

D. E. Broadbent, *Perception and Communication* (Oxford: Pergamon Press, 1958), p. 99.

D. E. Broadbent, in Cyril M. Harris, *Handbook of Noise Control* (New York: McGraw-Hill Book Company, 1957).

Wilson, *Noise—Final Report*, p. 12.

BENOX Report: An Exploratory Study of the Biological Effects of Noise (Chicago: The University of Chicago Press, December 1, 1953), p. 81.

D. A. Laird, "The Influence of Noise on Production and Fatigue, as Related to Pitch, Sensation Level, and Steadiness of Noise," *J. Appl. Psy.*, XVII (1933), 320.

H. C. Weston and S. Adams, Industrial Health Research Board, Reports Nos. 65 and 70 (London: Her Majesty's Stationery Office, 1932 and 1935).

S. S. Stevens, "The Effects of Noise and Vibration on Psychomotor Efficiency," Progress Report of Project II, March 31, 1941 (Washington, D.C.: National Research Council).

A. Carpenter, "Effects of Noise on Performance and Productivity," *The Control of Noise* (London: Her Majesty's Stationery Office, 1962), p. 301.

D. E. Broadbent, "Differences and Interactions Between Stresses," *Quart. J. Exp. Psych.*, XV, 205–11.

D. E. Broadbent and E. A. J. Little, "Effects of Noise Reduction in a Work Situation," *Occup. Psych.*, April, 1960, pp. 1–8.

Yasuhiro Nagatsuka, "Studies on Influences of Train Noise Upon Schoolchildren: V. On the Mental Works," *Tohoku Psychol. Folia*, XXIII (1964), 16–19.

The New Scientist, March 6, 1969.

Joyce Brothers, "Does Music Interfere with Students' Study?" *Chicago's American* (syndicated), October 14, 1968.

Anonymous, "Noise Helps Teen-agers Study," *Modern Med.*, June 6, 1968, p. 48.

Stanley Meisler, "How Little Noise Became Big—Subconsciously," Chicago *Sun-Times* (via Associated Press), January 31, 1960.

Interview with Dr. Gerd Jansen, in his office in Essen, Germany, April 11, 1968.

G. Jansen, *Int. Z. Angew Physiol.*, XVII (1959), 239.

Wilson, *Noise—Final Report*, p. 10.

D. E. Broadbent, "Non-Auditory Effects of Noise," *Advanc. of Sci.*, January, 1961, pp. 406–9.

"Study Indicates Plane Noise Can Add to Mental Problems," Chicago *Daily News*, December 15, 1969.

Millicent Brower, "Noise Pollution: A Growing Menace," *Saturday Review*, May 27, 1967, pp. 17–19.

Anonymous, "Noise—Something More to Worry About," *U. S. News and World Report*, September 23, 1963, pp. 64–66.

Von K. Bättig, "Der Lärm als präventivmedizinisches Problem," Sonderabdruck aus der Schweizerischen Medizinischen

Wochenschrift, 92, Jahrgang 1962, Nr. 36, Seite 1096, und Nr. 37, Seite 1123.

Fred Warshofsky, "What Sound Can Do to You," *Cosmopolitan*, July, 1961, pp. 52–57.

Private communication.

Chapter 6   What Noise Does To Your Body

Margaret Liley, M.D., and Beth Day, *The Infant World* (New York: Random House, Inc., 1967).

Lester W. Sontag, "Implications of Fetal Behavior and Environment for Adult Personalities," *Ann. N. Y. Acad. Sci.*, CXXXIV (February 28, 1966), 782–88.

Bertil Johansson, Erik Wedenberg, and Björn Westin, "Measurement of Tone Response by the Human Foetus," *Acta Otolaryng.*, LVII, 188–92.

Lester W. Sontag, "Effect of Noise During Pregnancy Upon Foetal and Subsequent Adult Behavior." Symposium on the Physiological Effects of Audible Sound (Extra-Auditory). 136th meeting of the American Association for the Advancement of Science, Boston, December 28, 1969.

Congressional Record, April 21, 1966 (Washington, D.C.), p. 8343.

Donald E. Broadbent, "Effects of Noise on Behavior," in Cyril M. Harris, *Handbook of Noise Control* (New York: McGraw-Hill Book Company, 1957), pp. 10–19.

BENOX Report, An Exploratory Study of the Biological Effects of Noise (Chicago: The University of Chicago Press, December 1, 1953).

A. F. Rasmussen, "Audiogenic Stress and Susceptibility to Infection"; Mary F. Lockett, "Effects of Sound on Endocrine Function and Electrolyte Excretion"; Amilcar E. Arguelles, "Endocrine and Metabolic Effects of Noise in Normal, Hypertensive, and Psychotic Humans." All at Symposum on the Physiological Effects of Audible Sound (Extra-Auditory), 136th meeting of the American Association for the Advancement of Science, Boston, December 28, 1969.

Leo J. Reyna, Ph.D., Alberto Di Mascio, Ph.D., and Norman Berezin, D.D.M., "Psychological Stress and Experimental Caries," *Psychosomatics*, VIII (May–June, 1967), 138–40.

James H. Winchester, "Is Noise Driving You Crazy?" *Science Digest*, LVI (August, 1964), 27–31.

Meyer Friedman, Sanford O. Byers, and Alvin E. Brown, "Plasma Lipid Responses of Rats and Rabbits to an Auditory Stimulus," *Amer. J. Physiol.*, CCXII (May, 1967), 1174–78.

J. W. Kakolewski and Y. Takeo, "Relationships Between EEG Patterns and Arterial Pressure Changes," *Electroenceph. Clin. Neurophysiol.*, XXII (March, 1967), 239–44.

William F. Geber, Ph.D., Thomas A. Anderson, Ph.D., and Bruce Van Dyne, M.S., "Physiologic Responses of the Albino Rat to Chronic Noise Stress," *Arch. Environ. Health*, XII (June, 1966), 751–54.

W. F. Geber and T. A. Anderson, "Cardiac Hypertrophy Due to Chronic Audiogenic Stress in the Rat, *Rattus Norvegicus Albinus*, and Rabbit, *Lepus Cuniculus*," *Comp. Biochem. Physiol.*, XXI (1967), 273–77.

UNESCO Courier, July, 1967.

C. Wiederhielm, "The Interstitial Space and Lymphatic Pressures in the Bat Wing," presented at the Pulmonary Circulation, a satellite conference of the Congress of the International Union of Physiological Sciences, Chicago, September 1, 1968.

G. Lehmann and J. Tamm, "Über Veränderungen der Kreislaufdynamik des ruhenden Menschen unter Einwirkung von Geräuschen," *Int. Z. Angew Physiol.*, XVI (1956), 217–27.

Interview in Dr. Jansen's office in Essen, Germany, on April 11, 1968.

G. Jansen, "Measuring the Physiological Effects of Noise," *Documenta Geigy* (special issue on noise), 1967.

Gerd Jansen, M.D., Samuel Rosen, M.D., J. Schulze, M.D., Dietrich Plester, M.D., and Aly El-Mofty, M.D., "Vegetative Reactions to Auditory Stimuli," *Trans. Am. Acad. Ophthal. Otol.*, May–June, 1964, pp. 445–55.

Y. P. Kapur, M.D., and A. J. Patt, M.D., "Hearing in Todas of South India," *Arch. Otolaryng.*, LXXXV (April, 1967), 400–406.

Interview in Dr. Kylin's office in Stockholm on April 16, 1968.

L. Rossi, G. Oppliger, and E. Grandjean, "Gli Effetti Neurovegetativi Sull'uomo di Rumori Sovrapposti ad un Rumore di Fondo," *La Medicine del Lavoro*, L (1959), 3–8.

Interview with Drs. Maugeri and Straneo in Dr. Maugeri's office at the University of Pavia, April 18, 1968.

G. Straneo and P. Seghizzi, "L'azione del Rumore sul Sistema

Vascolare Periferico, Nota II," *Folia Medica*, XLV (1962), 572–77.

Giovanni Straneo, "L'azione del Rumore sul Sistema Vascolare Periferico, Nota I," *Folia Medica*, XLIV (1961), 998–1009.

G. Straneo, P. Seghizzi, and M. Majeron, "L'azione del Rumore sul Sistema Vascolare, Nota III," *Folia Medica*, XLV (1962), 1009–15.

A. Taccola, G. Straneo, and G. C. Bobbio, "Modificazioni della Dinamica Cardiaca Indotte dal Rumore," *Lavoro Umano*, XV (1963), 561–78.

"Noise of Big Cities is Found to Cause Stress on Heart," *Medical Tribune*, March 29, 1965.

Chapter 7   How Noise Can Kill

UNESCO Courier, July, 1967.
Congressional Record, April 21, 1966 (Washington, D.C.), p. 8343.

G. Jansen, "Measuring the Physiological Effects of Noise," *Documenta Geigy* (special issue on noise), 1967.

Gerd Jansen, *Zur Nervösen Belastung durch Lärm*, Verlag, Darmstadt, 1967.

Moyra Patrick, "Pupilometry: Private Interim Report," November 11, 1967, Institute of Sound and Vibration Research, University of Southampton.

Daniel Kahneman and Jackson Beatty, "Pupil Diameter and Load on Memory," *Science*, CLIV (1966), 1583–85.

S. Maugeri, "Pathology of Noise," Congress of the Italian Society of Industrial Medicine, Palermo, October, 1967.

Charles H. Best and Norman B. Taylor, *The Physiological Basis of Medical Practice*, 8th ed. (Baltimore: The Williams and Wilkins Co., 1966), esp. pp. 142–43, 250–51.

E. Grandjean, "Biological Effects of Noise," *Proceedings of the Fourth International Congress on Acoustics* (Copenhagen: J. H. Schultz, 1962), pp. 109–14. Also, his discussion on the panel, "Effects of Noise on Man" at the National Conference on Noise as a Public Health Hazard, Washington, D.C., June 13–14, 1968.

Silvan S. Tomkins, *Affect, Imagery, Consciousness*, Vol. II (New York: Springer Publishing Co., 1963), p. 47.

Lord Horder, *Quiet*, I (July, 1937), 5.

Best and Taylor, *Psychological Basis of Medical Practice,* p. 250.

Theodore Berland, "Medical 'Miracles' with Ultrasound," *Family Circle,* LXIX (October, 1966), 47, 107–9.

Report on the Council on Physical Medicine and Rehabilitation, *J.A.M.A.,* CLVII (April 16, 1955), 1407–8.

M. Arslan, "An Improved Technique of the Ultrasonic Irradiation of the Vestibular Apparatus on Ménière's Disease, *Acta Otolaryng.,* LV (November–December, 1962), 467–72.

George C. Mohr, John N. Cole, Elizabeth Guild, and Henning E. von Gierke, "Effects of Low Frequency and Infrasonic Noise on Man," *Aerospace Med.,* XXXVI (September, 1964), 817–24.

Frank Dorsey, "Plan Machine That Kills With Sound," Dispatch from the London *Sunday Times,* in the Des Moines (Iowa) *Register,* April 19, 1967, p. 1.

John Dunning, "The Silent Sound That Kills," *Science & Mechanics,* XXXIX (January, 1968), 30–33, 76.

Best and Taylor, *Psychological Basis of Medical Practices,* pp. 85–86.

Robert C. Marsh, "Earmuffs, Please," Chicago *Sun-Times,* February 15, 1968.

"The Danger of Sounds We Cannot Hear," *UNESCO Courier,* July, 1967, pp. 28–89.

"Sounds That Lie Too Deep for Ears—Tornadoes, Tremors, Magnetic Storms," *Medical Tribune,* November 26, 1962, p. 26.

Chapter 8 How Noise Destroys

Robert J. Serling, *The Probable Cause* (New York: Ballantine Books, 1960), pp. 155–56.

Encyclopaedia Britannica (1964), II, 899.

Clayton K. S. Knight, *Plane Crash* (New York: Greenberg, 1958), p. 175.

Serling, *The Probable Cause.*

The New York Times, February 12, 1955, p. 33. (See also October 23, 1954, p. 33; and November 9, 1954, p. 55.)

Interview with Robert Crawford at the Institute for Sound and Vibration Research, University of Southampton, April 25, 1968.

Encyclopaedia Britannica (1964), IX, 113–15.

Werner Fricke and Richard K. Kaminski, "Airborne Noise, Its Simulation and Effect on Components," *Aero/Space Engineering,* XVIII (December, 1959), 47–53.

S. Boraas, W. Fricke, and B. Gaviller, "Calculation and Simulation of the Noise Environments of a Guided Missile for Testing of Components," 31st Symposium on Shock, Vibration, and Associated Environments, October 1–4, 1962, Phoenix, Ariz.

Werner Fricke and John R. Bissell, "Analytical and Experimental Studies of Sound Pressures in Ducted Propellers," 74th Meeting of the Acoustical Society of America, November 14–17, 1967, Miami Beach, Fla.

"Rocketry: Noise Problem Considered," *Science News,* XCIV (December 21, 1968), 619.

Richard D. James, "Busy Silent Partner: Ultrasound, an Old Idea, Wins a New Life in Home Appliances, Industry, Medicine." *The Wall Street Journal,* Friday, October 11, 1968, p. 34.

Encyclopaedia Britannica (1964), XXII, 676B.

James, "Busy Silent Partner."

Arthur M. Squires, in letter to *The New York Times,* dated August 2, 1967.

William R. Arnold (delivered by Major William McCormick), "Damage Experience," National Conference on Noise as a Public Health Hazard, Washington, D.C., June 13–14, 1968.

"Sonic Booms Shake Up Officials," *Science,* CLXI (July 26, 1968), 343.

"SST's Effect on Cathedrals," *Science News,* October 19, 1968.

Harvey H. Hubbard, "Sonic Booms," *Physics Today,* February, 1968, pp. 31–37.

Sonic Boom Experiments at Edwards Air Force Base, Interim Report (Arlington, Va.: National Sonic Boom Evaluation Office, 1400 Wilson Blvd., 1967), p. 22.

Ibid., p. 21.

Ibid., p. G-1-2-10.

Studies of Sonic Boom Induced Damage (NASA CR-227) (Washington, D.C.: National Aeronautics and Space Administration, May, 1965), pp. IV 1–3.

Structural Response to Sonic Booms (Final Report), (Oklahoma City: Andrews Associates Inc., February, 1965).

C. W. Newberry, "Measuring the Sonic Boom and Its Effect on Buildings," *Mat. Res. and Stds.,* IV (November, 1964), 601–11.

W. A. Ramsay, "Damage to Ottawa Air Terminal Building

Produced by Sonic Boom," *Mat. Res. and Stds.*, IV (November, 1964), 612–16.

Report on Physical Effects of the Sonic Boom (Washington, D.C.: National Academy of Sciences, February, 1968).

Cyril Stanley Smith, "Time Saved Versus Damage Made," *Physics Today*, June, 1968, p. 9.

Bo Lundberg, "The Menace of the Sonic Boom to Society and Civil Aviation," IVth International Congress for Noise Abatement, Baden-Baden, May 11–14, 1966.

"Correlation of Public Reaction to Sonic-Boom-Induced Property Damage," Fact Sheet (Cambridge, Mass.: Citizens League Against the Sonic Boom, 19 Appleton St., May 15, 1968).

PART TWO   Where Noise Comes From

Chapter 9   Our Noisy World

Robert A. Stevenson, Jr., "Underwater Television," *Oceanology International*, November–December, 1967, p. 32.

Column item in *Medical Tribune*, December 26, 1966.

Ronald McKie, *The Company of Animals* (New York: Harcourt, Brace & World, Inc., 1965), pp. 39–40, 47–48.

Johnny Hart, *B. C.*, Publishers Newspaper Syndicate, April 2, 1967.

Peter Sommer, "Noise—Eternal Scourge of Mankind," *Documenta Geigy* (special issue on noise), 1967.

Denzil Freeth, introductory address at symposium, The Control of Noise, National Physical Laboratory, June 26, 1961 (London: Her Majesty's Stationery Office, 1962).

Sommer, "Noise—Eternal Scourge."

Arthur Schopenhauer, *Essays*, translated by T. Bailey Saunders (London: George Allen & Unwin, 1951).

The Economist, London, March 2, 1968.

Robert C. Doty, "Rome to Put Drastic Curbs on Use of Vehicles in Central Area," *The New York Times*, July 29, 1968.

Interview in Professor Maugeri's office at Pavia, Italy, on April 18, 1968. Also, "Noise of Big Cities Is Found to Cause Stress on the Heart," *Medical Tribune*, March 29, 1965.

Leo L. Beranek, "Street and Air Traffic Noise—And What We Can Do About It," *UNESCO Courier* (special issue on noise), July, 1967, p. 14.

John D. Dougherty and Oliver L. Welsh, "Community Noise and Hearing Loss," *N. E. J. Med.*, CCLXXV (October 6, 1966), 759–65.

The New Yorker, September 10, 1966, quoted in Barbara J. Culliton, "Noise Menace Threatens Man," *Science News*, XC (October 15, 1966), 297–99.

Tony Embleton, "Urban Noise—Interior Sources," Seminar on Noise for Science Writers, sponsored by the American Institute of Physics and the National Association of Science Writers with the support of the National Science Foundation, Hotel New Yorker, New York City, April 18, 1967.

Leo L. Beranek, "Noise," *Scientific American*, CCXV (December, 1966), 66–76.

Michael Short, "Noise Expert Demands Less of It," Chicago *Tribune* (via Associated Press), April 23, 1967.

Arnold P. G. Peterson and Ervin E. Gross, Jr., *Handbook of Noise Measurement* (West Concord, Mass.: General Radio Company, 1967), pp. 4–5.

Alan Bell, *Noise—An Occupational Hazard and Public Nuisance* (Geneva: World Health Organization, 1966).

"It's a Historic Boom!" Associated Press dispatch from New York, published in the Chicago *Sun-Times* and elsewhere, November 10, 1967.

L. A. Steinberger, "Navy Carrier's Landing Deck Noisiest Place in the World," North American Newspaper Alliance dispatch from Baltimore, Md., December 14, 1966.

Walter W. Soroka, "Community Noise Surveys," National Conference on Noise as a Public Health Hazard, Washington, D.C., June 13–14, 1968.

Paul B. Ostergaard and Ray Donley, "Background-Noise Levels in Suburban Communities," *J. Acoust. Soc. Am.*, XXXVI (March, 1964), 409–13.

Sir Alan Wilson, and others, *Noise—Final Report* (London: Her Majesty's Stationery Office, 1963), pp. 118–19.

"Marvelous Menace," *Life*, January 31, 1969, p. 60.

Chapter 10   At Home and at Work

William and Allen Raphael, "Quiet, Dammit!" *Pageant*, November, 1967, p. 67.

Alan Bell, *Noise—An Occupational Hazard and Public Nuisance* (Geneva: World Health Organization, 1966), p. 11.

Paul Dunham Close, *Sound Control and Thermal Insulation of Buildings* (New York: Reinhold Publishing Corp., 1966), p. 35.

Lee E. Farr, "Medical Consequences of Environmental Home Noises," *J.A.M.A.*, CCII (October 16, 1967), 171–74.

Lee E. Farr, "The Trauma of Everyday Noise," Meeting of the American Medical Association at Portland, Ore., December 4, 1963, summarized in *Congressional Record*, House, April 21, 1966 (Washington, D.C.), pp. 8,350–51.

Anne Kelley, "Shocking Facts in Bilevel Noise Level," Chicago *Daily News*, undated (1968?).

Joseph Sataloff, "Acoustic Trauma in Children." *Ann. Oto., Rhino., and Laryng.*, LXI (March, 1952), 107–11.

Arnold P. G. Peterson and Ervin E. Gross, Jr., *Handbook of Noise Measurement*, 6th ed. (West Concord, Mass.: General Radio Co., 1967), pp. 119–20.

Close, *Sound Control and Thermal Insulation*, pp. 188–89, 196.

Jerry Gibbons, "Noise Levels of Some Air-Driven Rock Drills," *Noise Control*, November-December, 1960, pp. 247–49.

Robert P. Christman, Herbert H. Jones, and Ronald E. Bales, "Sound-Pressure Levels in the Wood Products Industry," *Noise Control*, September, 1956, pp. 33–39.

Interview with Dr. Kylin in his office at Stockholm, Sweden, April 16, 1968.

Sir Alan Wilson, and others, *Noise—Final Report* (Cmnd. 2056) (London: Her Majesty's Stationery Office, 1963), pp. 98–99.

N. Fleming, "Noise Problems in Factories," *The Control of Noise* (London: Her Majesty's Stationery Office, 1962), p. 235. (Proceedings of a conference held at the National Physical Laboratory on June 26–28, 1961. See Freeth reference, Chapter 9 of this volume.)

George Bugliarello, and others, "Noise pollution—A Review of Its Techno-Sociological and Health Aspects," Report to Resources for the Future, Inc., from the Biotechnology Program, Carnegie-Mellon University, February 1, 1968, Chapter 2.

Herbert H. Jones, "Noise—Its Effects, Measurement and Control." Unpublished.

Bell, *Noise—An Occupational Hazard*, pp. 101–2.

Wilson, *Noise—Final Report*, p. 87.

Industrial Acoustics Co., Inc., 341 Jackson Ave., New York, N.Y. 10054.

Congressional Record, House, August 4, 1966 (Washington, D.C.), p. 17,431.

Nicolas Slonimsky, "Sounds and Psyche," *Med. Opinion & Review,* December, 1968, pp. 38–45.

"Music and Eros," *SK&F Psychiatric Reporter,* undated, p. 3.

Marion Odmark, "Radio Generation Bugging Employers," *Chicago's American,* February 11, 1969.

Sam Blum, "Noise—How Much More Can We Take?" *McCall's,* January, 1967, p. 113.

Interview with Dr. Farr in his office at Berkeley, Calif., on May 12, 1968.

Chapter 11   On the Roads and Rails

Leo L. Beranek, "Street and Air Traffic Noise—And What We Can Do About It," *UNESCO Courier* (special issue on noise), July, 1967.

Herbert R. Hazard, "Propulsion Aspects of Transportation," *Proc. of the I.E.E.E.* (special issue on transportation), LVI (April, 1968), 531.

William W. Seifert, "The Status of Transportation." *Proc. of the I.E.E.E.* (special issue on transportation), LVI (April, 1968), 385–395.

"Chicago Traffic Heavier, Noisier than Ever Before," *Chicago's American,* October 3, 1966; "People in the News: Can't Hear If Cycle's Running," *Chicago's American,* February 14, 1969.

G. L. Bonvallet, "Outdoor Noise—What Is It?" *Proc. Fourth National Noise Abatement Symposium,* Illinois Institute of Technology, Chicago, October 23–24, 1953, pp. 1–9.

Laymon Miller, "Urban Noise—External Sources," Seminar on noise for science writers, New York, April 18, 1967. (See Embleton reference, Chapter 9 of this volume.)

David C. Apps, "Cars, Trucks, and Tractors as Sources," National Conference on Noise as a Public Health Hazard, Washington, D.C., June 13–14, 1968.

David C. Apps, "Automobile Noise," Chapter 31 in Cyril M. Harris, *Handbook of Noise Control* (New York: McGraw-Hill Book Company, 1957).

Lewis S. Goodfriend, "Control of Highway Noise," *Proc. First N.E. Conf. on Urban Planning for Environ. Health*, Tufts University, September 8–10, 1965.

Sir Alan Wilson, and others, *Noise—Final Report* (London: Her Majesty's Stationery Office, 1963), p. 44.

Francis M. Weiner, "Experimental Study of the Airborne Noise Generated by Passenger Automobile Tires," *Noise Control*, July-August, 1960, pp. 161–64.

Interview with Christopher G. Rice in his laboratory at the University of Southampton, April 25, 1968.

Jerome K. Brasch, "Vehicular Traffic Noise Near High-Speed Highways," *Sound and Vibration*, December, 1967, pp. 10–24.

"Noisy Motorcycles Most Popular," *UNESCO Courier*, September, 1967.

P. Hammarfors and A. Kajland, "Sound-Pressure Analyses of Noise from Motor Vehicles," *Acoustica*, XIII (1963), 258–69.

Erland Jonsson and Stefan Sörenson, "Förekomsten av bullerstörningar i samhället (existence of inconvenience through noise in society)," *Nordisk Hygienisk Tidskrift*, XLVIII (1967), 21–34.

William A. Jack, "Noise in Rail Transportation," Chapter 32 in Cyril M. Harris, ed., *Handbook of Noise Control*.

G. L. Bonvallet, "Outdoor Noise—What Is It?" pp. 1–9.

Vincent Salmon, "Noise in Mass Transit Systems," *Stanford Research Institute Journal*, Issue 16, September, 1967, pp. 2–7.

Seifert, "The Status of Transportation."

U.S. Bureau of the Census, *Pocket Data Book, U.S.A., 1967* (Washington, D.C.: Government Printing Office, 1966), p. 289.

Chapter 12   In the Air

William W. Seifert, "The Status of Transportation." *Proc. of the I.E.E.E.* (special issue on transportation), LVI (April, 1968), 385–395.

John O. Powers, "Airborne Transportation Noise—Its Origin and Abatement," Acoustical Society of America, 74th Meeting, Miami Beach, Florida, November 14–17, 1967.

"The Racket That Won't Go Away," *Business Week*, March 16, 1968, pp. 130–34.

Air Transport World, October and November, 1968, and February, 1969.

Joe Cappo, "The Jet Decade: History's Fastest," Chicago *Daily News*, October 25, 1968, pp. 3–4.

"Commercial Jets and Their Engines," *Air Transport World*, VI (February, 1969), 40.

Mabley's Report, *Chicago's American*, September 18, 1967, p. 3.

Aircraft Noise Abatement, Hearings before the Subcommittee on Transportation and Aeronautics of the Committee on Interstate and Foreign Commerce, House of Representatives, 90th Congress, First and Second Sessions, on H.R. 3400 and H.R. 14146; November 14, 15, 21; December 5–6, 1967; and March 19–20, 1968, pp. 15, 55.

Robert Sherrill, "The Jet Noise Is Getting Awful," *The New York Times* Magazine, January 14, 1968, pp. 24–25ff.

"Homes At the End of a Runway," London *Evening News*, April 24, 1968.

Federal Aviation Administration, Office of Noise Abatement, "The Aircraft/Airport Noise Problem and Federal Government Policy," December 15, 1967, p. 4.

Dorn C. McGrath, "Compatible Land Use," A.S.C.E./A.O.C.I., Joint Specialty Conference in Airport Terminal Facilities, Houston, Texas, April 14, 1967.

K. N. Stevens, "A Survey of Background and Aircraft Noise in Communities Near Airports" Washington, D.C.: National Advisory Committee for Aeronautics, Technical Note 3379, December, 1954.

Leo L. Beranek, Karl D. Kryter, and Laymon N. Miller, "Reaction of People to Exterior Aircraft Noise," *Noise Control*, September, 1959, pp. 287–95ff.

Alexander Cohen and Howard E. Ayer, "Some Observations of Noise at Airports and in the Surrounding Community," *Ind. Hyg. J.*, March-April, 1964, pp. 139–50.

Stanley R. Mohler, and others, "Aircraft Noise Measurements Near Washington National Airport," F.A.A., Washington, D.C., January 19, 1967 (unpublished).

Federal Housing Administration, *A Study—Insulating Houses from Aircraft Noise* (Washington, D.C.: Government Printing Office, 1966), Attachment A.

Leo L. Beranek, "Technical and Legal Factors Concerning Aircraft Noise," National Conference on Noise as a Public Health Hazard, Washington, D.C., June 13–14, 1968.

William J. Galloway, "Chairman's Introductory Remarks, Panel IV," National Conference on Noise as a Public Health Hazard, Washington, D.C., June 13–14, 1968.

Aircraft Noise Problems, Hearings before Subcommittees of the Committee on Interstate and Foreign Commerce, House of Representatives, 86th and 87th Congresses, Washington, D.C., 1959–1962, pp. 579–80, 582–83.

Federal Aviation Agency, *A Citizen's Guide to Aircraft Noise* (Washington, D.C.: Government Printing Office, 1963), p. 13.

Nicholas E. Golovin, "Noise and the Government," Science Writer's Seminar on Noise, New York, April 18, 1967. (See Embleton reference, Chapter 9 of this volume.)

Bo K. O. Lundberg, "The Acceptable Nominal Sonic Boom Overpressure in S.S.T. Operation," National Conference on Noise as a Public Health Hazard, Washington, D.C., June 13–14, 1968.

Karl D. Kryter, "Sonic Booms from Supersonic Transport," *Science,* CLXIII (January 24, 1969), 359–67.

William Hines, "A Victory Over the Sonic Boom," Chicago *Daily News,* January 13, 1969, pp. 3–4.

Henning E. von Gierke, "Effects of Sonic Boom on People: Review and Outlook," *J. Acoust. Soc. Amer.,* XXXIX, (1966), S43-S50 (Part 2).

H. W. Carlson and F. E. McLean, "The Sonic Boom," *Int. Sci. Technol.,* LV (July, 1966). Reprinted in *Sonic Boom Experiments at Edwards Air Force Base* (Arlington, Va.: National Sonic Boom Evaluation Office, 1967).

Galloway, "Chairman's Introductory Remarks."

Bo Lundberg, "The Menace of the Sonic Boom to Society and Civil Aviation," Fourth International Congress for Noise Abatement, Baden-Baden, Germany, May 11–15, 1966.

Kryter, "Sonic Booms."

Harvey H. Hubbard and Domenic J. Maglieri, "Noise Considerations in the Design and Operation of the Supersonic Transport," *Noise Control,* July-August, 1961, pp. 4–10.

Aircraft Noise Abatement, Hearings, p. 131.

John N. Cole and Robert T. England, "Evaluation of Noise Problems Anticipated with Future V.T.O.L. Aircraft," AMRL-TR-66-245, Aerospace Medical Research Laboratories, Wright-Patterson A.F.B., Ohio, 1967.

Werner Fricke and William Squire, "External Noise Fields of a Boost-Glide Hypersonic Vehicle," 28th Symposium on Shock,

Vibration, and Associated Environments, Washington, D.C., February 9, 1960.

"Airborne Noise—The Inside Story," *Noise Measurement* (General Radio Co.), (July, 1967), 1, 3.

Robert L. Wick, Jr., Lester B. Roberts, and William F. Ashe, "Light Aircraft Noise Problems," *Aerospace Med.*, XXXIV (December, 1963), 1133–37.

Jerry V. Tobias, "Cockpit Noise Intensity: Three Aerial Application (Crop-Dusting) Aircraft," *J. Speech Hrg. Res.*, June, 1968.

PART THREE   What You Can Do About It

Chapter 13   Keeping It Out of Your Ears

The New Yorker, September 10, 1966, quoted in Barbara J. Culliton, "Noise Menace Threatens Man," *Science News,* XC (October 15, 1966), 297–99.

Arthur Schopenhauer, *Essays,* translated by T. Bailey Saunder (London: George Allen & Unwin, 1951).

Millicent Brower, "Noise Pollution: A Growing Menace," *Saturday Review,* May 27, 1967, p. 17.

R. J. Minney, *Recollections of George Bernard Shaw* (Englewood Cliffs, N.J.: Prentice-Hall, Inc., 1969).

Dan Morganroth, "Noise Pollution: How We Can Solve the Problem Now," *Family Weekly,* September 15, 1968, p. 12.

Don C. Seitz, *Joseph Pulitzer, His Life and Letters* (New York: Simon and Schuster, Inc., 1924), pp. 13–15.

W. A. Swanberg, *Pulitzer* (New York: Charles Scribner's Sons, 1967).

George Horne, "Elizabeth 2 Covers 730 Miles on Maiden Voyage to New York," *The New York Times,* May 5, 1969.

"Ear Plugs or Pills, Advice to Sleepers," The London *Times,* April 27, 1968.

J. Zwislocki, "Ear Protection," *The Laryngoscope,* LXVIII (March, 1958), 486–97.

C. G. Rice and R. R. A. Coles, "Design Factors and Use of Ear Protection," *Brit. J. Ind. Med.,* XXIII (1966), 194–203.

R. R. A. Coles, "Control of Industrial Noise Through Personal Protection," National Conference on Noise as a Public Health Hazard, Washington, D.C., June 13–14, 1968.

Carl Zenz and Byron A. Berg, "Another Tool for Hearing Con-servation—An Improved Protector," *Am. Ind. Hyg. Assn. J.*, XXVI (March-April, 1965), 187–88.

W. I. Acton, "Effects of Ear Protection on Communication," *Ann. Occup. Hyg.*, X (1967), 423–29.

John L. Fletcher, private communication dated July 18, 1968.

Meyer S. Fox, "Noise Induced Hearing Loss—Role of Physician in Workmen's Compensation Cases," Sixth Congress on Environ-mental Health, American Medical Association, Chicago, April 28–29, 1969.

"Occupational Hearing Loss and High Frequency Thresholds," *J.A.M.A.*, CCI (July 10, 1967), 144.

W. Dixon Ward, "The Identification and Treatment of Noise-Induced Hearing Loss," *Ololaryng. Clinic N. Amer.*, February, 1969.

M. T. Summar and John L. Fletcher, "Long-Term Industrial Hearing Conservation Results," *Arch. Otolaryng.*, LXXXII (De-cember, 1965), 618–21.

Andrew Hosey and Charles H. Powell, eds., *Industrial Noise—A Guide to Its Evaluation and Control*, Public Health Service Publication No. 1572 (Washington, D.C.: Government Printing Office, 1967).

"Guide for Conservation of Hearing in Noise," *Trans. of Amer. Acad. of Ophthal. & Otolaryng.* (rev.), 1964.

Anonymous, *Noise and the Worker* (London: Her Majesty's Stationery Office, 1963).

Alexander Cohen, "Physiological and Psychological Effects of Noise on Man," *J. Boston Soc. Civ. Eng.*, LII (January, 1965), 70–95.

J. D. Ratcliff, "Quiet, Please!" *Reader's Digest*, December, 1961, pp. 123–26.

Mel Brdlik, "Ultrasonics: The Quiet Boom," *Dun's Review*, September, 1968.

Chapter 14   Building for Quiet

Paul Dunham Close, *Sound Control and Thermal Insulation of Buildings* (New York: Reinhold Publishing Corp., 1966), pp. 188–89, p. 196.

A Study—Insulating House from Aircraft Noise, H.U.D.T.S.-19

(Washington, D.C.: Government Printing Office, 1966), pp. 44–45.

"Indoor Noise Diminished by Outdoor Furnace," Chicago *Tribune,* January 20, 1968.

Leo L. Beranek, "Noise," *Sci. Am.,* CCXV (December, 1966), 66–76.

Construction Lending Guide, Section 106 (Sound Control) (Chicago: U.S. Savings & Loan League, 221 N. LaSalle St.).

"Wrap Yourself in Quiet," *Popular Mechanics,* September, 1965.

Sound Advice—A Guide to Controlling Noise in Your Home (New York: The Good Housekeeping Institute, 1967).

Raymond Berendt and George E. Winzer, *Sound Insulation of Wall, Floor, and Door Constructions,* National Bureau of Standards Monograph 77 (Washington, D.C.: Government Printing Office, 1964).

R. A. LaCosse, "Sound Materials Reduce Noise Flow," *Sound Ideas,* February (no year), pp. 13–15.

Noise Control with Insulation Board (4th ed.) (Chicago: Insulation Board Institute, 111 W. Washington St., 1967).

D. H. Lauriente and W. L. M. Phillips, "Architectural Applications of Lead for Noise Control," *J.R.A.I.C./L'R.A.C.* (Canada), May, 1966, pp. 50–53.

"Thin lead sheets, produced by a new process, are being used to deaden sound in buildings and machines," *Ind. Res.,* November, 1967, p. 47.

Acousta-Pane data sheets supplied by Amerada Glass Co., 2001 Greenleaf Ave., Elk Grove, Ill. 60007.

Data supplied by O. F. Wenzler, Manager Sales Technical Service, Libbey Owens Ford Glass Co., 811 Madison Ave., Toledo, Ohio 43624.

Construction Lending Guide.

Sound Advice.

Insulation Board . . . a 50 Year Start on Tomorrow (Chicago: Insulation Board Institute, 111 W. Washington St., 1964).

H. J. Purkis, "Sound Insulation and Absorption," Paper D-4, in *The Control of Noise,* Proceedings of a Conference held at the National Physical Laboratory on June 26–28, 1961 (London: Her Majesty's Stationery Office, 1962).

Close, *Sound Control and Thermal Insulation,* p. 192.

Sound Advice.

Robert W. Leonard, "Heating and Ventilating System Noise,"

Chapter 27 in Cyril M. Harris, ed., *Handbook of Noise Control* (New York: McGraw-Hill Book Company, 1957).

Close, *Sound Control and Thermal Insulation*, p. 194.

"Home 'First Aid' for Noisy Pipes," Chicago *Daily News*, January 26, 1968.

Close, *Sound Control and Thermal Insulation*, p. 194.

A Strategy for a Livable Environment, A Report to the Secretary of Health, Education, and Welfare by The Task Force on Environmental Health and Related Problems (Washington, D.C.: Government Printing Office, 1967), p. 18.

Chapter 15   Quiet by Design: At Home and at Work

Luman H. Long, ed., *The World Almanac* (New York: Newspaper Enterprise Association, Inc., 1968), p. 759.

"International Rise in Suicide," *Statistical Bulletin* (Metropolitan Life Insurance Co., New York), XLVIII (March, 1967), 4–7.

"A Quiet, Civilized Way to Mow," *Lawn Care Magazine* (O. M. Scott & Sons, Marysville, Ohio), September-October, 1968, p. 5.

Roderick Nordell, "Bubbling Vibrating Frequencies," *Christian Science Monitor*, April 12, 1968.

"Introducing the most proven NEW handpiece on the Market, the DENTISPLY BORDEN AIROROT II with Silencer Cartridge," Dentists' Supply Co. of N.Y., York, Pa.

"Garbage Can Noise Control," *Sound and Vibration*, February, 1969, pp. 6.8.

Duane Carlson, "Noise Control Program Is Quiet Success," *Mod. Hosp.*, CV (December, 1965), 82–85.

Fortune, November, 1967, p. 165.

"The First Quiet Portable Compressor," *Sound and Vibration*, III (May, 1969), 6–8.

Douglas Robinson, "New Cutter Is Tested to Enable Con Edison to Dig More Quietly," *The New York Times*, March 25, 1967, p. 49.

Laymon Miller, "Urban Noise—External Sources," Seminar for science writers, New York, April 18, 1967.

"Briefs," *Wall Street Journal*, April 4, 1968, p. 1.

Jack Mabley, "A Silent Drive for Progress," *Chicago Today*, I: 27 (May, 1969), p. 4.

Barbara J. Culliton, "Noise Menace Threatens Man," *Sci. News,* XC (October 15, 1966), 299.

James H. Botsford, "Control of Industrial Noise Through Engineering," *Noise as a Public Health Hazard,* Proceedings of the conference, A.S.H.A., Report 4 (Washington, D.C.: American Speech and Hearing Assn., 1969).

Private communications.

Ray Donley, "Non-Transportational Noise Control," Sixth Congress on Environmental Health, American Medical Association, April 28–29, 1969, Drake Hotel, Chicago.

Tony Embleton, Discussion at seminar for science writers held at the New Yorker Hotel on April 18, 1967, and co-sponsored by the American Institute of Physics and the National Association of Science Writers with the support of the National Science Foundation.

William C. Sperry and Guy J. Sanders, "Quiet Blades for 18-inch Rotary Type Power Lawn Mowers," *Noise Control,* May, 1959, pp. 162–67 (26–31).

Lewis S. Goodfriend, "Control of Noise Through Propaganda and Education," National Conference on Noise as a Public Health Hazard, Washington, D.C., June 13–14, 1968.

Interview with Dr. Alexander Cohen in his office in Cincinnati, February 14, 1968.

Leo L. Beranek, *Noise Reduction* (New York: McGraw-Hill Book Company, 1960).

R. E. Jelinek and K. S. Nordby, "Achieving Noise Reduction Economically," *Acous. Soc. Am.,* November 14–17, 1967, Miami Beach, Fla.

Sir Alan Wilson, and others, *Noise—Final Report* (Cmnd. 2056) (London: Her Majesty's Stationery Office, 1963).

Interview with Pierre Lenard in his office at O.N.E.R.A. near Paris, France, April 23, 1968.

Botsford, "Control of Industrial Noise."

W. I. Acton, T. W. Bull, R. A. Hore, and K. K. Schwarz, "Noise reduction in the circulating water pumphouse at Blyth 'B' power station," Paper 5, *Proc. Symp. Noise from Power Plant Equip.* (London: Institution of Mechanical Engineers, 1966–1967).

Interview with W. I. Acton in his office in Southampton, April 24, 1968.

Interview with Robert Crawford in his office at Southampton, April 24, 1968.

R. Crawford, "Noise of Rotating Spindles and Bobbins in a Textile Machine," *J. Sound. Vib.*, V (1967), 317–29.

W. Taylor, A. Clyne, and N. Jordan, "Noise Levels of a Wide Jute Loom With and Without Plastic Parts," *J. Textile Inst.*, LVIII (September, 1967), 377–84.

G. Berry, "Noise of Gears and Ball-Bearings," Paper C-1, *The Control of Noise*, Proceedings of a conference held at the National Physical Laboratory on June 26–28, 1961 (London: Her Majesty's Stationery Office, 1962).

E. M. Cantwell, "Noise Control in Underground Mines," Amer. Ind. Hyg. Conf., May, 1968, St. Louis, Mo.

Herman Seelbach, Jr. and Frederic M. Oran, "What to Do About Cooling Water Noise," *Htg., Piping, and Air Cond.* (reprint), 1967.

Frederic Oran, Herman Seelbach, and Robert Hochheiser, "Control of Centrifugal Fan Noise in Industrial Applications," *Air Cond., Htg., and Vent.* (reprint), 1967.

Ellis E. Singer, "Noise Is More Than a Nuisance," *Nat. Safety News* (reprint), 1967.

Andrew D. Hosey and Charles H. Powell, eds., *Industrial Noise—A Guide to Its Evaluation and Control*, P.H.S. Pub. No. 1572 (Washington, D.C.: Government Printing Office, 1967), Chapter 10.

Chapter 16 . . . On the Ground and In the Air

David C. Apps, "Cars, Trucks, and Tractors as Sources," National Conference on Noise as a Public Health Hazard, Washington, D.C., June 13–14, 1968.

Interview with Christopher G. Rice in his office at Southampton, April 24, 1968.

Alexander Cohen, "Location-Design Control of Transportation Noise," *J. Urban Planning and Dev. Div.*, A.S.C.E., XCIII (December, 1967), 63–86.

William S. Gouse, Jr., "Steam-Powered Automobiles Should Come Back," *Engineer*, IX (May-June, 1968), 22–26.

Editorial, *J.A.M.A.*, December 19, 1966.

"Exhaust-free," *Med. Trib.*, January 30, 1967, p. 13.

"Diesels Calmed by Foam," *Sci. News*, XCIII (March 23, 1968), 286.

Interview with Lee E. Farr, M.D. in his office at Berkeley, Calif., May 12, 1968.

"Clickety Clack Removed from Rail Travel," *Sci. Dimension,* I (April, 1969), 4–6 (National Research Council of Canada).

Peter A. Franken, "Transportation Vehicle Noise Control: Application and Acceptability," Sixth Congress on Environmental Health, American Medical Association, April 28–29, 1969, Drake Hotel, Chicago.

Civil Aviation Research and Development: An Assessment of Federal Government Involvement (Washington: Aeronaut. Space Eng. Bd., Nat. Acad. Eng., 2101 Constitution Ave., 1968).

William E. Burrows, "Hush-Hush Agent Helps Airlines Beat Noise Ban," *The New York Times,* October 20, 1967, p. 49.

Aircraft Noise Abatement, Hearings before the Subcommittee on Transportation and Aeronautics of the Committee on Interstate and Foreign Commerce, on H.R. 3400 and H.R. 14146, House of Representatives, Serial No. 90–35 (Washington, D.C.: Government Printing Office, 1968), pp. 36–37, 86.

Aircraft Noise Problems, Hearings before Subcommittees of the Committee on Interstate and Foreign Commerce, House of Representatives (Washington, D.C.: Government Printing Office, 1963), pp. 593–606.

John M. Tyler, "Control of Aircraft Noise at the Source," National Conference on Noise as a Public Health Hazard, Washington, D.C., June 13–14, 1968.

M. V. Lowson, "Reduction of Compressor Noise Radiation," *J. Acous. Soc. Amer.,* XLIII (1968), 37–50.

D. Chestnutt, "Jet Engine Inlet Noise Control," *Sound and Vib.,* II (December, 1968), 10–14.

R. A. Mangiarotty, "Acoustic Lining Concepts and Materials for Engine Ducts," *Acous. Soc. Amer.,* Philadelphia, Pa., April 8–11, 1969.

News Release No. 69–45 for April 8, 1969, McDonnell Douglas Corp., Santa Monica, Calif.

Robert Lindsey, "Engineers Eavesdrop on Boeing Jumbo Jet," *The New York Times,* March 2, 1969, p. 82.

Aircraft Noise Abatement, p. 72.

" 'Quiet' Plane Cost Queried," Chicago *Daily News,* May 14, 1969 (via United Press International).

"Noise Overboard," *Sci. News,* VC (March 1, 1969), 215.

"Design Out the Boom," *Ind. Res.,* August, 1968, p. 13.

Aircraft Noise Problems, pp. 362–63.

Aircraft Noise Problems, p. 600.

News release from The White House for March 22, 1967.

Jesse C. Burt, *Life & Health*, LXXXIV (March 30–31, 1960), 9.

Aircraft Noise Abatement, pp. 73–74.

Report of the Massachusetts Port Authority Relative to Noise Abatement and Rules Affecting the Health, Quiet, and Safey of New York, Chicago, and Washington Communities Served by Airports, Senate No. 1298. (Boston: The Commonwealth of Massachusetts, 1967), p. 25.

Cohen, "Location-Design Control," pp. 70–71, 73.

Fritz Ingerslev and Christian Svane, "Preliminary Studies of Sound Propagation in the Lower Layers of the Atmosphere," Sixth Int. Cong. Acous., Tokyo, Japan, August 21–28, 1968.

Interview in Volrath Holmboe's office at Bromma, Stockholm, Sweden, April 17, 1968.

Bo Lundberg, "The Acceptable Nominal Sonic Boom Overpressure in S.S.T. Operation," National Conference on Noise as a Public Health Hazard, Washington, D.C., June 13–14, 1968.

Interview in Bo Lundberg's office at Bromma, Stockholm, Sweden, April 17, 1968.

Jack Mabley, "Futuristic Plan for Chicago—and No Autos," *Chicago's American*, December 14, 1966.

Lewis S. Goodfriend, "Control of Highway Noise," *Proc. First New Eng. Conf. Urban Plng. for Environ. Health*, Tufts University, Medford, Mass., September 8–10, 1965.

Chapter 17   The People vs. Noise

Leo L. Beranek, "Noise," *Sci. Am.*, CCXV (December, 1966), 2–11.

Ernest S. Kettelson, "Inverse Condemnation of Air Easements," *Real Prop., Prob. and Trust J.*, III (Spring, 1968), 97–105.

Aram Glorig, "Industrial Noise and the Worker," National Conference on Noise as a Public Health Hazard, Washington, D.C., June 13–14, 1968.

Meyer S. Fox, "Noise-Induced Hearing Loss—Role of Physician in Workmen's Compensation Cases," American Medical Association's Sixth Congress on Environmental Health, Chicago, April 28–29, 1969.

Lewis S. Goodfriend, "Federal Regulation of Industrial Noise," *Sound and Vib.,* III (February, 1969), 11.

Lewis S. Goodfriend, "Time Extension on Federal Noise Regulation," *Sound and Vib.,* III (March, 1969), 17.

Interview with Surg. Comm. R.R.A. Coles in his office at Southampton, April 24, 1968.

Interview with Dr. Bengt Kylin in his office at Stockholm, Sweden, April 16, 1968.

"Soviet Tentative Standards and Regulations for Restricting Noise in Industry," compiled by I. I. Slavin, translated by Charles R. Williams, *Noise Control,* September, 1959, pp. 44–49ff., 308–13ff.

Heinrich Oels, "Noise Abatement and Measures to Combat Pollution of the Atmosphere," Monograph No. 26, Social Policy in Germany Series, published by the Federal Ministry of Labour and the Social Structure (Essen: Druckhaus Sachsenstrasse, 1964).

Alan Bell, *Noise, An Occupational Hazard and Public Nuisance* (Geneva: World Health Organization, 1966).

Richard V. Waterhouse, "Noise-Control Requirements in Building Codes," in Cyril M. Harris, *Handbook of Noise Control* (New York: McGraw-Hill Book Company, 1957), p. 40–1.

"Proposed Local Law Int. No. 436," New York: *The City Record,* VC (June 27, 1967), 2–147.

"Kennedy Favors Stronger City Noise Controls," *The New* York: McGraw-Hill Book Company, 1957), pp. 40–1.

Martin Hirschorn, "The New York City Noise Code" (Letter), *Sound and Vib.,* II (November, 1968), 6.

"Building code updated to keep Oak Park high standards," *Oak Leaves,* XCII (March 5, 1969), 1.

Paul Dunham Close, *Sound Control and Thermal Insulation of Buildings* (New York: Reinhold Pub. Corp., 1966), p. 196.

Private communication, dated February 20, 1968.

Residential Standards, Canada, 1965 (Ottawa: National Research Council), 3rd printing, including all corrections and revisions to December, 1967.

"Sound Insulation and Noise Reduction," Chapter 3 of *British Standard Code of Practice* (London: British Standards House, 1960).

Quality of Dwellings and Housing Areas (Stockholm: The National Swedish Institute for Building Research, 1967).

Waterhouse, "Noise-Control Requirements," pp. 40–3, 40–6.
Oels, "Noise Abatement and Measures to Combat Pollution,"
pp. 11–12.

Chapter 18   Cities vs. Noise

H. Wiethaup, "The Noise Nuisance and the Law," *Documenta
Geigy* (special issue on noise) (Basle: J. R. Geigy S. A., 1967),
pp. 7–8.
   Noise Abatement Act, 1960, 8 & 9 Eliz. 2, Chapter 68 (London:
Her Majesty's Stationery Office).
   Sir Alan Wilson, and others, *Noise—Final Report* (London: Her
Majesty's Stationery Office, 1963, reprinted 1966).
   Interview with Gordon L. Carey, Senior Executive Officer,
Ministry of Housing and Local Government, in his office at
London, April 26, 1968.
   Circulaire du Novembre 17, 1966, relative aux modifications à
apporter au règlement sanitaire departemental type, Article 103
bis (Paris: Ministère des Affaires Sociales).
   "French Move to Quiet Unnecessary Noises," Chicago *Sun-
Times* (via United Press International), December 27, 1966.
   Interview with Mlle. Germaine Moreau, Civil Administrator,
Environmental Hygiene, in her office at Paris, April 23, 1968.
   "The Campaign Against Noise in France," Information Sheet
No. 1069, April, 1968 (New York: Ambassade de France, Service
de Presse et d'Information).
   "More Cities Enact Noise-Control Laws, But It's Still Noisy,"
The Wall Street Journal, February 7, 1968, p. 1.
   James J. Kaufman, "Control of Noise Through Laws and Regu-
lations," National Conference on Noise as a Public Health Haz-
ard, Washington, D.C., June 13–14, 1968.
   Municipal Code of Chicago, Chapters 10.5, 27, 36, 99, 150, 188.
   Code of Ordinances, City of Memphis, Tenn., Chapter 24.
   "Memphis Curbing Noise Pollution," *The New York Times,*
May 18, 1969.
   "Anti-Noise Crackdown Works Quiet Wonder," Memphis *Com-
mercial Appeal,* December 9, 1965.
   "Quiet Is Rule in Memphis," *Manchester Guardian,* undated,
courtesy of M. Rodda.
   "Experts Combat São Paulo Noise," *The New York Times*
(via Associated Press), March 18, 1969.

G. L. Fuchs, "Cordoba (Argentina) Takes Noise Abatement by the Horns," *UNESCO Courier,* July, 1967, pp. 21–22.

"Rio winning its battle on street noise." Chicago *Sun-Times,* January 9, 1970.

"Wrong Note Struck as Bells Drown Out Anti-noise Defender," *The New York Times* (via Associated Press), January 28, 1969.

"8 Decibels Too Many" (with picture), *UNESCO Courier,* July, 1967.

Philip Shabecoff, "Variety of Noises Assails Tokyoites," *The New York Times,* September 8, 1968, p. 16.

Municipal Code of Chicago.

R. S. Forster, "Legislation Regarding Noise," in *The Control of Noise* (London: Her Majesty's Stationery Office, 1962), p. 328.

Constantin Stramentov, "The Architects of Silence," *UNESCO Courier,* July, 1967.

Martin Hirschorn, "The New York City Noise Code" (Letter) *Sound and Vib.,* II (November, 1968), 6.

"Motor Vehicle Noise Control," *Noise Control,* July, 1959, pp. 31–35 (231–35).

Heinrich Oels, "Noise Abatement and Measures to Combat Pollution of the Atmosphere," Monograph No. 26, Social Policy in Germany Series, published by the Federal Ministry of Labour and the Social Structure (Essen: Druckhaus Sachsenstrasse, 1964).

Martin Grützmacher, "Traffic Noise Problems in Germany," *Noise Control,* November, 1959, pp. 7–12ff., 339–44ff.

Interview with Mlle. Moreau.

"The Campaign Against Noise in France."

"Road Traffic: The Motor Vehicles Regulations, 1968, *Statutory Instruments,* 1968, No. 362 (London: Her Majesty's Stationery Office, 1968).

Gützmacher, "Traffic Noise Problems in Germany."

Oels, "Noise Abatement and Measures to Combat Pollution."

Theodore R. Kupferman, "Noise: The Need for Legislation and Technology," *Engineer, VII* (Autumn, 1966), 6.

William Bronson, "Ear Pollution," *Cry California* (Fall, 1967), p. 30.

Interview with Pierre Lenard in his office at O.N.E.R.A. Headquarters, outside of Paris, April 23, 1968.

The Wall Street Journal, February 7, 1968, p. 1.

Chapter 19 Legal Anti-Aircraft Weapons

James J. Kaufman, "Control of Noise Through Laws and Regulations," National Conference on Noise as a Public Health Hazard, Washington, D.C., June 13–14, 1968.

Ernest S. Kettelson, "Inverse Condemnation of Air Easements," *Real Prop., Prob. and Trust J.*, III (Spring, 1968), 97–105.

Item in *Rodale's Health Bulletin*, VI (March 9, 1968), 1.

Morris L. Ernst and David Loth, "Science and the Law," in *The 1969 Britannica Yearbook of Science and the Future* (Chicago: Encyclopaedia Britannica, 1968), pp. 87–88.

"Sonic booms or bangs," *Documenta Geigy* (special issue on noise), 1967, p. 6.

Sir Alan Wilson, and others, *Noise—Final Report* (London: Her Majesty's Stationery Office, 1963), pp. 17, 65, 67.

Communication from West German Consulate in Chicago.

Lyman M. Tondel, Jr., "Noise Litigation at Public Airports," *J. Air Law and Comm.*, XXXII (Dallas: South Methodist University School of Law, 1966), 387–407.

Charles M. Haar, "Airport Noise and the Urban Dweller," Practicing Law Institute Urban Renewal Seminar, New York, May 10, 1968.

Ezra J. Mishan, *The Costs of Economic Growth* (New York: Frederick A. Praeger, Inc., 1967), pp. 70, 174.

Haar, "Airport Noise."

Chapter 20 Conclusion: Make Yourself Heard!

Sam Blum, "Noise, How Much More Can We Take?" *McCall's*, January, 1967, p. 49.

David Binder, "Pilots Agree to Fly Higher Over Home of a Protester," *The New York Times*, March 1, 1967, p. 45.

John Connell, address at the International Congress for Noise Abatement, Salzburg, May 16–18, 1962.

Interview with John Connell at London, April 29, 1968.

O. Schenker-Sprüngli, "Down with Decibels!" *UNESCO Courier*, July, 1967.

Philip H. Dougherty, "Group on 6th Avenue Wants Muffling of Noisy Machines," *The New York Times*, May 13, 1965, p. 39.

"One Year Later, Progress Report" (New York: Citizens for a Quieter City, Inc., 1968).

Evert Clark, "Airports Forsake Anti-Noise Group," *The New York Times*, February 8, 1968.

APPENDIX D

GLOSSARY

Adapted from *Glossary of Terms Frequently Used Concerning Noise Pollution* and *Glossary of Terms Frequently Used in Acoustics*, with the permission of the American Institute of Physics.

$$((((((((((\;\cdot\;))))))))))$$

A-SCALE SOUND LEVEL (dBA)   The A-scale sound level is a quantity, in *decibels*, read from a standard *sound-level meter* that is switched to the weighting scale labeled "A". The A-scale discriminates against the lower *frequencies* according to a relationship approximating the auditory sensitivity of the human ear at moderate sound levels. The A-scale sound level measures approximately the relative "noisiness" or "annoyance" of many common sounds. See also *perceived noise level*.

ACOUSTICS   Acoustics is the science of *sound*, including its production, transmission, and effects (on people and devices).

ANALYSIS   The analysis of a *noise* generally refers to the composition of the noise into various frequency bands, such as *octaves, third octaves*, etc.

ANECHOIC ROOM   An anechoic room is a room whose boundaries (walls, ceiling, floor) absorb effectively all the sound incident on them, thereby affording essentially *free-field* (echo-free) conditions.

ARTICULATION INDEX (AI)   The articulation index is a numerically calculated measure of the intelligibility of transmitted or processed speech. It takes into account the limitations of the transmission path and the *background noise.*

AUDIOGRAM   An audiogram is a graph showing *hearing loss* as a function of frequency.

AUDIOMETER   An audiometer is an instrument for measuring hearing sensitivity.

BACKGROUND NOISE   Background noise is the total of all noise in a system or situation, independent of the presence of the desired signal. For example, in a living room the desired signal may consist of speech from conversation or from a television set. The background noise may come from room air conditioning, outside traffic, conversations in adjacent rooms, or other sources not directly related to the desired signal.

C-SCALE SOUND LEVEL (dB-C)   The C-scale sound level is a quantity, in decibels, read from a standard sound-level meter that is switched to the weighting scale labeled "C." The C-scale weights the frequencies between 70 Hz and 4000 Hz uniformly, but discriminates somewhat against frequencies below and above these limits. C-scale measurements are essentially the same as overall *sound-pressure levels,* which require no discrimination at any frequency.

COCKTAIL PARTY EFFECT   Anyone who has ever attended a cocktail party is aware of the fact that as people gather and time progresses, the noise level in the room gets louder and louder until finally the room is quite noisy indeed. By our usual notions of masking, it should be almost impossible to understand any of the conversation, yet we all know that people gather together in groups of two or more and carry on quite satisfactory conversations. This means that a human being is able in some way to focus his attention upon a desired source of sound, and to some extent ignore other masking sounds that may be present in the environment. This particular effect has been called the "cocktail party effect," and applies to any number of varied situations.

DAMAGE-RISK CRITERIA (HEARING-CONSERVATION CRITERIA) Damage-risk criteria are recommended maximum noise levels that for a given pattern of exposure, if not exceeded, should minimize the risk of damage to the ears of persons exposed to the noise.

DAMPING Damping is the dissipation of energy with time or distance. The term is generally applied to the attenuation of sound in a structure owing to the internal sound-dissipative properties of the structure or owing to the addition of sound-dissipative materials.

DEAD ROOM A dead room is a room that is characterized by an unusually large amount of sound absorption.

DECIBEL The decibel is a logarithmic unit of measure of sound pressure (or power) calculated according to a formula (e.g., see *sound-pressure level*). Zero on the decibel scale corresponds to a standardized reference pressure (0.0002 *Microbar*) or sound power (10^{-12} watt). Decibel is abbreviated dB.

DIFFUSE SOUND FIELD A diffuse sound field is one in which the time average of the mean-square sound-pressure level is the same everywhere and the flow of sound energy is equally probable in all directions.

DUCT LINING OR WRAPPING A duct lining or wrapping is usually a sheet of porous material placed on the inner or outer wall(s) of a duct to introduce sound attenuation and heat insulation. It is often used in air-conditioning systems. Linings are more effective in attenuating sound that travels inside along the length of a duct, while wrappings are more effective in preventing sound from being radiated from the duct sidewalls into surrounding spaces.

FILTER   A filter is a device that transmits certain frequency components of the signal (sound or electrical) incident upon it, and rejects other frequency components of the incident signal.

FREQUENCY   The frequency of a sine wave (of sound or electricity) is the number of times it repeats itself in each second. In *acoustics*, the unit of frequency is the cycle per second. In most European countries the cycle per second is called the hertz (Hz), and this term has recently been adopted in the United States.

Audio Frequency
An audio frequency is any frequency corresponding to a normal audible sound wave. Audio frequencies range roughly from 15 to 20,000 cycles per second.

Infrasonic Frequency
An infrasonic frequency is a frequency lying below the audio-frequency range. Vibrations in this frequency range can be felt but not heard. They have been used to produce unusual theatrical effects.

Natural Frequency
The natural frequency of a system is the frequency of free oscillation of the system. If a system has many degrees of freedom, there will be as many natural frequencies as there are degrees of freedom.

Ultrasonic Frequency
An ultrasonic frequency is a frequency lying above the audio-frequency range. Thus it extends from roughly 20,000 cycles per second upward.

HARMONIC   A harmonic is a sinusoidal quantity having a frequency that is an integral multiple of the *fundamental frequency*. For example, the first harmonic is the fundamental; the second harmonic has a frequency that is double that of the fundamental, and so forth.

HEARING LOSS (HEARING LEVEL) FOR SPEECH   Hearing loss for speech is the difference in decibels between the speech levels at which the average normal ear and the defective ear, respectively, reach the same intelligibility, which is usually set at fifty percent.

HEARING LOSS (HEARING LEVEL, HEARING THRESHOLD LEVEL)   The hearing loss of an ear at a specified frequency is the amount, in decibels, by which the threshold of audibility for that ear exceeds a standard audiometric threshold. Hearing loss and deafness are both legitimate qualitative terms for describing the medical condition of a moderate or severe impairment of hearing, respectively. Hearing level, however, should only be used to designate a quantitative measure of the deviation of the hearing threshold from a prescribed standard.

INVERSE-SQUARE LAW   The inverse-square law describes that acoustic situation where the mean-square sound pressure changes in inverse proportion to the square of the distance from the source. Under this condition the sound-pressure level decreases 6 decibels with each doubling of distance from the source. See also *spherical divergence*.

JET NOISE   Jet noise is the noise produced by the exhaust of a jet into its surrounding atmosphere. It is generally associated with the turbulence generated along the interface between the jet stream and the atmosphere.

LEVEL   In acoustics, the level of a quantity is the logarithm of the ratio of that quantity to a reference quantity of the same kind. The base of the logarithm is commonly 10. The reference quantity and the kind of level must be specified. The unit is generally the decibel. For example, one speaks of the "sound-pressure level in decibels referred to a reference of 2.0×10^{-4} *microbar.*" Zero level occurs when the sound pressure equals the reference pressure, 2.0×10^{-4} microbar.

LIVE ROOM   A live room is a room that is characterized by an unusually small amount of sound absorption.

LOUDNESS   Loudness is the intensive attribute of an auditory sensation, in terms of which sounds may be ordered on a scale extending from "soft" to "loud."

MACH NUMBER   Mach number is defined as the ratio of the speed of a moving element to the speed of sound in the surrounding medium.

MASKING   Each of us has had the experience of hearing a bird sing on a quiet Sunday morning in a rural area. Yet we well know that this bird could not be heard at noontime in the downtown portions of a large city. We explain this phenomenon by saying that the traffic noise in the city masks the song of the bird. Thus, masking is the process by which the threshold of audibility for one sound is raised by the presence of another, or masking, sound. To make the idea more quantitative, we can say that masking is the amount by which the threshold of audibility of a sound is raised by the presence of another masking sound. This increase in threshold of audibility is usually given in decibels.

MASS-LAW TRANSMISSION LOSS   The sound-transmission properties of a panel of a given mass per unit area and negligible stiffness are described by the mass-law transmission loss. In practice this mass law describes the performance of many wall structures below the critical frequency and above the lowest, highly-damped, panel-resonance frequency.

MICROBAR   A microbar is a unit of pressure commonly used in acoustics. One microbar is equal to one dyne per square centimeter.

MICROPHONE   A microphone is an acoustic transducer that responds to sound waves and delivers essentially equivalent electric waves.

NOISE   Noise is any undesired signal; thus, in acoustics, it is any undesired sound. By extension, noise is any unwanted disturbance within a useful frequency band, such as an undesired electric wave in a transmission channel or device. It is generally assumed that noise is an erratic, intermittent, or statistically random oscillation.

Ambient Noise
Ambient noise is the all-encompassing noise associated with a given environment, usually being a composite of sounds from many sources, near and far. Ambient noise can be quite distressing, as in a theater just before the curtain goes up.

White Noise
White noise is a random noise whose spectral density is substantially independent of frequency over a specified frequency range. Lately it is widely used in the random vibration testing of devices.

NOISE CONTROL   Noise control is the technology of establishing appropriate acoustical criteria to minimize noise, and of modifyng sources, transmission paths, and/or receivers of noise for the purpose of satisfying these criteria.

NOISE LEVEL   Noise level is simply the reading of a standard sound level meter when the excitation is that of the noise.

NOISE REDUCTION   The noise reduction of a structural configuration is the difference in the sound-pressure levels, expressed in decibels, on either side of the configuration. Noise reduction is often the quantity of practical engineering interest, while transmission loss is a more basic quantity associated with the physical construction of the structure. Under many conditions noise reduction can be related to transmission loss by a knowledge of the geometry involved and the acoustical absorption in the spaces under consideration. See also *sound transmission loss*.

OCTAVE BAND   An octave band is a frequency band with lower and upper cut-off frequencies having a ratio of 2. The cut-off frequencies of 707 Hz and 1414 Hz define an octave band in common use. See also *band center frequency*.

OSCILLATION   Oscillation is a general term which connotes a variation of some observable quantity about a mean value. Thus the voltage on the electrical mains in our homes will vary roughly between $+160$ and -160 volts, with a mean value of zero. A less regular oscillation is that experienced by a rider seated on the back seat of an automobile which is traveling over a bumpy road.

OVERALL SOUND-PRESSURE LEVEL   The overall sound-pressure level is the sound-pressure level measured in a broad frequency band covering the frequency range of interest. This band is often taken to extend from approximately 25 Hz to 10,000 Hz.

PERCEIVED NOISE LEVEL   The perceived noise level of a given sound is numerically equal to the sound-pressure level of a reference sound judged equally as noisy as the given sound. The units of perceived noise level are PNdB. Calculation procedures for perceived noise level utilize frequency-weighting techniques determined by laboratory and field judgment tests of various sounds.

PERCENT IMPAIRMENT OF HEARING (PERCENT HEARING LOSS)   Percent impairment of hearing is an estimate of a person's ability to hear correctly. It is usually based, by means of an arbitrary rule, on the pure-tone audiogram. The specific rule for calculating this quantity from the audiogram now varies from state to state according to a rule or law. (This is a very pathetic situation indeed.)

PHON   The phon is the unit of loudness level.

PITCH   Pitch is an attribute of the auditory sensation. It implies that a listener may order sounds on a scale extending from low to high pitch. Pitch depends primarily upon the frequency of the sound stimulus, but it also depends upon the sound pressure and the wave form of the stimulus. It is well known, for example, that given two sounds of exactly the same frequency in the upper audible range, the one which involves a higher sound pressure will appear to have a higher pitch.

PRESBYCUSIS   Presbycusis is the decline in hearing acuity that normally occurs as a person grows older.

RANDOM NOISE   Random noise is an oscillation whose instantaneous magnitude is not specified for any given instant of time. It can be described in a statistical sense by probability distribution functions, giving the fraction of the total time that the magnitude of the noise lies within a specified range.

RATE OF DECAY   Rate of decay is the time rate at which the sound-pressure level (or other stated characteristic, such as a vibration level) decreases at a given point and at a given time. The commonly used unit is decibels per second.

RESONANCE   Resonance is a term which is used to describe a particular interaction between a system and a simple harmonic excitation. More particularly, if the frequency of the excitation cannot be changed either up or down a small amount without causing a decrease in the response of the system, then a condition of resonance is said to exist. It will be noted that resonance depends upon the close matching of the frequency of an excitation to the characteristics of a system. One well known example of resonance occurs when two musical instruments, say violins, are placed on opposite sides of a room. If then a string of one violin is bowed and if the instruments are carefully tuned to each other, then the corresponding string on the other violin will be set into motion. This motion exists, of course, because of careful matching of frequencies associated with the excitation and with the system being excited.

RESONANT FREQUENCY   A resonant frequency is a frequency at which resonance exists.

RESONATOR   A resonator is a device that resounds or vibrates in sympathy with some source of sound or vibration.

REVERBERATION   Reverberation is the persistence of sound in an enclosed space as a result of multiple reflections after the sound source has stopped.

REVERBERATION TIME   The reverberation time of a room at a particular frequency is the time that would be required for the mean-square sound-pressure level, originally in a steady state, to decrease by 60 decibels after the source is stopped.

SHIELDING   Shielding is the process of providing attenuation of sound by interposing a wall, building, or other barrier between an acoustic source and a receiver.

SONIC BOOM   The sonic boom is the pressure transient produced at an observing point by a vehicle that is moving past (or over) it faster than the speed of sound.

SOUND   Sound is an oscillation in pressure, stress, particle velocity, etc., in an elastic medium, or the superposition (combination) of such oscillations. By extension, sound has also come to be associated with the auditory sensation evoked by this type of oscillation.

SOUND ABSORPTION   Sound absorption is the conversion of sound energy into some other form, usually heat, in passing through a medium or on striking a surface. Thus it is difficult to speak to a person sitting on the opposite side of a campfire, because of the absorption of sound by hot gases. We use sound absorbing materials on the walls of offices and theaters.

SOUND INTENSITY   The sound intensity in a specified direction at a point is the average rate of sound energy transmitted in the specified direction through a unit area whose surface is perpendicular to this direction at the point considered. The unit is generally watts per square centimeter or per square meter.

SOUND LEVEL   The expression "sound level" has a very particular technical meaning. There exists in this country a line of instruments whose performances are specified in an American Standard, and these are called "American Standard Sound Level Meters for the Measurement of Noise and Other Sounds." Now, each of these meters is equipped with three different electrical networks inside, which serve the purpose of weighting the frequency components in different manners. These networks are called Weightings A, B, or C. Now, a sound level is simply the reading of such a meter when subjected to a given sound. The level has meaning, of course, only if the particular weighting used at the time of reading the meter is specified.

SOUND-LEVEL METER   A sound-level meter is an instrument—comprising a *microphone,* an amplifier, an output meter, and frequency-weighting networks—that is used for the measurement of noise and sound levels in a specified manner.

SOUND-POWER LEVEL   The sound-power level of a source, in decibels, is 10 times the logarithm to the base 10 of the ratio of the sound power radiated by the source to a standardized reference sound power. The reference power must be explicitly stated. (The international standard reference sound power is 10^{-12} watt.) The sound-pressure level at a given position from a sound source is related to the sound-power level of the source by a knowledge of the directional characteristics of the source, the distance between the source and the receiver, and the presence or absence of reflecting surfaces, e.g., the ground or the boundaries of a room.

SOUND PRESSURE   The sound pressure at a point in a medium is the instantaneous pressure at that point in the presence of a sound wave, minus the static pressure at that point.

SOUND-PRESSURE LEVEL   The sound-pressure level, in decibels, of a sound is 20 times the logarithm to the base ten of the ratio of the pressure of this sound to the reference pressure. The common reference pressure for acoustics in air is 2.0×10^{-4} microbar. In English units this quantity is approximately 4.2×10^{-7} pounds per square foot.

SOUND TRANSMISSION COEFFICIENT   The sound transmission coefficient of a structural configuration is the fraction of incident sound energy transmitted through it.

SOUND TRANSMISSION LOSS (TRANSMISSION LOSS, TL)   The sound transmission loss of a structural configuration is a measure of sound insulation. Expressed in decibels, it is 10 times the logarithm to the base 10 of the reciprocal of the sound transmission coefficient of the configuration. See also *noise reduction.*

SPEECH-INTERFERENCE LEVEL (SIL)   The speech-interference level of a noise is a calculated quantity providing a handy guide to the interfacing effect of a noise on speech. The speech-interference level is the arithmetic average of the octave-band sound-pressure levels of the noise in the most important part of the speech-frequency range. The levels in the three octave-frequency bands of 600–1200 Hz, 1200–2400 Hz, and 2400–4800 Hz are commonly averaged to determine the speech-interference level.

SPEED (VELOCITY) OF SOUND IN AIR   The speed of sound in air is 344 m/sec or 1128 ft/sec at 78° F.

SPHERICAL DIVERGENCE   Spherical divergence is the condition of propagation of *spherical waves* that relates to the regular decrease in intensity of a spherical sound wave at progressively greater distances from the source. Under this condition the sound-pressure level decreases 6 decibels with each doubling of distance from the source.

THRESHOLD OF AUDIBILITY   The threshold of audibility for a specified signal is the minimum effective sound-pressure level of the signal that is capable of evoking an auditory sensation in a specified fraction of the trials in a battery of listeners. The characteristics of the signal, the manner in which it is presented to the listener, and the point at which the sound-pressure level is measured, are all important in determining just what the threshold of audibility is for the given signal.

THRESHOLD OF DISCOMFORT   The threshold of discomfort for a specified signal is the minimum effective sound-pressure level of that signal which, in a specified fraction of the trials by a battery of listeners, will stimulate the ear to a point at which the sensation of feeling becomes uncomfortable.

THRESHOLD OF PAIN   The threshold of pain for a specified signal is the minimum effective sound-pressure level of that signal which, in a specified fraction of the trials by a battery of listeners, will stimulate the ear to a point at which the discomfort gives way to definite pain that is distinct from the mere non-noxious feeling of discomfort.

WAVELENGTH   The wavelength of a periodic wave (such as sound in air) is the perpendicular distance between analogous points on any two successive waves. The wavelength of sound in air or in water is inversely proportional to the frequency of the sound. Thus the lower the frequency, the longer the wavelength.

INDEX

$((((((((((\ \cdot\ ))))))))))$

359